"Dr. Yaqoob has years of tutoring experience and it shows. He takes math-concerned parents by the hand and shows them how they can help their child with math. Concepts that parents never quite 'got' or barely remember are grist to the mill. Practical help for the parent with no time!"

Prof. Barry McKernan (former student), City University of New York (CUNY), and American Museum of Natural History, New York, USA.

What Can I Do

to Help My Child with Math When I Don't Know Any Myself?

Tahir Yaqoob, Ph.D.

Copyright © 2011 Tahir Yaqoob. All rights reserved.

Front and back cover art, copyright © 2011 Tahir Yaqoob.

Additional supplementary material is available at
http://www.helpyourchildwithmath.com.

A publication of New Earth Labs™ (education and outreach division),
P. O. Box 5672, Baltimore, MD 21210. http://www.newearthlabs.com.

No part of this book may be reproduced, translated, distributed, transmitted, or stored in a retrieval system, by any means whatsoever, without the permission of the copyright holder. Brief excerpts (totalling less than one page) may be quoted in literary review articles without permission. While the techniques described in this book have been successful for the author, results will vary. No guarantee or warranty is made, implicit or explicit, on any results that might be obtained from applying the techniques. The author's opinions and statements made in this work are associated with the author alone, and are not endorsed by any institution that the author is affiliated with, nor any institution that is mentioned in this work.

ISBN: 978-0-9741689-0-6

Cataloging data:

What Can I Do to Help My Child with Math When I Don't Know Any Myself?
Tahir Yaqoob.
Includes index.
Keywords: 1. Parenting; 2. Study guides; 3. Test preparation; 4. Mathematics (grade school); 5. Self help.

Acknowledgments

I would like to thank all of my students, spanning a period of over more than 25 years, for teaching me how to teach, and much more. I also thank my wife and kids for an endless stream of ideas, for all of their contributions to this book, and for putting up with the antisocial behavior while it was being written. Finally, thanks to my teachers who gave their dedication and inspiration, in person, or in print.

Contents

Preface		**1**
1	**Foundations**	**5**
	1.1 What This Book Is For	5
	1.2 How to Use This Book	6
	1.3 The Dreaded "Why Do I Need to Know This?"	11
2	**Developing Intuition**	**23**
	2.1 Intuition Can Be Learned	23
	2.2 Case Study: The Calculus Student Who Forgot Her Multiplication Tables	25
	2.3 The Calculator Reflex	27
	2.4 The Money Rule	28
	2.5 Developing a Habit of Looking for Mistakes	31
	2.6 Developing Skills in Estimation	34
	2.7 Oral Drills	37
	2.8 Skills That Online Math Aids Can and Cannot Provide	41
	2.9 Application-Oriented Teaching and Motivation	47
3	**Daily Power Tips**	**49**
	3.1 Date It to Organize It	50
	3.2 Materials and Supplies Check	52
	3.3 What Did Your Child Study Today?	52

3.4		Studying Techniques and the Study Environment	53
3.5		Homework Checklist	55
3.6		Administering Oral Drills	56

4 Graphs and the Graphing Calculator — 59

- 4.1 Hand-Drawn Graphs ... 59
    - 4.1.1 Scale, Axes, and Resolution ... 60
    - 4.1.2 Hand-Drawn Graphs: Basic Checklist ... 61
    - 4.1.3 Advanced Graphing Errors ... 62
- 4.2 The Graphing Calculator ... 71
- 4.3 What Can a Graphing Calculator Do That a Regular One Cannot? ... 71
- 4.4 The Major Pitfalls ... 72
    - 4.4.1 Poor Rendering of Essential Features of Graphs ... 73
    - 4.4.2 The Display's Aspect Ratio ... 79
    - 4.4.3 Strategy ... 82

5 Tutoring Options and How to Optimize the Return on Limited Funds — 85

- 5.1 I Wish I Could Afford Private Tutoring ... 85
- 5.2 Independent Tutor versus Tutoring Agency ... 86
- 5.3 Cost-Effective Tutoring Options ... 89
    - 5.3.1 Tutoring Worksheet ... 93
- 5.4 How to Find a Suitable Tutor ... 96
    - 5.4.1 Using an Agency ... 96
    - 5.4.2 Finding and Interviewing an Independent Tutor ... 98
- 5.5 Targeted Tutoring ... 104
    - 5.5.1 Resolving Issues with Problematic Topics ... 105
    - 5.5.2 Diagnostic Testing ... 108
    - 5.5.3 Exam or Test Preparation ... 110
    - 5.5.4 Graphing and the Graphing Calculator ... 113

		5.5.5 Interpretation of Key Phrases in Questions 115
		5.5.6 Customized Oral Drills 115
	5.6	Case Study: The Student Who Dropped From a Grade B to a Grade C 116
	5.7	How to Get the Most Out of Tutoring 119

6	**Ingredients for Exam Success**	**121**
	6.1 Maximizing Exam and Test Performance 121	
	6.2 Concentration and Distractions 123	
	6.3 Maintain Accessibility to Topics That You Already Covered 123	
	6.4 Don't Spend Too Much Time on Your Favorite Areas . . . 125	
	6.5 The Wall Sheet: a Powerful Memory Aid 125	

7	**Reviewing for Exams**	**129**
	7.1 Set Goals and Get Focused at Every Study Session 129	
	7.2 Nurture Your Active Memory 130	
	7.2.1 Passive and Active Memory 130	
	7.2.2 Active Memory Can Be Trained 130	
	7.3 Don't Just Think It! Write It! 133	
	7.4 Discipline and Motivation 134	
	7.5 Active Memory for Proofs and Derivations 135	

8	**Simulated Exams and Tests**	**137**
	8.1 The Vital Importance of Simulated Exams 137	
	8.2 Set Yourself TIMED Exams 138	
	8.3 How Often Should You Do Simulated Exams? 139	
	8.4 Do Multiple-Choice Exams Even If They Are Not Required 139	
	8.5 Mental Preparation 140	
	8.6 Is It Worth Paying for Exam Preparation Courses? 141	

9	**Multiple-Choice Exams**	**143**
	9.1 Three Key Tips for Multiple-Choice Exams 143	

	9.1.1 The Techniques for Elimination 145
	9.1.2 The Mechanics of Guessing 148
9.2	The "Big-Name" Advisers' Strategy 150

10 Strategies During Exams 155

10.1 Read the Paper Slowly, Comprehend Each Question 155
10.2 Decide on the Order of Attack 155
10.3 Know and Understand the Critical Keywords in Questions 156
10.4 Pay Attention to the Points Scheme and Stick to Time . . . 156
10.5 Force Yourself Out of Being Stuck 157
10.6 Graphs 158
10.7 Don't Blow It on Neatness 159
10.8 Write Down SOMETHING 160
10.9 Dealing with Blackouts 161
10.10 The Nightmare Calculation 162
10.11 Show Every Step 162

11 The Parental Crib Sheet 165

A Oral Drills 323

A.1 Elementary-School Level 327
A.2 Middle- to High-School Level 341
A.3 Precalculus and Calculus 363

Index 369

Preface

No parent needs to be told how critical it is for their kids to succeed in math, stay on top of it, stay motivated, and indeed to attain the best possible level of achievement. Whether a student is in the elementary grades or at high-school level[1], making sure that their kids are achieving a sufficiently high standard in math is a constant source of stress for every parent. I have tutored and mentored students at all levels for over 25 years, and time and time again I have come across the classic dilemma that parents have. That is, in an ideal world, every parent would like to spend time with their kids to help them achieve their full potential in math, but how? The reality that parents run into is that once the student reaches 7th to 8th grade or so, most parents would have to spend time first reviewing or relearning the material themselves because it has been too long since they studied that material in school or college themselves. Unless a parent uses the math regularly in his/her profession, he/she would have to spend a considerable amount of time refreshing his/her memory and relearning the material *continuously*, at a faster pace than his/her child. Indeed, there are plenty of books out there which go about trying to teach parents the material again, presumably with the aim that parents can then help by providing supplemental tutoring to their children themselves. But how many people really have time for that? The school pace is *extremely fast*. In my experience, the severe time constraints that parents have make it absolutely out of the question for most

---

[1] For readers outside the United States, grades 1 to 12 correspond roughly to ages 6 to 18, plus or minus one year at each end of the range.

parents to relearn the material in order to help their kids (excepting parents in technical and/or particular teaching professions). If you are a parent who *does* have the time to provide supplemental tutoring, you are very fortunate, and if you want to relearn the material you should get hold of one of those other books, or even a textbook. Even so, you may find this book to be a helpful supplement as I have written down what I have learned from tutoring and mentoring for more than 25 years. It may turn out that all you need are brief "memory joggers" to recall entire topics without much further work in order to help your child with math, in which case you may also find this book helpful because of the "parental crib sheet" that I have included. If you are a homeschooling parent you may find this book helpful as a reference tool. Or perhaps you are a grandparent who has a bit of time to help your grandchild with math. Time spent in this way can be fun and a very rewarding bonding experience. It may even be an unexpected activity if mom and dad have instructed, to your horror, that your grandchild must be returned to them with all homework completed.

This book is primarily aimed at the majority of parents, who barely have enough time to read for pleasure, let alone teach themselves math! The book came about because of a common type of question originating from parents themselves. Parents of students I have taught have repeatedly asked me what they can do to help their kids with math given that they have "forgotten it all" themselves, and given that there is no way they will ever have the time to relearn the material themselves. If you have experienced the perfectly normal loss of memory of how to do the math that your kids are doing in school, and you want to know what you can do, this book is for you. There is actually *a lot* that you can do, and you may be surprised to realize just how much you can do. I have written down in this book what I have learned from tutoring and mentoring over the last 25 years, and it is my goal to empower you with the knowledge to significantly improve your child's *performance and motivation* in math. The book contains information that is relevant for all levels from 1st to 12th grade, but I will point out those situations that are specific to only certain ranges in grade level.

As part of the program, one of the things that I would like to do for you is to give you the tools to be able to engage your child in a meaningful conversation about what he/she studied in math on a given day, without requiring you to read anything more than that which is in this book. You will never have to solve a math problem. I will use nontechnical language that is *in context* and that assumes no prerequisite specialized knowledge. In contrast, getting information from the internet "in context" is extremely difficult, especially for mathematical topics. There is absolutely no uniformity in the academic level of the information. For example, have you *seen* the Wikipedia entry for "rational number"? In grade-school math this is a very simple concept but the Wikipedia entry consists of a large amount of gobbeldygook written for mathematics professors or researchers. For grade-school level most of the information in that Wikipedia entry is completely useless. Yet, a Wikipedia entry on a different topic may consist of only a couple of lines of poor quality information. The internet has no uniformity in the quality of information. Moreover, the "heavyweight" websites are given a blanket high ranking by the search engines regardless of whether a particular page has an inferior quality of information compared to a smaller website that has a higher quality of information. On the other hand, for this book the primary audience, namely you, the overworked parents who want to help their kids with math, is very clearly defined. I can therefore tailor information to your exact needs. Having just mentioned the disadvantage of information on the internet, a *focused* website, on the other hand, *can* be extremely useful and there *are* some very useful resources catering to our common goals. This book does in fact come with a website[2] that contains material complementary to the book. The website also provides links to other carefully selected internet resources. Different material on the website for this book is targeted for parents, students, and tutors. I will refer to the website at various relevant points in the text. Fi-

---

[2]http://www.helpyourchildwithmath.com

nally, I thank you for giving me the opportunity to share my experiences with you and I hope that this book will help you and your kids achieve your goals.

Chapter 1

Foundations

1.1 What This Book Is For

I have already talked about the purpose of this book in the preface, but here I will give a little more background about the motivation behind the book. Early in my experience with tutoring students in their homes, I came across a common concern that the students' parents would express. It was phrased in a variety of ways but always along the lines of, "How can I help my child with math? I don't remember how to do any of the stuff my son/daughter is doing." Of course, I knew that the parents were perfectly capable of refreshing their memories or learning the material again. We all know that this is in practice usually out of the question simply from the point of view of the required time commitment. There are already not enough hours in the day to manage the myriad of demands of work, family, and life in general. There is often an associated sense of guilt on the part of the parents. They feel that they should know the material and that they should be able to do it. However, this guilt has no foundation because it is perfectly natural to forget even the basic math if it is not used everyday. Only a tiny fraction of the adult population uses and applies math on a regular, daily basis, beyond simple percentages and fractions. Do you know anyone who, for example, solves algebraic equations, or writes down geometric proofs on a daily basis?

Every child is of course unique and a single set of strategies may not work for every child if those strategies are not tailored to the individual. However, the techniques and strategies that I describe in this book (in their appropriate domains) have worked for the majority of my students. As a parent you know the unique characteristics and abilities of your child so use your judgement in applying the techniques that are described. Some of them may work, some of them may not. You may also find that some of the techniques described in this book conflict with current teaching philosophies in general and/or the teaching philosophy of your child's school teacher, or teachers. However, I emphasize again that what I describe in this book is based on many years of experience with using techniques that have consistently delivered successful results. On the other hand, part of your strategy as a parent, if necessary, will be to "hand your child back" to his/her teachers. You cannot afford to throw away such an enormous resource. In general, teachers have chosen their profession because they are passionate about teaching and because they have a genuine desire to impart knowledge and skills to their students. Teachers generally put up with poor salaries, and yet exhibit extraordinary dedication to what is a very weighty responsibility, namely the education of your child. If the advice and techniques described in this book conflict with the methods and philosophies of your child's school teachers, and if you believe that the methods in this book could help your child, you must find a way of reconciling the different approaches. Methods and philosophies in this book that seemingly conflict with those of your child's teachers are not necessarily mutually exclusive. Again, exercise your judgment.

1.2 How to Use This Book

This book is divided into three parts. Part 1 (chapters 1 to 5) concerns the essential strategies that you as a parent can use to help your child with math. I suggest reading all of it, regardless of the grade levels of your kids. Some of the material may only be useful later for higher grade levels, but there is a lot of information that is relevant to all grade levels that is difficult to separate out. In part 1 of the book I also discuss in considerable detail what options might be available to you for getting help from a math tutor. I strongly recommend reading this section even if you think you would never be able to afford tutoring. You may be surprised to find that you *can* afford tutoring on a limited budget. Moreover, even if you can only afford a few lessons, I will describe specific ways in which a limited number of lessons should be used in order to produce the highest return. I will refer to this as "targeted tutoring," and the section of the book that details the "targeted tutoring" topics (§5.5) should be useful to you as a parent, whether you decide to get help with tutoring or not.

After having read part 1 of the book, you will be able to begin implementing a plan, while reading part 2 of the book. Part 2 of this book (chapters 6 to 10) describes techniques for exam success and for studying for exams and tests. Whilst some of these are well known, some may be new to you. Although many of them seem obvious, students who struggle with tests and exams do not apply all of the techniques that they could be using, even though they may be aware of them. You should convey and share what you learn in part 2 with your child (not all in one go, but spread out over time). If your child is in 8th grade or above, he or she should read part 2 himself/herself, after which it would be a good idea to discuss with each other what you have both read. Many of the techniques and strategies discussed in both part 1 and part 2 involve ongoing activities that are designed to enhance various skills over time. Your role as a parent will vary for each activity and will be discussed in the relevant places. Your role will be more interactive for part 1 than for part 2. For the latter, with respect to the study skills and exam preparation techniques, your role will be principally that of advising and enforcing (the correct habits and techniques).

Part 3 of the book (chapter 11) is what I call the "parental crib sheet."

One of the the most important factors that I will discuss in this book is to develop a habit of *regularly* talking to your child about what he/she has been doing in math. Understandably, many parents are afraid of doing this because they fear that they may know little or nothing of the topic, hindering the ability to follow up with anything sensible, in answer to questions such as "What did you do in math today?" However, it is important to realize that in order to have a meaningful and genuine conversation with your child about a particular math topic you don't need to know the rigorous definitions or the gory technical details concerning a topic. If you have the time and inclination for rigorous definitions and gory details then you should go and study a mathematics textbook. If not, as is the case for the majority of parents, my "parental crib sheet" will provide you with the information that you need to at least start a meaningful conversation with your child. The crib sheet is essentially a glossary of commonly used terms in grade-school math that you can use as a reference at any time. However, there is a *big* difference between my crib sheet and the "math dictionaries" that you will find on many websites on the internet.

Each entry in my crib sheet has been very carefully crafted to explain things in a nontechnical manner, in the framework of the appropriate context for your purpose, yet without sacrificing accuracy. The crib sheet will help you to gain some kind of clue as to what your child may be talking about and to be able to respond in a meaningful way. Sometimes all you need is a quick memory jogger to bring back things you thought you had forgotten, and in fact you may be able to recall more than you anticipated after a helpful nudge from the crib sheet. Perhaps your memory will even be jogged enough for you to be able to help your child yourself with a complete homework problem (for example), without any further effort. Since many of the strategies in this book emphasize communication with your child, even a minimal, but functional, understanding of what he/she may be talking about will go *a very long way*. Part of the reason for this is, of course, that your child will know that you are taking a genuine interest in what he/she is doing.

What I am really talking about with respect to the crib sheet is the nature of knowledge itself. Allow me to explain by means of an analogy. Consider a situation in which you take your car into a garage for repair. The mechanic may tell you that your timing belt needs replacing. If you don't know what a timing belt is, you might ask your mechanic to explain, and he/she may tell you in a brief sentence or two. You will likely be satisfied with this minimal information and understanding because it actually tells you *a lot*. You need to know *nothing* about how to replace the timing belt, what it is made of, or where you would get one. You don't even need to see it. Yet the little bit of information that the mechanic gave you has gone a long way to reassure you that you understand something very fundamental about what is wrong with your car. Part 3 of this book, the crib sheet, serves exactly such a purpose. The crib sheet covers concepts and material for your child's entire tenure at school, from 1st to 12th grade.

You may wonder why, in this age of the internet, the crib sheet in part 3 of this book is not redundant because you could just look up anything on the internet. You are welcome to use the internet for this purpose if you have the time to sort through the multitude of results, many of which may be completely out of context, and/or may be of low or questionable reliability. Chances are that you don't have the time to do that. As I mentioned in the preface of this book, the Wikipedia page for "rational number" consists of a large quantity of what can only be described as gobbeldygook written for mathematics professors. Yet "rational number" at grade-school level, all the way up to 12th grade, is an extremely simple concept. The Wikipedia page is the top result in a *Google* search for "rational number," the last time that I checked at the time of writing. Try it and see for yourself. There is absolutely no uniformity in the academic level of information and knowledge on the internet. There cannot be any because of the nature of the monster. Smaller websites, which may have a higher quality of information on a particular topic than a "heavyweight" website, are being bumped down in ranking by the search engines. This is wrong and it actually contradicts the purported mission of the search engines. It is based on the false assumption that a website that is an internet "heavyweight" has a high quality of information on *every* page and/or topic. In contrast, the crib sheet in part 3 of this book provides a quick and easy reference that will give you results that are *in the context that you need them, and in a form that is tailored for you*.

Although the information in the crib sheet is nontechnical, practical, and free of gobbeldygook, great care has been exercised to ensure that it is *accurate*, and that definitions and explanations reflect the true meaning of words and concepts. The work in sorting, organizing, and *expressing* the knowledge has already been done for you. That is, after all, what books were designed for. Somebody (yours truly in this case!) has already done the work for you. Another use of the crib sheet that you may find beneficial and interesting is that of simple, casual browsing. The crib sheet is by no means exhaustive but I hope it will go a long way towards helping you to help your child with math. Despite the nonuniform nature of information on the internet that results from a search, as you are aware, there are many focused websites which do aim at giving you preprocessed information. Some websites are much better than others, and sorting out what is good and bad in itself requires effort. Since websites come and go, I will not mention any specifically in this book (since such information can quickly go "out of date"), but instead I refer you to the website that comes with this book (http://helpyourchildwithmath.com). This website contains different resources targeted for parents, students, and tutors, as well as some links to selected resources on other websites. Notification of the possible benefit of internet resources will be provided at appropriate places in the text of this book.

Finally, the appendix consists of a set of oral drills that are designed to develop mental math skills, as well as parent/child communication. Detailed instructions on how to use them can be found in §2.7 and §3.6, and in the appendix itself.

1.3 The Dreaded "Why Do I Need to Know This?"

Shortly after becoming a graduate student in Leicester, England, survival issues dictated that I needed to supplement my income. As every student knows, the term "income" in this context has only a limited interpretation as it is not a wage (a more appropriate term would be "a trickle of funds to feed the debt"). So I applied for a part-time teaching job at a local college across town. The job entailed teaching classes of 18- to 21-year-old students who were taking courses that were predominately related to lithography and photography. I was to teach them science and math as part of their studies. At that time I had acquired only some limited teaching experience, tutoring individual students, and I barely had any experience teaching classes. So I was rather apprehensive at the job interview. However, to my amazement I was offered the job and I was quite thrilled, not only at the prospect of increasing the trickle of funds, but I had a genuine interest in sharing my excitement about science and math in a teaching environment. Years later, in hindsight of course, I realized that the college must have been desperate to hire somebody cheap who looked like they might be able to make a half-baked attempt at teaching those kids science and math.

However, soon after I began teaching the classes I ran into a brick wall. The students were only a year to three years younger than me, they were as scruffily dressed as I was, and by the third class they had become rowdy and uncooperative. I felt that I had no authority over these kids, who were essentially the same age as me. The reason for the rowdiness and the lack of cooperation was actually very simple and the students expressed it themselves. "We are going to be photographers and/or lithographers. Why do we need to know this stuff? This is a waste of time." Add to these a range of expressions along similar lines. I tried to explain to them that in order to understand the chemistry behind photography and lithography they needed to understand the foundations of chemistry and physics and that they needed to understand the math in order to be able to do the chemistry and physics. They were emphatically unconvinced. They argued that while a little bit of chemistry might be helpful, they failed to see the purpose of learning things like atomic physics, Newtonian mechanics, calculus, and a long laundry list of other topics. In fact they argued that almost the entire curriculum was of no use to them. "We did not sign up for this, and we will be perfectly capable of doing photography and lithography without knowing any of this, thank you very much." Things got so bad that some of the students would literally not touch any of the equipment during an entire laboratory class, when they were supposed to be doing a physics experiment. They would disrupt others who *were* trying to do something, frequently verbalizing (loudly) their frustration with "Why do we need to do this? I don't need to know this."

Feeling like a total failure so soon after taking up the teaching job, I tried to figure out where I was going wrong. Up to this point I had naively thought that the majority of the population is, by nature, interested in science and math, especially those people who are engaged in activities that involve interesting physical processes like photography and lithography. Why would anyone *not* be interested in wanting to learn more science and math? One day I was cycling across town from class back to my own university, pondering the problem again. Then it suddenly came to me, and to this day I still remember the feeling during that "Eureka moment." They were right! They don't need to know! They *don't* need to know any of that stuff! They don't need to know atomic physics, Newtonian mechanics, or calculus. They don't need to know electromagnetism. They don't need to do any physics experiments. They don't even need to know the periodic table! They are going to be perfectly good photographers and lithographers without coming to my class and without knowing any of the stuff I'm trying to teach them. No wonder I haven't been able to convince them that they need to know this stuff, I thought. They are right! *They don't need to know.* Why was I trying to convince them that they do? I had lost their respect because I was trying to convince them of something that is fundamentally not true. Furthermore, I realized that all along, I myself did not really believe that the students needed to "know that stuff" either, and perhaps they picked up on that.

Having run into this marvelous revelation, I was so happy that by now my cycling had become quite vigorous. But then I slowed down as I realized that I was still faced with a major problem. I still needed to teach that class because I needed the money. I still needed the students to cooperate. I still needed to regain their respect. Moreover, although I had discovered that I did not want to tell the students that they *needed* to "know that stuff" because I didn't believe it myself, I still *wanted* them to "know that stuff." I wanted them to get good grades and come out of college with the best qualifications and skills. Somehow there was a disconnection and I tried to figure out what it was. I asked myself, *"Why* did I want them to learn the science and math? Why does the education system want them to know that stuff?" The one thing that was very clear was that I had to find some honest answers that myself and my students believe to be true without having to be persuaded. I knew that one of the key payoffs of learning math and the sciences, aside from the actual content, is that these subjects, in a variety of ways, help to nurture and develop many different kinds of analytic and mental skills, techniques and capabilities. Such skills may be indirectly useful in real life, divorced of the original content or purpose.

By way of analogy, suppose that you decide to regularly use free weights to exercise your biceps and triceps to increase muscle strength. Then one day you take a job that involves lifting heavy sacks of potatoes. Of course, all the training with the free weights will have served you well and will help you perform your job with greater ease, and perhaps help you to perform better than you would have done without the previous training. The brain and a myriad of mental skills and abilities also benefit from training. You may never again do a calculus problem after leaving school but the skills that you developed in the process of learning calculus and doing calculus problems may actually serve you and help you indirectly in a completely different activity, without you even being aware of it.

But here's the problem: the analogy of training the physical body to improve performance in other physical tasks is very transparent and obvious. On the other hand, the connection between learning various skills in science and math with real, practical benefits in cognitive abilities in real life is really not very transparent at all. I knew that I would be unable to convince the students on this basis alone because it is hard to prove with concrete and concise examples. Even if I were able to convince the students of the truth of the basic proposition, they may not care, and may argue that they won't need the purported nebulous cognitive skills, or that they could acquire them later, along with the actual knowledge content of the subjects (science and math). I needed to find a way to relate what I was trying to teach the students, to photography and lithography, in a way that was virtually self-evidently true.

Clearly, I had to dig and search deeper for an answer. I asked myself, "If I were one of the students, how would I benefit from knowing that stuff if I was ambivalent about it?" Then came the second "Eureka moment." *I* would feel that I am a *better* photographer and/or lithographer if I "knew that stuff." Every endeavor, every profession is competitive. Everyone wants to be the best at what they do and everyone wants to outsmart and outperform the competition. Furthermore, *I* would feel more enriched, and more empowered, to perhaps come up with something new, compared to a photographer and/or lithographer who didn't "know that stuff." My cycling had again become quite vigorous and I soon got back to my office, but I couldn't wait until the next class to test out my new hypothesis. Not only did I think I had come up with an idea of how to regain respect from the students, and regain control of the class, but, if my hunch was right, I may have discovered a reason why somebody should be motivated to learn something that may have little obvious, direct benefit. But I couldn't be sure until I tested it out in the trenches.

The next class came around, and at the beginning of the class I told the students the bottom line, without the details of how I had come to my conclusions. I told the students something along the lines of what follows. "I've been thinking about what you have been saying and I realized that you are absolutely right: you *don't* need to know this stuff. You don't need to know any of this to be able to do photography or lithography. You don't need to come to my class at all. But here's the thing: if you don't learn this stuff, you'll just be average at what you do. To be *good* at what you do, you *do* need to know this stuff. Don't you want to be *good* photographers and lithographers? Don't you want to stand above the rest and be proud of being the best? Don't you want to come up with something new, something that somebody else might not have thought of? It's entirely up to you, it's in your hands." The students were actually listening and taking it in, and they raised no objections. The results were absolutely astounding, and I couldn't quite believe it myself. From that time onwards, the entire class gave me their full cooperation, and I never had a problem with them ever again. Even the students who refused to touch the laboratory equipment cooperated, and eventually they even showed some enthusiasm for the experiments. The rowdiness was history. In fact, I was impressed by how the entire class actually became quite conscientious.

Since that breakthrough, over a period of more than two decades, I have observed the same principle over and over again. I have never had a problem with gaining the respect and cooperation from either individual students, or from a class, whether I was teaching math, physics, chemistry, or biology. In hindsight the reason is quite obvious. Everyone respects honesty: it is a basic human trait. The students knew that I truly believed they were right in that they didn't really need to know most of what I was trying to teach them, but they also knew that I truly believed that I wanted to help them to improve themselves so that they could achieve their full potential in whatever profession they were going to go into. I was happy because I could be freely honest and not feel like a phoney, trying to convince the students of something that I didn't ultimately believe myself. Nobody wants to be just average, and everybody wants to be the best that they can be. That is another basic and very universal human trait, and it is a powerful motivator. It is so basic and universal that I didn't even have to provide any further justification or explanation to that rowdy college class because every single person understood, and could relate to that fundamental truth.

Now let's come back to the central question of this book: "What can I do to help my child with math if I don't know any myself?" The lesson from the anecdote described above should be clear. Why do we try to convince our kids that the math that they learn over many years at school will be *literally* useful to them? The kids very quickly come to know that this is absolutely not true. Just consider what they observe around them. They do not in general see adults around them using math. For the majority of kids, whose parents are not in a profession that utilizes math everyday, teachers are the only adults that the kids see using math on a daily basis. Parents helping them with math homework are other exceptions that they see. Even most parents who are in a technical profession do not use most of the math that is taught at school. When was the last time *you* saw an adult merrily passing the time doing a geometrical proof? When was the last time *you* saw an adult enjoy doing a "sum to infinity?" Or solving a quadratic equation? Compound on top of that, the fact that compared to when you and I were at school, the kids of today know that if anything needs to be calculated, they can just go to the internet, and somebody, somewhere will have made available a tool to do the job, and to do it in a manner that will require minimal thinking.

Most adults do not use math in everyday life beyond percentages and simple fractions. This is perfectly natural and normal. If *we*, the adults, barley do even basic things like percentages every day, there is not much of a reason to expect a kid to be motivated to do it. The point is that the kids are not dumb. They are smart. If math were really as fun as adults tell the kids, we should not be surprised if the kids think there is a basic dishonesty there because they do not observe adults merrily having fun with math in their daily lives.

You, as a parent may think that you may be able to explain to your child the indirect benefits of learning and becoming proficient at the math they are going to learn in their school career. You may try to explain that even though he/she will never, ever have to do a geometrical proof, or solve a quadratic equation by hand after he/she leaves school, the cognitive skills that are learned in the process will be useful. Good luck to you. The chances of success are extremely slim, as I explained with my anecdote about the college students. It is hard enough to convince adults, let alone children. This is because it is very difficult to directly demonstrate and prove that the wide range of topics that are taught in math will be of any practical use in real life. You may be able to do this with a particular topic, relating it to a particular profession or hobby that may be important and exciting to a child at a particular time. But in general you will have a hard time. Chances are that you may not even be convinced yourself, and your child will pick up on that. You have to be honest with yourself and your child. When you do this you are likely to see a turnaround in the attitude of your child and in his/her receptiveness to learning the math and becoming good at it, just as I did with my unruly college students.

It is likely that I have told you nothing new. You know this already, really. So, be honest. Tell your child, well actually, you're right. Most of the math that you learn in school will *not* be *directly* or *literally* useful to you. Almost all of the math that you learn in school will never, ever be used by you again after you leave school. Obviously, addition and subtraction, and multiplication will be useful everyday. But you may be able to get by without ever having to do fractions and percentages, because we have calculators and computers. As for everything else that you learn in math, you will probably never need to recall and use it, unless you go into a profession that does need you to know those things. But, if you want to do more than just get by, if you want to be more than just average, if you want to be proud of being the best that you can be, then you need to learn all that math and be good at it. If you want to be better than everyone else at what you do, and if you want to be able to compete for the best jobs, you need to learn all of "that stuff." If you want to be able to come up with new and creative ideas in whatever you do, you need to learn all that math because new ideas often have their roots in unexpected connections that are impossible to predict. If you learn all that math, the door will be opened to enjoying and taking pleasure in things that may be completely unrelated, but which you may not otherwise have been aware of. Needless to say, in addition to all of this, the *methods and procedures* of thinking, problem solving, and reasoning, will absolutely be useful to you in countless ways.

Is math fun? Can math be made to be fun for someone who doesn't think so? These are critical questions in the context of our discussion. The answer is unique for each child, and a system that tries to enforce or foster a uniform attitude will fail. I have worked with the entire spectrum of students, from those who absolutely love math, to those who hate it (the latter group will *never* think math is fun). I genuinely empathize with each person's attitude towards math because *each one is correct*. I empathize with those for whom math is fun, because for some people the unique stimulation, the challenge, and the satisfaction gleaned from problem solving *is* fun. But I also genuinely empathize with those who hate math, because it is dry, allows no room for human emotion, and is stifling to certain types of creativity. For these people math is boring, tedious, uninspiring, and a chore. However, that most certainly does not mean that people who hate math cannot do it, or cannot be good at it. They can. In my experience it is actually more common for someone to be predominantly a "math hater" than a "math lover." This makes perfect sense to me because natural selection did not rely on humans being able to solve quadratic equations. It is perfectly OK to hate math. What you should do is talk to your child and discuss how he/she feels about math, where he/she sits on the spectrum from "math hater" to "math lover," and then find a way to *genuinely* empathize with his/her position. If *I* can find that empathy for both sides, then so can you.

For a child to know that it's OK, and not unusual to hate math is a critical step in the process of "handing your child back" to the teacher, and thereby helping your child with math. If you establish that your child will never think that math is fun, the next step after empathizing with it is to then agree on why you both still need to work towards putting in the best effort to improve the math skills and aim for the best possible grades, whilst still being at liberty to hate math. *You* know your child best, but one possibility is to discuss the fitness training analogy again. Do athletes think that the warm-up exercises are fun? Do they think that all the training exercises are fun? The grueling push-ups? The assault courses? Maybe some of them do. But some of them don't, and yet they still have to do them, whether they like them or not, because of the *desire to reach the end goal*. With math, in the context of the big picture, you should talk about what those end goals are.

Do *I* think math is fun? By the time I finished high school I had done math, further math, and higher math. If the school had any kind of math to offer, you can be sure that I did it. Decades later, I use math in my research and teaching almost everyday. On some days it is simple math, on other days it is much more advanced (the kind in which a single equation can take up half a page or more). Did *I* think math was fun at school? Do I think math is fun now? The answer to both questions is sometimes. Obviously, for some fraction of the time, I must have found math to be fun. But sometimes it was tedious, sometimes boring, sometimes frustrating, and sometimes it was just plain uninspiring, because of the lack of opportunity for certain kinds of creativity. All of these attitudes prevail with me today and are just as appropriate as they were then. This is how I can genuinely empathize with every child's unique perspective towards math (which itself cannot be described by a single adjective), because math is all of the things I have mentioned. A person may harbor different proportions of those attitudes, or all of them, and those attitudes may vary erratically, or uniformly with time. It is a grave mistake for society to present kids with an oversimplified and "either/or" attitude towards math, denying that a single person can have a very complex perspective that doesn't even have to be constant in time.

By all means use any available tools to encourage your child to make math more fun, such as computer software and applications, which are now very widely available (but note the caveats discussed in chapter 2 and chapter 4). However, the bottom line is not to force it. The key is to be honest. In between the two extremes of the "math lover" and the "math hater" is an entire spectrum. As I have already mentioned, your child sees a world in which most adults are *not* having fun with math. A child observes that most adults don't use math in their everyday lives at all, and in fact he/she may have realized the dark, secret, and horrifying truth. That is that many adults don't actually like it either. Perhaps you are one of the adults who *does* like math and are willing to actually help your child with math by supplemental teaching. Or perhaps you are willing to relearn the math and then help your child by supplemental teaching. However, the chances are, if you are reading this book you don't have time. Very few people have time to tutor their kids, let alone time to relearn a subject in order to tutor their kids.

The lesson from this chapter is one of the most important ones in this book. That is, the first step in helping your child with math is to "hand your child back" to his/her teacher by ramping up motivation levels to the best that can be achieved, doing so by engaging in an honest discussion that is genuinely empathetic. If this can't be done you may as well not read the rest of the book because it is critical. Remember the story about the disobedient and uncooperative college class that I related to you earlier in this chapter. In the beginning I was wasting my time and I was not able to teach that class anything until that critical point, when I told them that I understood why they thought they didn't need to learn what I was trying to teach them. That empathy was not faked, it was genuine. The students would have known right away if it was faked, and there would have been no result.

As I said earlier, your child's teachers constitute the single most valuable resource that you and your child have, and one of your goals should be to inspire your child with a renewed approach that is more receptive to learning math, taking advantage of the available talent that is already on offer. Extraordinary teachers are all around you, and I would hazard to guess that they constitute a majority (so by "extraordinary" here, I really mean that they are extraordinary people). Generally speaking, teachers have chosen to make it their mission in life to help students learn, and to help them reach their full potential, despite incredible challenges. In the following chapters I hope to show you additional ways that you, as a parent, can help your child. You will also learn how your child can help himself/herself as a result, and how this can increase the value and benefit of what your child's teachers can do for him/her.

Chapter 2

Developing Intuition

2.1 Intuition Can Be Learned

It is a common myth to think that if one is not born with some kind of innate ability to excel in math, then it is not worth putting in the effort to try. It is a myth to think that there are those who are "good at math" and those who are not. This myth really has no basis for truth, and belief in the myth can be extremely detrimental to a child's performance in math, to the extent that the perception of futility is defeating. Of course it is true that some people do seem to have a particular aptitude for math. But that is true of any subject. Unfortunately, belief in the myth for math, as opposed to other subjects, seems to have much more of a negative effect than it does for other subjects. For example, somebody who wants to learn playing the piano may be well aware that he/she is not "a Mozart," and will never be "a Mozart," but that does not usually prevent him/her putting in maximal effort to learn the piano. Yet the same person may put in less effort into learning math, with the "excuse" that he/she is "not good at it." Think about it: the legacies of "grand master" figures in music and the arts do not prevent a person putting in a maximal effort to be the best that they can be, but people are more likely to have a negative attitude about their abilities for math. It is important to regard math on a par with other subjects and drop the myth that math is somehow different or more difficult than other subjects, or that fewer people can be "good at math." How is it possible to decide that one is "not good at math" before learning it, and before being *taught* the thinking skills that are required? The entire purpose of learning a subject is to acquire those skills *over time*, and thereby become competent at it. Yet many students (and parents) insist on believing that somehow, some people are born with a special set of skills that enable them to be "good at math" *straight away*. *I* certainly was *not* born with those skills. I had to learn them, practice them, cultivate them, and I had to work hard at it. Taking things to a more advanced level, I was not for example, born with the skill and intuition to solve university-level math and physics problems. The intuition and skill had to be learned. Yes, the *intuition* had to be *learned*.

    Math is like any other subject or endeavor in that the intuition and skill has to be learned and cultivated. Many parents and students think that intuition for math cannot be learned. It is simply not true. I have taught many students over the years, and have found it a great pleasure to be able to teach them *intuition*, and to see that intuition grow and develop, and to witness students then understanding how they can continue cultivating intuition themselves. As I mentioned, I had to go through that myself as a student. From grade school through to college, I did not understand everything straight away. On the contrary, new material was almost never intuitive. I had to work at it. It took time and effort and some figuring out of how to overcome the challenges and hurdles (see part 2 of this book for more details on techniques). I still managed to get top grades. By the time I left high school I had obtained an "A" grade in the most advanced high-school math exam available in England at that time ("S" level, Higher Mathematics), and I also passed the entrance exams for admission to the University of Oxford to study physics. Much credit is due to the extraordinary encouragement, dedication, and commitment of my teachers who took the time to give a few of us extra tuition after school. They did not have to do that, they did it voluntarily. At first I told my teachers I didn't want to take the University of Oxford entrance exam. It was too hard, I told them. They insisted that I could do it. In the end, I thought, "They have more experience then me, maybe they are right." I trusted them and I passed the exams.

The lesson from all this is that you have to build confidence and trust in your child, explaining to him/her why you believe he/she can succeed. This is age-old advice, and you have of course heard it before in many other contexts. However, the reason why I am telling you is that you may not realize just how much of a negative attitude *you* may be harboring about a person's ability to succeed and excel in math. You are, after all, a product of the same cultural forces. You must search within yourself and get rid of those negative attitudes and come to an understanding that they are unfounded. Think about what I have said about music and the arts. It simply does not make sense that math should be different. Yes, different parts of the brain are involved, but that in itself proves nothing. The problem lies with *expectation*. We don't expect a child to pick up a violin and become a virtuoso without practicing and *cultivating* the skills. Yet we expect a child to be introduced to new concepts in math and "get it" straight away.

The important thing for you to put into practice right away is to tell your child, if relevant, to stop using the phrase "I'm not good at math" and replace it with "All math skills can be learned and I can improve them all the time." In this chapter I hope to be able to show you some of the ways that you, as a parent, can help your child to develop intuition for math.

2.2 Case Study: The Calculus Student Who Forgot Her Multiplication Tables

Many years ago I was working with a bright and conscientious 12th-grade student studying calculus. I'll call her Kate, although that is not her real name. During a tutorial I asked Kate to solve a particular calculus problem in front of me. The problem involved first breaking down an algebraic expression into a number of simpler factors. The process involves a little bit of trial and error until the right factors are found (there is no set recipe for it). The trial-and-error process usually involves mentally multiplying pairs of integers and then adding the same integers in the pair, to see if a solution is possible with that pair of integers. The student struggled with it and was unable to do it, but it was in fact something an 8th-grade student should have been able to do. The student was unable to even attempt the calculus problem because she got stuck on this first stage. At first I was puzzled why Kate was stuck because she had up to then been very good at tackling calculus problems in general. I tried to give a clue and asked her, "What is 12 times 7?" This particular student was very good about calculators and did not try to grab one. However, I was absolutely horrified that she was completely stumped by the simple question. I was saddened at the realization that this bright and very capable 12th-grade student was unable to do a calculus problem because she had forgotten her multiplication tables, something that should have been second nature to her at least ten years earlier. However, Kate was honest with me and to herself, and I requested that she relearn her multiplication tables before the next lesson, and I told her that I was going to test her next time. Needless to say, this was embarrassing for her, but she understood that it was holding her back with 12th-grade math. The conclusion from this case study is so important that I will summarize it in boldface in the next paragraph.

There are many situations in advanced math topics, aside from the example that I have just given, for which forgetting how to do basic mental arithmetic (and how to do it quickly) can be a severe hindrance, but it may not be directly obvious to the student or teacher.

Obviously, the same lesson applies to less advanced topics as well, but the underlying message is the same. That is, speed, proficiency, and accuracy in basic mental arithmetic should be maintained *at all times*. It is common for a student to neglect the "simple stuff," especially when he/she has moved on to advanced topics, and not realize how much it is affecting overall performance in math. Oral drills, of the kind in appendix A of this book, should be used for regular *maintenance*, after they have been mastered the first time. I will say more about the oral drills in §2.7 and §3.6.

2.3 The Calculator Reflex

Over the years, from experience with one-to-one tutoring, I have noticed that students have evolved a new reflex that is becoming more and more commonplace. It consists of an extremely rapid motor response of one of the upper limbs when asked a simple arithmetic question. The limb reaches out to a nearby calculator at a speed approaching that of light, without intervention or engagement of the brain. When I first started to observe this remarkable phenomenon I was, aside from being alarmed and disappointed, curious to investigate the severity of the problem. So one day during a tutorial I asked a 9th-grade student, "What is one times zero?" Sure enough, the student's hand impulsively zipped towards the calculator. Fortunately, by this time I had evolved my own calculator reflex and managed to grab the calculator before the student did. With the calculator firmly in my possession, I shook my head and said, "What is one times zero?" The silence was heavy. The student was lost and could not answer the question. I had to tell him, and explain the answer. This was a student who was perfectly capable of understanding advanced concepts in algebra II but had forgotten how to do simple multiplication, and it was implicitly hindering his ability to be proficient at solving algebra problems. Unfortunately, this is an extremely common problem.

2.4 The Money Rule

I came across a very curious phenomenon early on in my teaching endeavors, and both parents and students should take full advantage of it. I found that if I asked a student a mental arithmetic question, especially one involving fractions, the student might struggle and struggle, and possibly give up, yet adding one simple word to the sentence would immediately, and rather miraculously, prompt the student to give the correct answer. That word is "dollar" (obviously you should use whatever currency is relevant for your country). I was astounded when I first came across this, and I have since verified that it seems to be a universal phenomenon. For example, I might ask a student, "What is three-halves minus a quarter?" The student may be completely stumped. Yet if I asked, "What is three-halves of a dollar minus a quarter of a dollar?" the student would often be able to immediately respond with, "A dollar and a quarter." This proves that the student already had the mental faculties and "wiring" in his/her brain to do the calculation, but the relevant part of the brain was not called up when the question was asked in abstract form.

I have found that the student is usually gobsmacked when he/she realizes that just inserting one word into the question can make such a disproportionate difference to him/her being able to do the mental calculation. I find this phenomenon very interesting, and it has many ramifications. It proves, in general, that *the way* in which materials and/or problems are presented to a student can make a disproportionate difference to the student's performance, which have nothing to do with the student's intrinsic ability. You, as a parent, can take full advantage of this, and use it to help your child with math. One obvious way that you can do this is to incorporate the "money rule" into the oral drill practice, whenever necessary (see §2.7 and §3.6). Some problems may not be amenable to applying the money rule, but you will always be able to think of at least one other way to present the same problem, if not more. You will find that analogies using time or sport are also effective because again, the mental faculties are already there, and practice is needed in accessing them in a different context. Eventually of course, once the student opens the pathways to accessing these underutilized faculties, he/she will no longer need to explicitly use the analogies. This entire phenomenon is an excellent illustration of how simple mental activity can lead to fast and irreversible improvement in performance in math.

As another concrete example, suppose your child is stuck on a problem that asks, "What average speed must a car travel at to cover 400 miles in 8 hours?" The question could be rephrased as, "If I spent $400 in 8 days, how much on average, did I spend per day?" A student will typically be able answer the second question quicker than the first. Yet the two questions are mathematically identical. Demonstrating the mathematical equivalence of problems like these and opening those mental pathways is something that you as a parent can easily help your child with. You will be amazed by the leveraging effect it has because once those pathways are opened, your child will experience benefits that are not even directly related to the specific kinds of problems that were used to open those pathways.

As you know very well, every parent naturally imparts to their kids a huge range and variety of skills and knowledge well before the kids go to school. This includes the money-counting skills that you teach your kids when you are out and about, shopping, or engaging in other activities, and you do it without even thinking because it is so natural. This is, I believe, the origin of the "money rule," and one of the reasons why it works, because the "wiring" has been set up by *you* even before school. Of course, it is a two-way process, often prompted by questions from the kids themselves. So why not go one step further? When you are out and about and talking to your kids, go beyond what you would normally talk about in terms of numeracy. You probably already go beyond money, but "push the envelope" and go further than you normally would.

Don't underestimate what your child is capable of, but *stretch* to what he/she is capable of. You will know if and when you have stretched too far, but most parents don't stretch far enough. You see, when you are talking to your child about numeracy while you are engaging in everyday activities, *it is in context*, and you should not pass up such golden opportunities to make use of the receptiveness of your child to learn. Such situations are *not abstract*. Once a math problem is abstracted, it is as if a giant gate closes, blocking off access to certain mental faculties. It requires training to keep those gates open. Taking advantage of situations that are not abstract, and that are in context, is an important means of transitioning smoothly to the abstract domain. In such "real-life" situations your child *is interested and asking questions!* How different is that from "Why do I need to know this?" The topics that a child will be interested in, and that are suitable for you to develop numeracy with on a par to money, are virtually endless. You have to find what is age-appropriate (there is really no age/grade limit for this) and what is of particular interest to your child if he/she is older. For the younger kids there is a host of universal topics in addition to money and shopping that you may not have considered using, such as gasoline, friends, birthdays, mail, weather, and temperature, to name only a few.

Finally, I will describe a powerful activity that you can do with your child, especially if he/she has studied, or is in the process of studying, fractions at school. Go to the bank, or rummage around the house, and get one hundred pennies. Also collect four quarters, ten dimes, and twenty nickels. Now play around with the hundred pennies, organizing them into various piles, attempting to make piles that each have an equal number of pennies. Place the higher denomination coins against each pile in order to remind yourselves of the number in each pile and its value. In this way your child will quickly develop an intuition for the decimal equivalent of fractions, and get a "feel" for various common fractions, including the addition of simple fractions and their decimal equivalents. For example, you could divide the hundred pennies into four equal groups, with the equivalent larger denomination coin placed next to each pile of pennies. The student will be able to see that one-fourth is equivalent to twenty-five parts of one hundred. Addition of fractions can be illustrated by moving different piles of coins next to each other.

You can go on to illustrate how an attempt to divide the hundred pennies into three equal piles leaves one penny left over, and you can explain that you would need to divide the final penny into three if you wanted to create three equal piles. Obviously, there are many more examples that you can easily explore. You can get even more sophisticated and play with *three* groups of one hundred coins to illustrate, for example, the addition of one-quarter and one-third. To do this you would divide one set of one hundred pennies into four piles, and the second set into three piles (perhaps using three pieces of paper to represent one-third of a penny). Then you move one pile from each of the above groups next to each other and add the number of pennies. This immediately gives you the decimal equivalent, but then you can challenge your child to estimate the fraction. Next, you go to the third set of one hundred pennies and use a trial-and-error procedure consisting of dividing the pennies into a varying number of groups (starting with say, eight). At each trial you ask how close can you get to (approximately) 58 pennies by choosing a number of these groups. You should find that six groups of ten pennies is a good estimate (i.e., $6/10$, or $3/5$), as is seven groups of eight pennies (i.e., $7/12$).

2.5 Developing a Habit of Looking for Mistakes

The two examples I described above (in §2.2 and §2.3), in which loss of proficiency in something very basic has a knock-on effect in degrading proficiency in more advanced topics, are illustrations of a common problem. I have observed the same phenomenon at various levels, going all the way up to college and Ph.D. level. It is not always the calculator or computer that is the culprit. It may not even be simple arithmetic that has been compromised. It could be a basic set of facts or principles that the student learns early on in a course of study, but then loses sight of those foundations by the time he/she gets close to completing the course. This then ultimately is reflected in some way as a hindrance with the more advanced material. The lesson to learn from this is that no matter what grade your child is in, never assume that the basic skills and fundamentals are sound. Just as the body needs regular maintenance, so does the brain!

Now let us return to the calculator, for there is one more severe problem in addition to the reflex action. Essentially, what has happened is that students are losing the ability to think about whether or not the answer they see on the little window of the calculator is nonsense. Never mind that the wrong key may have been hit by accident. Students are trusting everything that the calculator throws out at them. The quick, mental "sanity check" has been tossed out of the metaphorical window. I have seen this time and time again and a mistake like this can be disastrous, especially at the beginning of solving a math problem. Yet most of the time, simple "sanity checks," consisting of even a moment's reflection on the calculator's output, could have caught a problem and rectified it. I am not just talking about advanced calculator functions, but even simple arithmetic. Hitting the wrong key is a common cause of error, but not the only one. Another common cause is the improper use of parentheses in more complicated calculations. Even if the student properly understands the use of parentheses, it is easy to make mistakes. There are other types of common mistakes that involve graphing calculators and I will talk about these in chapter 4.

Trusting calculators and trusting one's ability to press the right keys accurately are not the only sources of error. It is normal for mistakes to be made by even the best students, when solving any kind of math problem, even in the traditional way. The key is to catch the mistakes before finishing with the problem. The ability to do frequent "sanity checks" is a skill that should be developed and cultivated. In fact it is absolutely critical if a student is to achieve his/her full potential and get the best possible grades in math. Ignoring the "sanity checking" process and the self-scrutiny skill may bring a student down by an entire grade or more. It makes no sense to put so much effort and time into studying hard, only to throw it all away because of the inability to catch mistakes. A student who does not put time into developing these skills is not being fair to himself/herself. The self-checking should be *an integral part of problem solving*. As a parent, this is a tangible and extremely effective way that you can help your child with math, without getting involved in the details.

Aside from regularly conveying the message to your child, you can help your child to develop the habit by talking about his/her homework on a regular basis. You can ask to look over the homework after your child has completed it, and then ask him/her whether he/she has checked the working and determined whether each answer seems reasonable. You do not need to understand how to solve the problems yourself and you do not need to go over the problems in any detail.

For some types of problems you will be able to determine yourself if an answer is *unreasonable* without working through the problem, or knowing how to work through it. For example, for a calculation of the area of a complex shape you will be able to tell if the answer is unreasonably large or small. For more abstract problems it will not be so obvious. It would be a good use of spending a small amount of money to have a tutor come for two to three lessons to help with teaching all the different techniques for "sanity checking" various types of problems (see chapter 5). It never ceases to amaze me how often students will neglect to see, even in the most obvious cases, that a particular answer simply cannot be correct. They are usually in a mad rush to get to the next question and be done with it. You should make the homework discussion as brief as possible because your child will already be tired and bored of the homework, and will be anxious to move on to doing other things. There are more tips on what you can do to check homework in chapter 3.

2.6 Developing Skills in Estimation

This is another skill that I think is so critically important, but yet again, it is rarely developed either in school or out of school. It also ties into what I have just said in §2.5 about developing "sanity-checking" and self-correction skills. In addition, the mental processing power that results from the practice of coming up with *approximate* answers to fairly difficult arithmetic problems is extremely far-reaching. The skill developed even at elementary-school level will stay with the student all the way to the end of his/her school career and beyond. If the practice is maintained all the way through school (with increasingly more complex problems) the result will be correspondingly more powerful. Estimation exercises are something I regularly do with students from elementary level all the way to Ph.D. level, in order to train them in developing intuition, usually in the form of oral drills (supplemented, for more advanced work, with written drills). This is a very powerful and high-return activity that you, as a parent of an elementary-school to high-school student, can easily and very effectively help your child with. Here I will simply illustrate with three examples, one for elementary-school level, one for middle-school level, and one for high-school level. There are some more examples in the oral drills designed for this purpose in appendix A of this book, on pages 339, 352, 358, and 360. Some of the questions in these estimation drills are more difficult and challenging than the three examples given below. Further general discussion on oral drills can be found in §2.7 and §3.6.

- **Elementary**

    Roughly what do you need to multiply 4 by to get 19? (Response time should be about 2 seconds or better.)
    Even if an elementary-school student has not explicitly covered division, this is fine, and it will help him/her to become comfortable with division when he/she has to do it. For this example the student should already be familiar with the multiplication tables of 4

and 5. The type of problem illustrated by this example practices mentally going through the first few lines of a multiplication table, invoking a trial-and-error procedure, and implementing a "mental decision tree." This is much more powerful training compared to simply asking, "What do you need to multiply 4 by to get 20?" since the student may simply recall the answer from memory.

- **Middle**

  Roughly what is 5/9 plus 1/5? The estimate is to be a simple fraction not a decimal. (Response time should be about 3 seconds or better.)

  Even though the question states that the answer should be a fraction, there is no rule against doing the estimation in decimals and then converting back, if that is easier. The student can use the money rule (§2.4), and reason that $1/9$ is about 11 cents, so $5/9$ is about 55 cents. A fifth of a dollar is 20 cents. So the sum is 75 cents, making the answer *roughly* $3/4$. This estimate is much faster than mentally doing the formal addition of fractions, which would give an exact answer of $34/45$ (equivalent to a decimal value of 0.7556). In any case, the question asked for a *simple* fraction. Note that the money rule could be used by an elementary-school student to estimate sums and differences of fractions even before the student has formally studied the addition and subtraction of fractions. For example, a student could estimate that $1/2$ plus $1/3$ is approximately equal to $4/5$ because 50 cents plus 33 cents is 83 cents, which is approximately $8/10$, or $4/5$.

- **High**

  Is $461 \times 12 \times 87$ smaller or larger than a half a million? (Response time should be about 2 seconds or better.)

  The student should reason that 12×87 is roughly $10 \times 100 = 1000$. Then, if 461 were instead 500, the answer would be half a million. But 461 is sufficiently smaller than 500 to make the answer less than half a million. (Note that this question is for illustration purposes and is in fact a bit too easy for high-school level, but the estimation oral drills on page 360 are more challenging.)

I will reiterate a point made in the second example because it is so important. That is, don't invent a rule that doesn't exist! If a student is asked to come up with an answer (or estimate), either orally, using mental arithmetic, or in writing, and the question does not state *how* to get the answer, then the student should use whatever method is easiest and quickest to get the result. That sounds obvious but you will be surprised how often a student will not use an allowed method, under the false assumption that a particular method is not allowed. A good general example that frequently comes up in tests at various levels of difficulty (from elementary-school to high-school level) is the numerical ordering of fractions. The student is given two or more fractions, which must be placed in a correct ascending or descending numerical sequence. This type of question is particularly common in standardized aptitude tests. Usually, no restriction is placed on the method. If it is a multiple-choice question, then there is definitely no restriction on the method. Under such circumstances, it is not illegal to convert the fractions to approximate decimal equivalents first. This can *sometimes* be much quicker than trying to manipulate all the fractions to have the same common denominator, which is what many students will try to do, thinking that converting to decimal equivalents is illegal in this type of question. In fact, a student may have been taught by a teacher that such a question *must* be done by getting all the fractions to have the same denominator. However, if the question places no restriction on the method, then a better and quicker route to the answer is not illegal.

So, the process a student should follow for ordering a set of fractions should actually be a flexible, case-by-case approach, following a few simple guidelines. First, if relevant, the student should immediately separate those fractions that are "top-heavy," and therefore greater than 1, from those that are less than 1, and this can be done by inspection. Next, the student should see if any of the fractions can easily be determined by inspection to be greater than, or smaller than a half. For example, 3/8 is obviously less than a half, and 5/9 is clearly greater than a half. Therefore 5/9 is greater than 3/8. Similar logic could be applied to determine whether a fraction is less than or greater than a quarter, and three-quarters. Next, the student should determine if any of the fractions *can* be rewritten to have the same denominator as another fraction in the list, simply upon inspection. Then, the student should do any necessary conversions of fractions into *approximate* decimal equivalents, and usually these can be done by inspection.

2.7 Oral Drills

Oral drills, which you can administer, are a powerful means of training the mind for improved mental agility, and for developing speed and accuracy. With appropriately chosen content for the drills, a student's "sanity-checking" ability can be greatly increased. The kind of skills imparted by the oral drills that I am talking about are learned, and no student should be excused from doing them, even if the student is getting top grades in math at the moment. In principle it is possible for a student to train himself/herself, but it is rare for a student to voluntarily do that, and it is harder to do it alone. Therefore you can play a critical role in helping your child develop the necessary mental agility by means of practicing oral drills with him/her.

A set of oral drills that you can administer on a regular basis is given in the appendix. You don't actually need to understand all of the material in these drills yourself. The answers are given with the drills, so all you need to do is ask the questions and communicate to your child whether the answer is right or wrong. Your role here is very important because it is something that you will be doing together with your child, and you will be discussing how he/she is doing and how speed and proficiency is developing and progressing. The topics of the drills are very simple. You should examine the drills themselves in the appendix for details. The time spent on each drill need not be very long and only approximately 10 to 20 minutes per session is recommended. Be aware that making a session any longer than this is likely to be counterproductive. The key is to make the process regular, and to repeat the drills over and over (in multiple sessions), in order to improve the success rate, in terms of speed, accuracy, and proficiency, until each drill is mastered. Whether the drills are done everyday or not will depend on individual circumstances and progress in each session. The more frequent the sessions are, the better, but if it is not possible to practice everyday then obviously something is better than nothing. The notes for each drill in the appendix describe expected outcomes in terms of response-time goals required before a drill can be said to have been mastered. After mastering each drill, it can then be practiced only occasionally, in particular just before exams.

The drills in the appendix are organized approximately by grade level using the three categories of elementary school, middle school, and high school. Start with developing *proficiency and speed* in basic multiplication at grade-appropriate levels and response times. There are also some exercises in the reverse of multiplication (breaking a number into two factors that multiply to give the number), as well as some exercises in squares of numbers and square roots. There are drills for practicing fractions and percentages at different levels of difficulty. In addition, there are some more advanced drills that are appropriate for precalculus and calculus students. The material covered by the set of all drills is very limited, but exhaustive coverage is *not* their purpose. Rather, the purpose is to get you started, so that you have a rough idea of how to compose your own drills on a particular topic, using material from your child's textbook (for example). If you are not comfortable with doing this yourself, in chapter 5 I will talk about how to get affordable tutoring help for this and other common needs.

Do not be fooled by the simplicity of the oral drills. Although the drills cover only a tiny fraction of what a student is supposed to know, and they are just a start, the topics that *are* covered are absolutely fundamental. I cannot overemphasize how developing speed and accuracy in these drills will go a very long way towards helping your child with math for years, even after he/she leaves school. At the very least, it absolutely makes sense that the less time a student spends on the "easy stuff" in an exam, the more time he/she has left to figure out the "hard stuff." Sadly, I see too often such a simple principle unappreciated by students all the way from elementary school up to the Ph.D. level. Once again, you as a parent can be pivotal in helping your child with math without "knowing any yourself," by instilling this principle over and over again. Yet the principle is so obvious in some sense, that it is repeatedly ignored by students to their peril.

Of course, part of the problem is that the drills do appear to be too easy. *You* might even think they are too easy. It is a big mistake to think so. Your job in getting your child to cooperate with the drills will be a difficult one because he/she is likely to think that some of the drills are patronizing and insulting. In fact the drills look so easy that your child, and at first perhaps you, may have a hard time seeing how they can help, let alone help profoundly. The key is of course developing speed and accuracy to the point where conscious thought processes are substantially bypassed, as is the case for something like driving a car. After learning to drive, part of the process becomes hardwired into the brain so that you don't have to consciously think of every detailed part of the task. That hardwiring is what you and your child are aiming to get out of the drills. In the same way that you can look at a driving test layout and say that it's easy, you can do that with the drills. But reserve judgment until you have made a serious attempt to do them properly.

So, be prepared to hear all kinds of objections. "I know this already. I can already do these quickly. I'm already good at these. How is this going to help?" You have to explain to your child that even if he/she is already good at these, if he/she could do the exercises two to three times faster (accurately), *it will leave more time in an exam situation to do the harder problems.* It will also increase the likelihood of getting the harder problems right because the drills help to develop an intuition for being able to spot mistakes. Isn't it better to be able to do the "easy stuff" more accurately and quickly without much thinking, and to then consequently be in a better position to do the "harder stuff" more accurately and quickly as well? Why throw away points in an exam by taking too long over the "no-brainer" material?

The leveraging power of the oral drills in improving grades in math across the board is enormous. I often use drills like the ones in the appendix (and more advanced, topic-specific ones) in my tutorials with students. The attitude that you should take towards persuading your child to cooperate with the drills will obviously depend on many factors. Let's face it, it is boring and tedious doing these drills. But they must be done. The end goal in the "big picture" should be the motivating factor. Anybody who wants to do anything worthwhile has to go through some sort of rigorous training, not all of which is fun and exciting. Math is no exception. If you like, you can implement a reward system. You know your child best, and you will be able to figure out what works.

With an older student you may be able to skip the multiplication drills, but don't *assume* that the student's competence is satisfactory in this area. Remember my story about the bright calculus 12th grader who had forgotten her multiplication tables (§2.2)? If your child has a problem with proficiency in multiplication it will likely show up elsewhere and at that point you will have to explain that you both need to backtrack and work on the multiplication. If you are not comfortable with administering the drills yourself, or if you meet with too much resistance, encourage your child to do the oral drills with a friend. The friend could also benefit from reciprocation.

For the older students who present a high resistance to the oral drills, I strongly encourage you to be persistent in finding some way for your child to benefit from them. The oral drills concerning estimation exercises are particularly critical, and actually, the middle-school and high-school estimation drills *are hard and challenging* (see pages 358 and 360). I simply cannot overemphasize the high-leveraging and far-reaching effects of these estimation drills in particular. The estimation drills are especially important for enhancing intuition, and the capabilities to spot mistakes in one's own work, and I have already talked about the central role that these two skills play in a student's performance in math. All of the oral drills have been carefully designed and crafted. If the drills (and extensions of them) are mastered, you will be astounded by the improvement in performance (speed and accuracy) in solving a huge range of math problems that may have nothing to do with the actual content of the drills.

If you continue to meet with resistance to the oral drills, consider having a local college student to help out (see chapter 5 on tutoring). If you can't afford to pay a student, consider offering a good hearty meal in exchange for a session. College students are always hungry, especially for home-cooked food, and will often go to great lengths to avoid spending money on food (as opposed to other things). I will discuss in chapter 5 the "ins and outs" of how to go about finding a suitable tutor that you can afford, and how to make optimal use of tutoring, especially if you can only afford a limited amount of it.

2.8   Skills That Online Math Aids Can and Cannot Provide

You are most likely aware that these days there are a vast number, and a variety of, lets say, math aids available in the form of software tools and internet resources. You may be wondering whether these could help as much, or more than, the methods I have discussed. The answer is not simple. There is no doubt that such tools can be extremely valuable and helpful. By all means use whatever you can that works with the particular needs and personality of your child. You won't know until you try because every child is unique. Moreover, I encourage you to use as many different techniques as possible, find the ones that work best, and use them.

However, you must remember that there are some *critical skills that cannot be developed and improved by software or online resources*, simply because of the very nature of those tools. I have touched on the most important of these skills already and I will come back to this issue now. The most important of these processes is that of working out a written solution that involves multiple steps, developing an intuition for spotting mistakes along the way, and correcting them to reach the final solution.

Learning how to tell if you have veered off the correct path to the solution to a problem is as much a part of the problem-solving process as knowing how to solve the problem in the first place. This simple and straightforward fact is so underappreciated that I will repeat myself. It is common to think that making mistakes and veering off the path towards the correct solution to a problem is a temporary state of affairs that will soon be eliminated with practice. It is not true. *Making mistakes is part of the problem-solving process and knowing when you have made a mistake, or obtained an unreasonable answer, is part of the problem-solving process.*

No matter how good you are at solving a problem, the possibility of making a mistake will always be there. Now, you may argue that software or similar tools could in principle help to develop the necessary skill and intuition. You may argue that a software tool could lead a student through a step-by-step process and produce a loud beep every time the student makes a mistake or veers off the path. Let me ask you this: when your child is sitting in the examination room, is there going to be a loud beep every time he/she makes a mistake or veers off the correct path? No, of course not. The student must absolutely develop ways to spot his/her own mistakes. In a test or exam situation nobody is going to ring a buzzer. This skill of tracing back and finding your own mistakes *is* one of the skills that *will* be important and of *practical use* in later life because the process is similar, whether or not it is a math problem. You and I know only too well that nobody is going to ring a warning buzzer when a mistake is made in real life.

Let me also tell you about my own circumstances. I often have to solve math or physics problems as part of my research. If I am going to solve a problem of any substance tomorrow, say, even if it involves techniques and methods that I have been using for decades, I can predict that I will very likely make a mistake before coming to the solution. But I also know that I will be able to realize that I have made a mistake, hopefully without wasting too much time on the wrong path. Ten years ago it would have taken me longer to figure out when I had veered off the path, and twenty years ago it would have taken me even longer. You get the idea.

Earlier, I discussed how most of the actual math content that kids learn in school will never be used in real life by most of the kids. Well, you as an adult are only too well aware that the aspect of developing the skill and intuition to know when you have made a mistake is precisely the kind of skill that *is* useful in real life, professional or otherwise. The quick "sanity check," the rough estimate, the look and feel of a solution in relation to other solutions to similar problems, are all valuable practical skills.

Any software engineer will tell you that a major part of software development is the debugging: writing the initial code is relatively easy, but finding the mistakes and flaws, and iterating to make everything work and function as intended is the hard part, and it often constitutes the main substance of the work. That's just one example. You will be able to think of hundreds more, and as you do, you will realize that almost everything we do that challenges us involves a similar process. This sort of thing is precisely what you should be telling your child if he/she quizzes you along the lines of "Why do I need to learn something that I'm never going to use?" Isn't the answer easy now? Then fold in the perseverance that is required to solve a stubbornly difficulty problem. Essentially everything that you will do that is meaningful and challenging to you will benefit from the skills that you learn from solving math problems, if you develop those skills.

There is another important thing to remember about software math aids. Most of them work on *visual* cues, although some do have restricted audio cues. However, it is vital not to neglect cues that are not machine-made. The oral drills can provide certain benefits that a machine cannot, one of them obviously being the engagement with a real human. More importantly, the oral drills provide no "safety nets," or "mental crutches." No calculators are allowed and no writing is allowed. The brain goes into "free fall," and the student is forced into forging mental pathways that may not have been there before, or were "shaky" at best. This is especially true of the "estimation skills" oral drills (see pages 339, 352, 358, and 360), which can be *very hard and challenging* at first, but extremely rewarding when they are mastered. The oral drills are discussed further in §3.6 and in the appendix). Software aids cannot replace oral drills delivered by a human, it is as simple as that.

Nevertheless, the software aids are still useful for building speed and efficiency, triggered by artificial cues, as long as it is remembered that this is only a part of what is needed. You can easily demonstrate differences for yourself by taking some of the questions that your child might be practicing with a software aid, and testing your child orally, noting the difference in results (accuracy and response time) for the same questions.

It is difficult to come up with recommendations of what is good and not so good in terms of software aids in general, but my general advice would be to assess the *efficiency* of the aid. Figure out from the typical amount of time that a child will spend with the aid and what the net outcome (in a "best-case scenario") is likely to be. Is the amount of time expended worth the return? Could more be gained in less time by other methods that do not involve any software or computers? All too often I see instances of "technology in teaching" or "technology in the classroom" when there is no real justification for it. Advantages over other methods have to be *demonstrated* and not simply *assumed*. In this respect, a "research shows..." type of statement has no value if no details on the study are provided, since there is no information on the parameters, the methodology, or the measurement tools and criteria. Sometimes technology is used simply because there has been a blanket "mandate" from higher up in the command chain in an institution, and not because it is better suited for a particular purpose. As far as "technology in the classroom" goes, sometimes it is better suited for a particular purpose than other methods, sometimes it is neither better nor worse, but sometimes it *is* worse than other methods.

Related to the software tools discussed above, there is plenty of software that is in the form of an actual game, albeit designed to help with math skills. Again, there are cues in this type of setting that are different to other methods, and actually different to what might be useful in real life. Similar comments apply to the "online homework" tools that come with some textbooks these days. The mental processes compared to writing out extended solutions completely by hand are different. It is difficult to assess the impact on what is lost if traditional methods are abandoned, but you should be wary of it. What is clear, and always has been, is that anything that detaches a student from the actual subject matter and content, takes the student one step away from developing intuition. It is the "detachment factor" that is difficult to assess in some cases.

I very often see advice given to parents that essentially amounts to the philosophy that motivating a child to perform better in math is as simple as making math fun, culminating in the conclusion that math games are a major solution to the problem. However, an important factor to bear in mind is that math games (whether they are computerized or not) only ever address very elementary skills, and cover only a very tiny portion of the material that a student must learn during his/her entire time at school. Thus, even if games are successful in improving your child's performance in math, they can only ever be a temporary measure that is relevant only for a relatively short fraction of the time that your child is at school. You cannot therefore rely on games for long-term motivation. For example, it is very unlikely that a 12th-grade calculus student is suddenly going to become inspired and motivated from the memory of a game that he/she played ten years earlier.

A teacher once said to me, after returning from a very large national math teacher's "expo," that it was "like being in an amusement arcade," referring to the overwhelming noise and colorful lights emanating from large numbers of computer games and applications. That says it all. It is a fact that countries that currently rate highest in international math literacy levels rated highly well *before* the ubiquitous use of "technology in the classroom." Math literacy was not achieved by turning the classroom into an amusement arcade. It is another fact that "technology in the classroom" has not propelled the countries that rate poorly in math literacy "through the roof." Some people argue that "rote learning" methods are responsible for high performance in math in countries with high math literacy levels, and "we don't believe in that." This argument does not "fly" because, compared to other subjects, there is relatively very little "rote learning" to do in math. High performance in math is about understanding concepts, developing intuition, and problem solving. A student can do all the "rote learning" that is necessary and yet still be unable to solve math problems. I have witnessed this many times.

One type of internet resource that has become widely available in recent years is the video tutorial. There are many websites now that offer free video tutorials on a large range of topics in math, covering the entire range in grade level. These are certainly worth checking out, especially if your child has missed some classes. However, if the relevant classes have not been missed, studying with videos can be more time-consuming than studying from books. As a parent you can help by determining when the use of video tutorials is appropriate, case-by-case. Some links to video tutorials can be found at http://www.helpyourchildwithmath.com. Since a major downside of video tutorials is that the student cannot interrupt in order to ask questions, one possibility is for you to play the role that the video tutor cannot. This would be feasible if you watch the video with your child, and if you already know the material, or else if the video is enough of a memory jogger for you to be able to answer any questions that your child might have. You may not, of course, know in advance whether you will be able to answer a particular question, but why not just try it?

2.9 Application-Oriented Teaching and Motivation

Although I have said that parents and teachers should be honest with students about how much of the math that they learn at school will be *directly* useful to them after school, I am not advocating purely abstract teaching of math. On the contrary, math should be taught in the context of applications whenever possible, because it is naturally more interesting and motivating for most students than a purely abstract approach. What you can do to help, as a parent, is to leverage your child's interests and hobbies. What are the things that your child is most passionate about? Math has such a vast arena of applicability, from sports to astronomy, that the chances that people have written about the connection between math and a particular topic are very high. Encourage your child to read such material (preferably books), as it will provide motivation and inspiration for the math itself. If the available material is too difficult for your child to read because it is beyond his/her grade level, then I suggest that *you* read it yourself and then discuss and talk about what you learned with your child.

School math textbooks have improved significantly over the last couple of decades, in terms of adopting a more application-oriented approach. However, there is room for much more improvement. In particular, in the capacity of both a professional astronomer, and a math educator, I can tell you that a large proportion of kids of all ages find astronomy inspiring and fascinating. It is an important fact that astronomy is capable of demonstrating the direct application of a huge range of math, from the very elementary topics to the most advanced topics that students must learn at school. I therefore find it shocking that students' natural, and apparently ubiquitous, curiosity about space science is still heavily underutilized in the school math curriculum and in school math textbooks. Certainly, there has been considerable progress in incorporating advances in astronomy into the science curriculum, but such applications have yet to make their way explicitly into the math curriculum.

Direct incorporation into the math curriculum is manifestly different to incorporation into the science curriculum. Most surprising is the fact that the current teaching of geometry in schools makes very little use of astronomical applications, yet many aspects of geometry permeate astronomy in very fundamental ways. The current geometry curriculum consists of a long string of boring proofs, theorems, and abstract calculations, rarely with inspiring contexts and applications. It is not necessary to compromise rigor and content if interesting applications are introduced, so the fear of sacrificing rigor and content cannot be the reason for the lack of progress. I hope this situation will change in the near future, especially as over 500 planets outside our solar system have now been identified, and the very first Earth-sized, possibly habitable, planets have been discovered. As a parent, you don't have to wait until the time that the applications aspect of the math curriculum becomes less boring for kids. Utilize what you know already to inspire and motivate. Then learn more, together with your child. You can find some useful pointers on the website http://www.helpyourchildwithmath.com.

Chapter 3

Daily Power Tips

In this chapter I will talk about what you, as a parent, can do on a day-to-day basis to help your child with math without knowing how to do the math yourself. If you *do* know the material, all the better for you and your child, but the purpose of this book is to first and foremost help the majority of parents, who are no longer familiar with most of the material. I will emphasize again that many of the things that I will talk about may seem obvious, but their importance should not be underestimated. As simple as some of the activities and procedures may seem, I have found that they are *very often not implemented.* Ignoring one item may have a small impact, but the compounded effect of ignoring many of the items can have very detrimental results. Once poor results set in, a student can become discouraged and disinterested in the work, and from there spiral down into further poor performance, setting off a vicious cycle. A key point to remember, which you should teach your child, is that *clarity of thinking* (for solving a math problem) can be directly and very powerfully impacted by the *clarity of implementation.* For example, trying to solve a problem with a blunt pencil, drawing a diagram that is too small, or laying out the working of a problem in a muddled fashion, can all result in muddled thinking, which makes it hard or impossible to catch mistakes.

While some of the advice in this chapter is aimed primarily at the younger students (8th grade and below), for the older students you should (subtly) check whether they are "healthy" in each "department." You could also administer the oral drills (see §2.7, §3.6, and appendix A) that are appropriate according to the student's particular weaknesses (you may not know what these are until you try all the relevant oral drills). The older student will object strongly to the oral drills but you must be persistent (see discussion in §2.7). Remind him/her about the case of the calculus student whose performance in calculus was compromised because she had forgotten her multiplication tables (see §2.2). Also explain that the oral drills are a good excuse for personal interaction, which is hard to come by these days with everybody being so busy. If you still encounter resistance, you could suggest, as I mentioned previously, that your child get together with a friend and administer the oral drills to each other.

Remind your child also that one of the aims of the oral drills, which seem deceptively simple, is to develop and improve speed. This is especially important for an older student, who may think that the oral drills are too easy and that he/she has already mastered the skills.

Every minute that a student saves in an exam by doing the easy and "bread-and-butter" material FAST is like gold dust for making more time for the harder problems.

Finally, have the older student read part 2 of this book, which describes study techniques and exam preparation techniques in more detail. For the younger student, read part 2 of the book yourself and disseminate the advice on a regular basis.

3.1 Date It to Organize It

All too often I come across students whose folders are stuffed with a chaotic bundle of worksheets, handouts, and other material. When it comes to putting these loose sheets into the folder into some kind of order, any mortal would have difficulty figuring out the order in which they should go. How is it possible to review a subject when the notes and worksheets are messed up? How is it possible for the mind to create that critical map and network for the material, something that is required in order to solidify understanding and mental processing of a subject? How can you, as a parent, keep up with not only what your child has been studying, but *when* a topic was covered in relation to other topics, if the folder is a mess?

Keeping the work organized is a minimal, yet critical step towards improving a student's performance in math (and of course in any other subject). We all know that some people are better organizers than others. I am not a great organizer myself. However, the good news is that you or your child don't need to be "super-duper" organizers. There is something extremely simple that a student can do which will make a huge difference. That is, whenever he/she receives *any* piece of paper from school whatsoever (worksheets, notes, quizzes etc.), he/she should put a date on it. You can help your child to make it a habit to do this *every single day*. He/she should *put a date on every single piece of paper (or group of papers), including any additional notes of his/her own, and on all homework assignments, as soon as the material is in his/her hands!* If not immediately, it should certainly be done by the end of the day. Even if only two or three days pass without doing this, the task will again becoming daunting and before you know it, that folder will be a mess again. At least if every single scrap of paper has a date on it, any backlog in organization will be a "no-brainer" to fix. That way a student can put stuff away into a folder in at least *roughly* the right order. After all, how many pieces, or groups, of paper for one subject can a student get from school on a given day? Rarely more than ten. You have probably witnessed yourself the enormous amount of time wasted as a student tries to figure out where even one piece of "stray" work should fit in the folder.

3.2 Materials and Supplies Check

Younger students will often not tell you if they have lost something or if they have "run out" of something, and they will try to get by without the missing item rather than tell you. Obviously, you cannot ask all the time, but keep an eye out for clues. For example, lines drawn without a ruler may indicate that the ruler is lost. Graphs drawn with a pen rather than a pencil may indicate that there are no pencils. The sudden appearance of thick writing and/or illegible graphs may indicate that a pencil sharpener has been lost.

3.3 What Did Your Child Study Today?

Make a point of asking your child as regularly as possible what he/she studied in math on a given day, or what he/she has been studying recently. Many parents shy away from this because they are not sure what to do with the answer, often because they may be apprehensive of finding out that they do not know anything about the topic. However, after asking the question, you may not actually have to do anything with the information. The fact that you have asked conveys to your child that you are taking an interest in what he/she is doing in math, and it will go a long way towards building the child's confidence for the subject, and for maintaining a conscientious and consistent input of effort. Your child may not want to get into explanations of what the topic entails, but now you have the crib sheet in part 3 of this book to help you at least attain a basic understanding of the topic (also see discussion in §1.2). The crib sheet has been especially designed for you, for the specific purpose of disseminating enough information on a topic so that you can at least begin to engage in a meaningful conversation with your child about what he/she is studying.

You may actually be surprised about how knowledgeable your child is, and that *starting* such a conversation is sufficient for your child to teach *you* about the topic. You may already know something about a particular topic, or you may have completely forgotten everything about it, the information having been buried in the murky depths for years. You should not feel embarrassed about looking it up in front of your child; in fact you can turn it into a joint activity. With nonmath or nonscience subjects I often tell my kids that I studied "that topic" a long time ago but have no clue anymore about it, and I ask *them* to give me a brief reminder (they don't always have the patience to do so). Being older, we have the excuse that our memories have been beaten down! The information in the crib sheet is nontechnical, devoid of unnecessary details that you don't need to know, but sufficient in accuracy and depth to give you a working understanding of what your child is doing in math. In other words, the information has been tailored and carefully crafted for the exact context that you need it. The crib sheet covers material from 1st grade all the way to 12th grade. As I mentioned at the beginning of this book, it is generally not recommended to do the lookup on the internet (unless you are looking at a specific, focused website) because there is so much information that is out of context and sometimes of questionable reliability, that it is very time-consuming and tedious.

You should also regularly ask your child if there was anything he/she studied on a given day that he/she found difficult and/or didn't understand. Most of the time no action will be required, aside from recommending that he/she tell the teacher. Make a note of it, and if there are frequent issues then consider contacting and/or meeting the teacher, or getting help from a tutor (see chapter 5, which describes in detail how this can be done, on a very limited budget if necessary).

3.4 Studying Techniques and the Study Environment

This section is mostly for the younger students (8th grade and below). For the older students the advice on study techniques in part 2 of this book is more appropriate, especially with respect to self-study and preparation for exams.

You are already probably aware of the need to respect the fact that concentration can only be maintained for limited periods at a time. There is a tendency, when one concentration period comes to an end, for a person to get distracted and flounder rather than take a short break and start again. There are of course many factors that can affect how long a typical concentration period is, obviously including the level of fatigue. Your child may not be aware of this so ensure that he/she gets to know himself/herself well enough to recognize the different phases of concentration periods and to be able to relate them to how tired he/she is.

If the homework seems to be taking too long, try to figure out why. The following may sound obvious but it is important to systematically ascertain which factors are relevant, by elimination. Your child may not know himself/herself well enough in this respect, so you may have to "passively" observe a couple of homework sessions (which may not be so easy, however). Are there distractions that could be the culprit that could be eliminated (for example, noise, or a desk facing a window)? Is there excessive fatigue from trying to fit too many activities in the day (in which case consider whether something should be eliminated). Or is it because your child is having difficulty with understanding the work? I will say more about what to do if this is the case in chapter 5, but if your child is doing fine with the homework but underperforming in tests, there is one more thing you can do. That is, take previous relevant pieces of homework (which should now be easy to find if you have followed the advice in §3.1), and have your child do some of them again even if he/she got an excellent score the first time. You will have to make a photocopy to cover up the answers and working so that only the questions show on the paper.

Your child will likely object very strongly to the assignment, so you will have to work at some persuasion techniques and/or a reward system. I also recommend that you stay in your child's room and passively supervise whilst he/she is doing the work (read a book or something). If he/she gets really stuck, allow him/her to take a quick look at the original solution, then put it away and try again. This technique of trying to recall, taking a quick look, and trying again (in several iterations if necessary) is extremely powerful for building long-term memory and mental skill. I will say more about this in chapter 7 (particularly in §7.2).

3.5 Homework Checklist

Even if you are familiar with the material in the homework, you are very unlikely to have time to check everything in meticulous detail. However, you can go a long way with a few key checks. First of all, ask your child if he/she has checked whether any of the answers or solutions seem blatantly unreasonable. If he/she says that has not been done, hand the homework back and ask to see it again when it is done (it should not take very long so you can wait while it is being done). In chapter 2, I discussed the techniques that a student should develop for enhancing intuition, estimation skills, and the ability to find his/her own mistakes. If you have not already read chapter 2, you should do so before continuing.

Then go through the following checklist. Again, many of these things are obvious, but having them all written down will ensure that you don't miss anything yourself.

- Were any of the questions inadvertently missed?

- Is the work neat and legible enough? If not, it will have to be done again. Was the work done with a sharp enough pencil?

- Are the diagrams and labels large enough?

- If there are any graphs, do they conform to the graph checklists in §4.1.2 and §4.1.3?

- Is the layout of the working orderly? It is common for a student to start off with large writing, not anticipating the number of steps required for a solution, and then run out of space. Consequently, the student will jump from one side of the page to the other, and possibly back again, trying to squeeze everything into tiny spaces. This sort of thing inevitably leads to muddled thinking, mistakes, and incorrect solutions because it is difficult to maintain continuity in thinking from one step to the next. It is also very difficult to spot mistakes, both while the solution is being written out, and while tracing back afterwards. If this has occurred you must request that the work be done again from the beginning, erasing the previous attempt if it has to be done on a worksheet. This time the problem is to be done with smaller writing, laying out each step logically from left to right, top to bottom, without jumping back and forth from one place on the paper to another.

3.6 Administering Oral Drills

I have already talked about the motivation and technical details for administering oral drills in §2.7. These should be done as and when necessary. There may be a shortage of time during the week but if your child is underperforming, the oral drills should be given a high priority and should be done as frequently as possible. If your child is doing fine but wants to raise his/her grades and performance level, the drills could be done at weekends if it is not possible to fit them in during the week. The drills (in the appendix) are organized roughly by school academic level (elementary-school, middle- to high-school levels, and a set for precalculus and calculus students), as well as by topic. Some of the drills are harder than others. Each drill has an approximate response-time goal and each set should be practiced until the goal is achieved or surpassed to your satisfaction. After that, each drill can be used occasionally for *maintenance*. Each drill only has a limited number of questions but you can make up more questions of a similar nature if necessary (perhaps with the help of a teacher or tutor). New drills can be also be made on additional topics, as appropriate. Refer also to the discussions in §2.7 and §5.5.6.

Chapter 4

Graphs and the Graphing Calculator

In this chapter I will cover both hand-drawn graphs and the graphing calculator. The latter is only needed for algebra II and above, although I understand that some schools in the US are now requiring that a graphing calculator be purchased for algebra I. However, there is nothing that is covered in algebra I that cannot be done without a graphing calculator.

4.1 Hand-Drawn Graphs

One of the most common areas in which a student will let himself/herself down and unnecessarily throw away points in assignments and exams is the neglect of some basic graphing essentials. There are many types of graphs but there are many skills common to all of them. You may recall the most common types of graph, which I list below:

- bar graph
- histogram
- line graph
- pie chart
- box and whisker plot

- scatter plot

In the spirit of the title of this book, I am not going to go into details about all of these different types of graphs if you have forgotten things yourself (although some details are provided in part 3 of this book, the crib sheet). In my experience, most students have a good understanding of the mechanics of the graphs that they study, and your child can probably do a pretty good job of explaining things to you if you have forgotten. What the students have difficulty with is interpreting the question, translating unfamiliar data into a graph, and indeed, interpreting the results.

A natural tendency is for a student to read the question and immediately jump into constructing the graph. What the student *should* do is browse the data, ingest the data, think about the data, and then read the question again in the context of having mentally scanned and processed the data. For hand-drawn graphs there are rarely going to be more than 20 or so data points. When browsing the data, the student should be looking for getting a sense of the numerical ranges of each set (or group) of data points. The student should also be thinking about what the numbers mean in the context of the question while scanning the data. In some cases there may be a pattern that emerges even from a quick scan.

4.1.1 Scale, Axes, and Resolution

For graphs that require numerical values on the axes (line graphs, scatter plots, histograms, bar graphs) a major problem area is that the scale and tick marks on the axes are poorly chosen. The student should calculate, using the minimum and maximum range of the data, what correspondence there should be between intervals in the data and intervals on the graph paper (boxes, tick marks, or actual length measurements). Any special instructions in the question should be taken into consideration (for example, whether an axis is to be started at the value of zero, even if the minimum value of the data is far away from zero). If the smallest tick mark or box on the graph paper is too small there will be cramming of data points, resulting in a mess. Judgement should be exercised by the student in deciding upon the optimal scaling. If it turns out to be a poor choice, the student should not hesitate to erase the graph and start again. Mistakes are often made in calculating the scale factor. If the student is having problems with the axes and scaling you should have him/her practice additional problems of a similar type. You may be able to make these up yourself or find similar problems in a textbook. Alternatively, practice with setting up graphs correctly would be an excellent use of what I call "targeted tutoring." A couple of lessons in this area will have a large, long-term payoff, which is especially important if your funds are limited. See chapter 5 (§5.5) for a more detailed discussion of targeted tutoring.

4.1.2 Hand-Drawn Graphs: Basic Checklist

There are other common problems with hand-drawn graphs and these are summarized in a checklist below. Each of the items is fairly obvious but they can all become compounded, resulting in large and unnecessary losses in points and performance.

- Was the pencil used sharp enough?
- Is the graph large enough, with no excessive cramming of writing or data points?
- If relevant, was the choice of scaling reasonable? Are there any particular regions of the graph for which the cramming of data points is still a problem?
- Is there a title on the graph?
- Are *all* straight lines drawn using a ruler or straight edge?
- If relevant, are the axes clearly labeled (i.e., annotated by labels that indicate what each of the axes represents)?

- If relevant, are the tick marks sloppy (i.e., scribbled rather than neatly marked, short, vertical or horizontal ticks)?

- If relevant, are there a sufficient number of numerical values written along the axes? For bar graphs, is there an identification displaying what each bar represents?

- If there are additional labels or annotation, are they neat and legible? For pie charts, is the annotation too small for the size of the circle and segments?

- For pie charts the circle should not be drawn by hand. Either a compass or a template should be used. Angles should be measured accurately, and segment lines should be drawn with a ruler or other straight edge.

- If relevant, check that the data points are neat and not "blotchy." They should either be marked by crosses, empty circles with a dot in the middle, and/or they should conform to any special instructions in the question.

- If relevant, if any data points need to be joined (or overlaid) with a smooth curve, check that the curve is in fact smooth and not disjoint.

4.1.3 Advanced Graphing Errors

In this section I will discuss some advanced graphing techniques, and then I will discuss further common mistakes that students make in hand-drawn graphs. From the earliest studies in math, students are required to *sketch* graphs of *functions*. The graphs become more and more complex as the student progresses to more and more advanced math, and in the later years a student should be able to sketch graphs without necessarily using graph paper. The graph may or may not be part of a larger question. The purpose of these sketches is to demonstrate certain key features of the behavior of the graph. It is important to realize that a hand-drawn graph need not be "perfect" in terms of artistic quality. The important thing is that the key features should be shown, and they should be shown correctly. This is especially true when a sketch is required to be rendered on plain, "ungridded" paper that is not graphing paper. I will not go into great detail because students usually have a pretty good idea of the mechanics, which they can explain to you. However, I will tell you enough for you to be able to check for mistakes, and to enforce implementation of the correct methods, asking the student to repeat the work if necessary. The most important features that are usually requested to be displayed in the graph of a function are listed below. Some of them may not be relevant for every graph since the list is meant to cover the most complex cases. Note that the list of items below covers points *in addition* to the basics already discussed in §4.1.1 and §4.1.2. I will illustrate the common mistakes with examples to clarify the items described in the list below.

- Whether or not the curve (or curves) cross or touch either or both of the horizontal and vertical axes should be clearly demonstrated.

- Whenever relevant, the points at which the axes are crossed by the function usually need to be marked. By this I mean that the numerical values of the horizontal and vertical coordinates on the horizontal and vertical axes respectively need to be marked.

- The manner in which the graph behaves at the extreme ends in the horizontal directions (left and right) *and* at the extreme ends in the vertical directions (top and bottom) needs to be clearly demonstrated.

- The positions and/or equations of straight lines called *asymptotes* (consult the crib sheet in part 3 of this book), should be clearly marked. Usually the *asymptote* lines are horizontal or vertical but they could alternatively be slanting. Not all functions have *asymptotes*, but for those that do, the graph of the function can get closer and closer to an *asymptote* but never reaches it (by definition of an *asymptote*). The curve (or curves) should never touch the *asymptotes*, but should *approach* them without touching. In some cases the curves may *cross* an *asymptote* but, by definition, the graph must turn back again, and there has to be a region where the function approaches the line again but never reaches it. There is a subtle difference between *crossing* an *asymptote* and *touching* it.

- The places where the curve "turns around," forming a "hump" or a "valley," should be smooth and not "pointy," unless the actual function is "pointy" in those places. The student usually knows if it should or should not be "pointy," but is often sloppy in sketching. The value of the horizontal coordinate on the horizontal axis corresponding to each hump and valley usually needs to be marked. Sometimes the vertical coordinate at the "hump" or "valley" also needs to be marked.

An important thing to remember is that the graph of some functions is broken into two or more disjoint pieces. I will now, just briefly, go *against* the title of this book somewhat, and illustrate with an example, so I will need to get into some technicalities. It is difficult to illustrate what you should be looking for without going into some detail. The example I will discuss will also serve to help illustrate some common difficulties that students experience with a graphing calculator that will be discussed later in §4.4.

Let's sketch the graph of a particular function as an example. We will graph the values of the function (*output*, or y) on the vertical axis against values of the *input* (or x), on the horizontal axis [1]. Figure 4.1 shows a hand-drawn graph of the function. This is an example of one of the most

---

[1] For those who are interested, the function is $y = 2 + [2/(1 - x^2)]$.

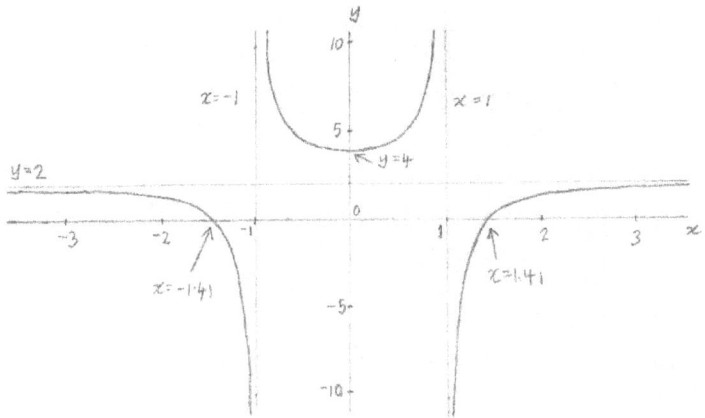

Figure 4.1: A hand-drawn graph illustrating all of the essential features of the graph of a particular function (see §4.1.3). In figures 4.2 to 4.9 the same graph is drawn with different (deliberate) errors that correspond to common mistakes that students make, and that lead to unnecessary loss of points. These common mistakes also lead to a hindrance for developing intuition for understanding the graphs of functions in general. *Note that this graph, and all the other graphs shown in figures 4.2 to 4.9, and in figure 4.13, should be clearly annotated with a title that is appropriate for the context of the particular question that is being answered with the graph.*

difficult types of function that students are given and have a lot of trouble with, both by means of hand drawing, *and* by means of a graphing calculator. The graph has two vertical *asymptote* lines (marked with $x = -1$ and $x = +1$), and one horizontal *asymptote* line (marked with $y = 2$). Take a good, careful look at figure 4.1 and then compare it with each of the graphs that follow (figures 4.2 to 4.9). These latter graphs are plots of the *same* function, but with *deliberate mistakes* that are commonly made by students, and I will discuss each in turn. The mistakes should be easy for you to identify and spot in your child's work. Remember that the example function shown here is one of the most complex that is likely to be encountered, so not all of the mistakes shown here will be relevant for simpler graphs. However, the mistakes shown in graphs A, B, D, F, and H are relevant for *any* kind of graph. I have placed images of small hands on some of the plots to point to the specific locations of the deliberate errors.

- **Graph A** (Figure 4.2): In this graph the axes were not drawn with a ruler.

- **Graph B** (Figure 4.3): In this graph the horizontal and vertical axes are not labeled (in this case they should be labeled with "x" and "y" respectively).

- **Graph C** (Figure 4.4): In this graph some of the curves touch one of the *asymptotes* (in this case the horizontal line marked $y = 2$). By definition, the graph of a function should *never* touch an *asymptote*. Rather, the function should approach the *asymptote*, never reaching it (although the *asymptote* may be *crossed*).

- **Graph D** (Figure 4.5): In this graph the valley and some of the other parts of the curves are too "pointy" and not smoothly curved.

- **Graph E** (Figure 4.6): In this graph the numerical values of the horizontal and vertical *asymptotes* are not marked.

- **Graph F** (Figure 4.7): In this graph the places where the curves cross the x and y axes are not marked.

- **Graph G** (Figure 4.8): The mistake in this graph is very subtle. On the right-hand and left-hand sides of the graph the curves should always be getting closer to the horizontal *asymptote*, but in this example they are actually turning *away* again from the *asymptote*.

- **Graph H** (Figure 4.9): This graph is way too messy. Some of the annotation is illegible and a blunt pencil was used. This graph would lose a lot of points for lack of clarity and neatness because the information being conveyed is not clear and some of the information may as well be missing.

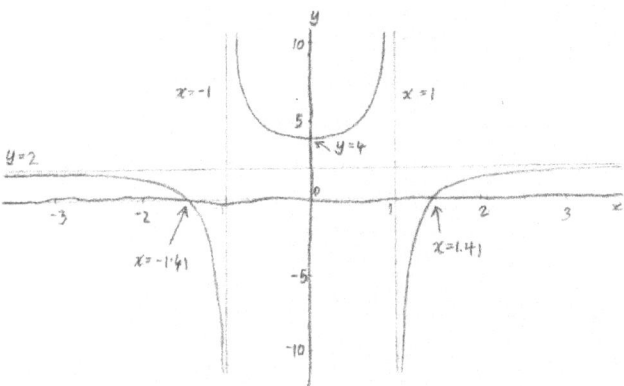

Figure 4.2: **Graph A**: A hand-drawn graph illustrating a common mistake (see §4.1.3). In this graph the axes were not drawn with a ruler. The corresponding graph without mistakes is shown in figure 4.1.

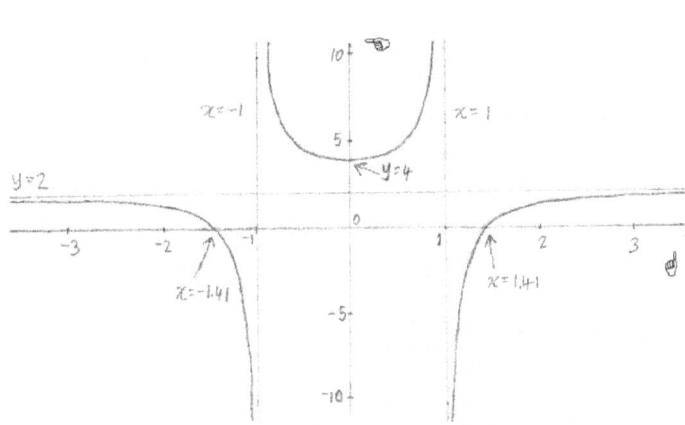

Figure 4.3: **Graph B**: A hand-drawn graph illustrating a common mistake (see §4.1.3). In this graph the horizontal and vertical axes are not labeled (in this case they should be labeled with "x" and "y" respectively). The corresponding graph without mistakes is shown in figure 4.1.

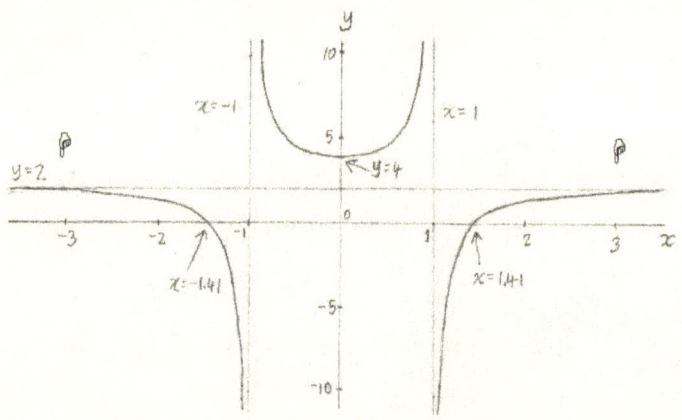

Figure 4.4: **Graph C**: A hand-drawn graph illustrating a common mistake (see §4.1.3). In this graph some of the curves touch one of the *asymptotes* (in this case the horizontal line marked $y = 2$). By definition, the graph of a function should *never* touch an *asymptote*, but should instead approach it without ever reaching it (although it may cross the line and *then* approach it). The corresponding graph without mistakes is shown in figure 4.1.

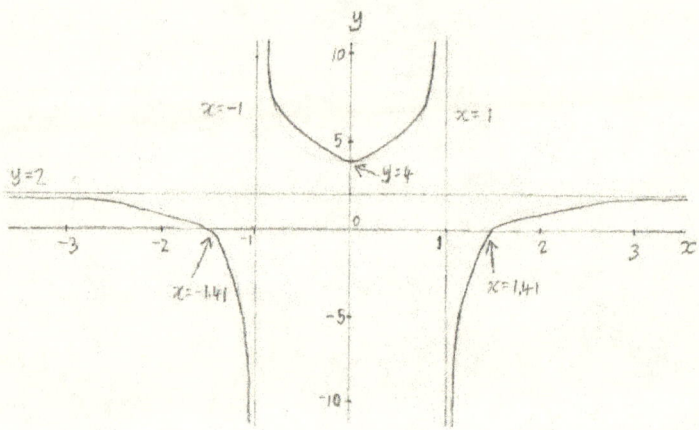

Figure 4.5: **Graph D**: A hand-drawn graph illustrating a common mistake (see §4.1.3). In this graph the "valley" and some of the other parts of the curves are too "pointy" and not smoothly curved. The corresponding graph without mistakes is shown in figure 4.1.

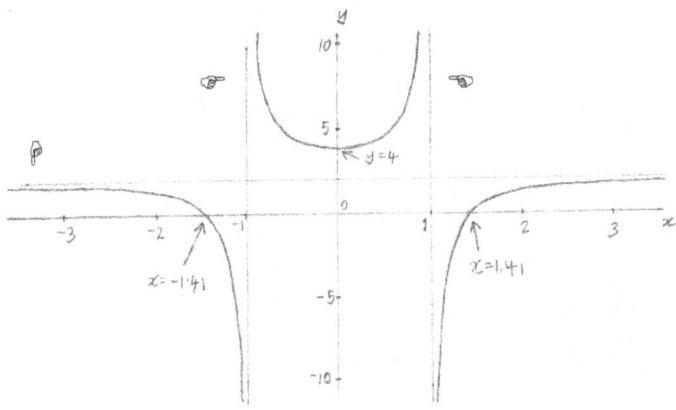

Figure 4.6: **Graph E**: A hand-drawn graph illustrating a common mistake (see §4.1.3). In this graph the numerical values of the *asymptotes* are not marked (compare with the correct graph in figure 4.1).

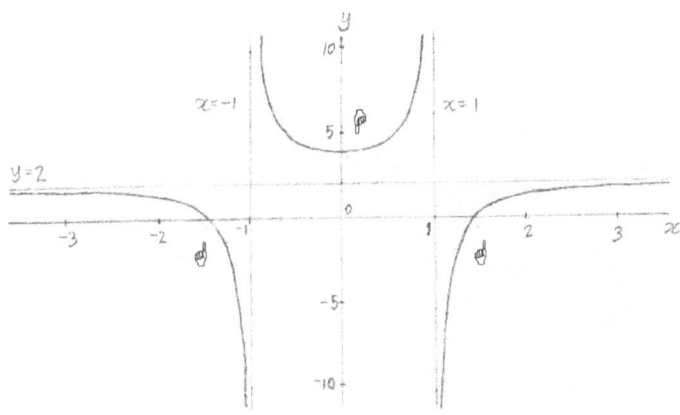

Figure 4.7: **Graph F**: A hand-drawn graph illustrating a common mistake (see §4.1.3). In this graph the places where the curves cross the x and y axes are not marked. The corresponding graph without mistakes is shown in figure 4.1.

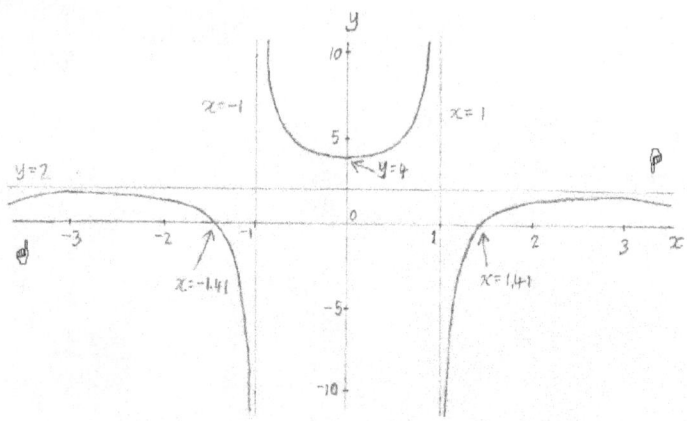

Figure 4.8: **Graph G**: A hand-drawn graph illustrating a common mistake (see §4.1.3). The mistake in this graph is very subtle. On the right-hand and left-hand sides of the graph the curves should always be getting closer to the *asymptotes*, but in this example they are turning away again from the horizontal *asymptote*. The corresponding graph without mistakes is shown in figure 4.1.

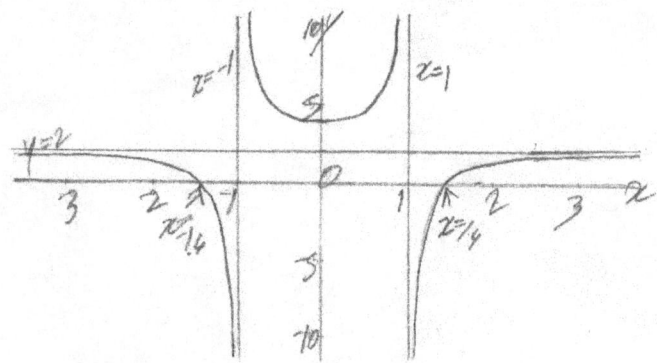

Figure 4.9: **Graph H**: A hand-drawn graph illustrating a common mistake (see §4.1.3). This graph is way too messy. Some of the annotation is illegible and a blunt pencil was used. This graph would lose a lot of points for lack of clarity and neatness because some of the information being conveyed is ambiguous and/or not clear. Compare with the original (correct) graph in figure 4.1.

4.2 The Graphing Calculator

Despite costing over a hundred bucks and having what seems like hundreds of keys and functions, the graphing calculator is not to be feared. The first thing that you should find reassuring is that, in my experience, I have found that students pick up very quickly on the mechanics of how to use a graphing calculator, and they usually know how to access all the relevant functions. You should not need to learn how to use it yourself and you should not be embarrassed about not knowing how to use it. Instead, you should be encouraged by the fact that you can help your child with using the graphing calculator in a very big way *without knowing how to use it*. Having said that, there is a convenient resource on the website http://helpyourchildwithmath.com for both parents and students, in the form of pointers to memory joggers for how to perform various tasks on specific graphing calculators. Although every graphing calculator model comes with a thick manual, I find that students do not study the manual. These manuals are generally very dry, terse, and extremely boring, so I don't blame them.

4.3 What Can a Graphing Calculator Do That a Regular One Cannot?

The first major question (and indeed, concern) that parents have, after forking out the requisite small fortune is, "What does it do that can't be done with a twenty-buck device bought from the pharmacy?" I list below the main attributes of the more expensive machine that are relevant.

- This one is obvious: it can graph functions. Moreover, it can graph *several functions overlaid on top of each other*. There are tools for various types of *analysis* of the graphs.

- It can be used to evaluate complicated functions and expressions for given input values. These functions and expressions can be stored for repeated, multiple evaluations.

- It can handle operations with things called *complex numbers* (consult the crib sheet in part 3 for more details if you want to).

- It can also *solve equations* and yield the coordinates of locations where graphs of functions cross each other.

- It can trace graphs with a cursor, displaying the numerical values of both the input and output of a function, at the position of the cursor.

- It handles *lists* of data and can compute a variety of statistical quantities from the data. It can also perform *statistical analysis* on the data, including "hypothesis testing," and fitting theoretical models to data.

- It can do *matrix calculations* and solve *matrix equations*. Matrices are multidimensional arrays of numbers that have special rules for addition, subtraction and multiplication. Consult the crib sheet in part 3 of this book for more details if you are interested.

- It can do calculus (to a limited extent). You don't really need to know what this entails: your child will probably be able to explain it to you if you need to know.

- It is a small computer. It has its own language that you can write programs in, and you can have it do entire suites of calculations using its intrinsic functions. This capability is often not used in the school curriculum, however.

4.4 The Major Pitfalls

Having just explained how the graphing calculator is superior to the non-graphing calculator, I will now tell you that everything a student is required to do for school work with the graphing calculator can be done by hand. It may take a lot longer, but it can be done. (Recall that you and I even had to evaluate trigonometric functions without a calculator by looking them up in tables.) I will go further and say that I have found that most of the difficulties that students have with a graphing calculator can be traced to not having developed enough intuition for the material first. In my opinion the graphing calculator is introduced too early in the course, well before students have developed the necessary intuition for the new material. Students will take everything that they see on the screen of the calculator too literally. They are too trusting of the calculator, and of themselves. They often ignore the possibility that they may hit the wrong key, put parentheses in the wrong place in an expression, or make a host of other simple mistakes in usage.

In §2.5 I already talked about developing intuition for what to expect of solutions to a given type of problem and developing the skill and habits to know when a mistake has likely been made, and to look for those mistakes. It is absolutely imperative to develop this kind of skill for working with the graphing calculator as well. The best thing that you can do to help your child with graphing calculator difficulties is to have him/her repeat selected problems (from classwork, assignments, or homework) that were destined to be done with the graphing calculator, *by hand*. Not all of the problems will be amenable to being done by hand in a reasonable amount of time of course, so you will have to determine, together with your child, which ones are.

4.4.1 Poor Rendering of Essential Features of Graphs

Aside from the inability or unwillingness on the part of the student to assess the reasonableness of answers that the graphing calculator spews out, another major area of difficulty relates to the actual graphing capability of the graphing calculator. Time and time again, students are perplexed and thrown off by taking what they see on the screen too literally. They fail to realize the limitations of the graphing calculator in displaying the true nature of functions because of four factors, which I list below. A fifth factor will be discussed in §4.4.2.

1. The finite (and rather small) number of pixels on the screen causes poor rendering of a graph.

2. The finite numerical resolution also compromises the rendering of a graph, as well as the analysis of the graph. The numerical resolution refers to the number of points at which a function is evaluated (it is not necessarily evaluated at every pixel). The numerical resolution is adjustable, but a student may not be aware that the relevant settings are inappropriate and/or inadequate.

3. The zoom settings, or window settings, of a calculator refer to the ranges of the horizontal and vertical axes of the graph in terms of the minimum and maximum values on each axis that display in the window. The appropriate zoom settings to answer a particular question for a particular graph (it may be different for different questions about the same graph) should be selected. The zoom settings also affect the accuracy with which a graph is rendered, so they affect the severity of the two problems mentioned above. More details on this are given below.

4. The inability of the graphing calculator to properly handle a "divide by zero" (or *infinity*) compromises the rendering of certain types of graphs. In the graphing mode, a graphing calculator will *not* necessarily issue any warning when a "divide by zero" exists in the graph, and the calculator will simply join points on either side of the infinity, which is *wrong*. This is rarely appreciated by students. Although it is usually possible to select a graphing mode that does not join any of the calculated points on the graph with line segments, such a

choice can be *worse* for students attempting to interpret the graph (I will say more on this below).

All four of the above factors lead to the fact that some features of a graph could be missed or completely misinterpreted. To show you what I mean, I will illustrate the problem using the graph of the function that was used in the examples in §4.1.3 (see figure 4.1). Shown in figure 4.10 is a screen shot of that *exact function*: compare this with the hand-drawn version of the same function in figure 4.1. The hand-drawn graph (figure 4.1) and the calculator graph (figure 4.10) look nothing like each other do they? What went wrong? The calculator graph is a mess. Many of the lines that should not be joined together or should not be touching do appear to join or touch in the calculator version. Moreover, the calculator version of the graph seems to "stop" before it reaches the bottom and top of the window.

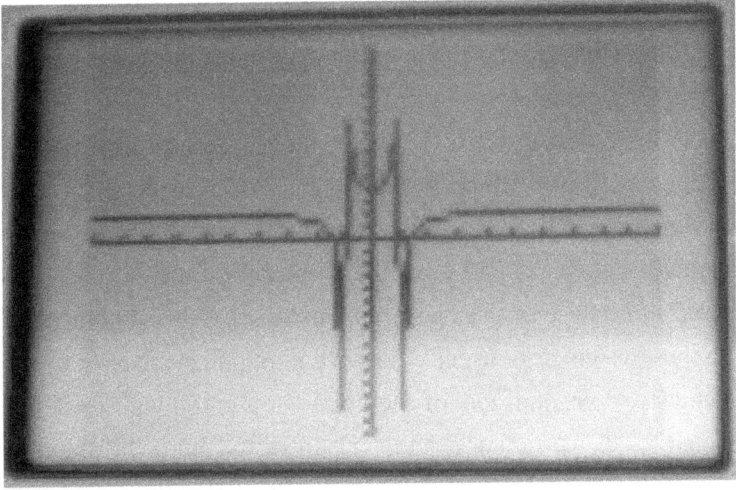

Figure 4.10: Illustration of how a graphing calculator can plot the graph of a function incorrectly (see §4.4). The function that is plotted is *identical* to the one plotted in figure 4.1 (without the *asymptote* lines), so the two graphs should be similar, but they are not. Notice how the graphing calculator has truncated the function in the vertical direction because it does not properly handle points where the function becomes infinite. Combined with the effects of pixelation (finite resolution), the distortions of the graph are intolerable.

The first thing to realize is that the calculator will simply use the zoom settings that were set whenever the calculator was previously used (even if it was switched off after the previous use). The zoom settings are way more critical than students realize. In theory, if the calculator was "perfect," the zoom settings should not matter. However, graphing calculators have severe limitations and the zoom settings are absolutely critical. Even if a student manually adjusts the zoom settings, if he/she is graphing a new and/or unfamiliar function, he/she will not know in advance how *particular* zoom settings will affect a *particular* graph. In other words, even if a student manually adjusts the zoom settings, the graph displayed on the screen could still be wrong. Yes, the graph displayed by the graphing calculator in figure 4.10 is *wrong* and the hand-drawn one is correct. Finding appropriate zoom settings requires a *trial-and-error* procedure, and an overwhelming number of students fail to appreciate this, despite many hours of learning in the classroom. For some functions, the graph displayed by the graphing calculator will *never* be completely correct for *any* zoom settings.

Now, using our example function, let's try adjusting the zoom settings on the graphing calculator to zoom in a bit (strictly speaking we are adjusting the window coordinates). The result is shown in figure 4.11 (note that independent zoom/window settings can be set in the horizontal and vertical directions). This new graph (figure 4.11) is a bit better. However, the calculator's ability to plot this kind of complex function is *still severely compromised* because of the four problems listed above. I point out again that graphing calculators usually do have a graphing mode that instructs the calculator to *not* join *any* of the points in a graph with lines (consult the manual for the particular calculator). In such a mode the graph will be displayed as a set of "dots." This can actually present more of a problem for the student if he/she is not familiar with the behavior of the graph of the equation that is being plotted because the number of "dots" displayed depends on the display settings. Consequently, it may still not be obvious to the student what the graph should look like, due to the possible ambiguities

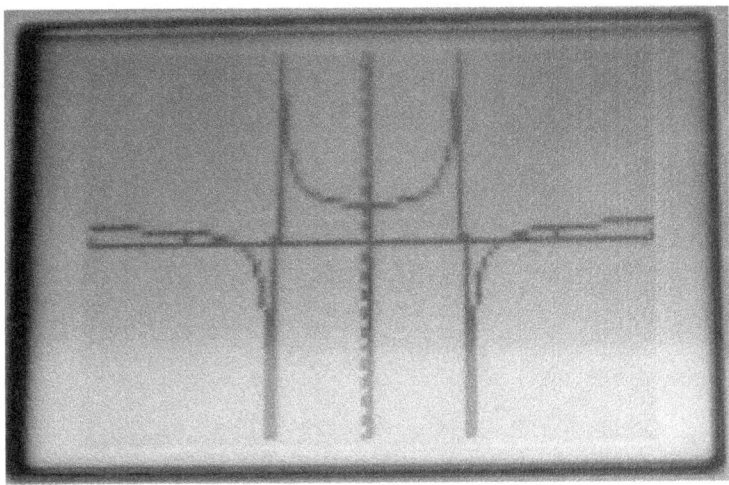

Figure 4.11: Illustration of how a graphing calculator can plot the graph of a function incorrectly (see §4.4). The function that is plotted is *identical* to the one plotted in figure 4.1 (without the *asymptote* lines), so the two graphs should be similar, but they are not. Compared to the graph in figure 4.10, the graph shown here is better because the zoom settings (horizontal and vertical axes minimum and maximum values) of the calculator have been adjusted. However, the representation of the graph at the vertical *asymptote* positions is still wrong and intolerable.

in the rendition of the graph. In other words, if a student is graphing a particular function for the first time, the student is unlikely to be familiar with the behavior of the function, so how is he/she expected to know in advance what the correct calculator settings should be? Even if the student adjusts the calculator settings, how will he/she know that the displayed graph is correct and free of errors and/or inaccurate rendition?

Unfortunately, the inexperienced student often thinks that what the calculator shows is literally what the graph is supposed to look like. The limited number of pixels, the limited numerical resolution, and the poor handling of infinities compromises the calculator's ability to accurately portray the graph. This, together with careless use of the display settings can lead the unaware student to draw wrong conclusions and make incorrect deductions, ultimately leading the student to deduce wrong answers to questions

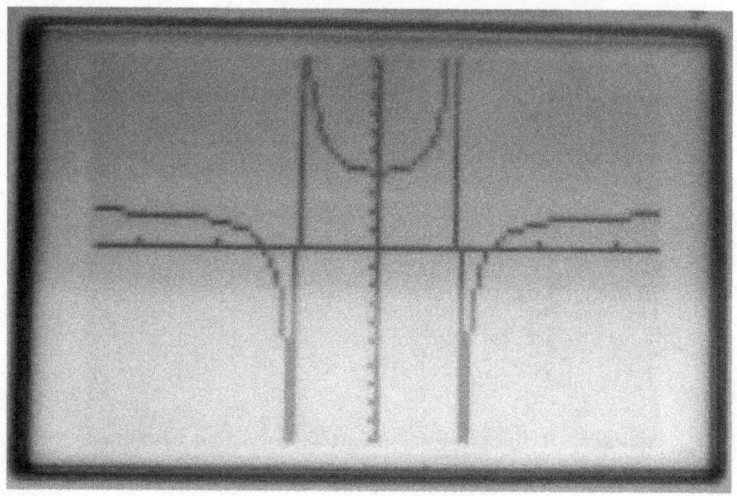

Figure 4.12: Illustration of how a graphing calculator can plot the graph of a function incorrectly (see §4.4). The function that is plotted is *identical* to the one plotted in figure 4.1 (without the *asymptote* lines), so the two graphs should be similar, but they are not. Compared to the graphs in figure 4.10 and figure 4.11, the graph shown here is better because the zoom settings of the calculator have been further adjusted (notice the gap in the curve near the right-most vertical "line," which is better than the situation near the left-most vertical "line"). However, the representation of the graph at the vertical *asymptote* positions is still wrong and intolerable.

concerning a function and its graph.

The zoom settings on the graphing calculator allow, to some extent, mitigation of the graphing limitations, but the problem is that the more that you zoom in, the smaller is the portion of the graph that can be displayed. Figure 4.12 shows another graph, again of the *same function*, that was made using the graphing calculator by further adjusting the zoom settings. There is some more improvement: for example, you can see that the curve in the top right-hand quadrant now shows a gap (near the vertical "line"), but the curves in the other three quadrants are still touching when they should not be. You really have to know what part of the graph to zoom in to, according to the particular question about the graph that you want to answer. You can see, therefore, that it is essential that the student endeavors to develop an intuition for the functions that are to be graphed *before* using the graphing calculator to plot these functions. Otherwise, how would the student know which parts of the graph are artifacts of the graphing calculator, and which parts are genuinely correct?

When I show students these limitations of the graphing calculator, they are most often hearing about them for the first time, and they are perplexed as to why such a fancy and expensive calculator is so poor at plotting certain kinds of functions, and why it has the limitations that I have outlined above. The fact is, a graphing calculator *is* poor at graphing certain types of functions. Those functions are *better drawn by hand*, or with a computer. Believe it or not, a graphing calculator is a very poor choice of tool for plotting graphs of all except the simplest of functions. It is an excellent tool for many other types of analysis of functions and data, but the graphing calculator, despite its name, is not good for graphing. Yet the curriculum requires students to graph functions with a tool that it is actually not well-suited for the job. Given that it is required by the curriculum however, we have to work with it.

As a final illustration, in figure 4.13, I show the same function again, this time plotted using a computer. You can compare this with figure 4.1 and figures 4.10 to 4.12. You will easily agree that the graphing calculator shows by far the poorest rendition of the function.

4.4.2 The Display's Aspect Ratio

There is another problem for the unwary student, in addition to the issues that I have talked about above, and it is the fifth factor mentioned in §4.4.1. One of the best ways to illustrate the problem is to simply enter the equation of a circle into the graphing calculator in order for the calculator to plot a simple circle (or use the "circle" function of the calculator). I have done that for you and the result is shown in figure 4.14. You can see immediately that instead of showing a circle, the calculator has plotted something

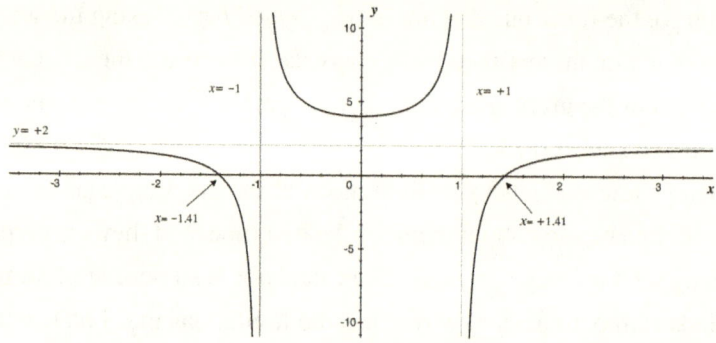

Figure 4.13: A graph of the *same* function that is plotted in figure 4.1, and figures 4.10 to 4.12, but this time the graph shown here was generated by using computer software. Contrast the accuracy and precision of this computer-generated rendition with the distorted (and incorrect) graphs produced by a graphing calculator, in figures 4.10 to 4.12.

that looks like an ellipse. It has squashed the circle! Remember that the calculator will simply use the current window settings for determining the minimum and maximum values of the horizontal and vertical axes. In producing the plot for figure 4.14, the horizontal minima and maxima of the window settings were not equal to the vertical minima and maxima. So you might think that symmetry would be restored, and the circle would be plotted to actually look like a circle, by making the horizontal and vertical window settings equal to each other. I have done this for you, and the result is shown in figure 4.15. Again, you can see immediately that the graph still shows a squashed circle and not an actual circle! It is better than the plot in figure 4.14 but the distortion is still severe and intolerable. Notice also that the finite image resolution makes both plots look terrible in terms of the lack of smoothness of the curves.

What is happening? Why is the circle distorted? The answer is that the graphing calculator forces the *scaling* of the horizontal and vertical axes to conform to the *aspect ratio of the physical display device*, if the correct "zoom" *mode* has not been selected. What I mean by this is that no matter what window settings you use for either axis, the tick marks on

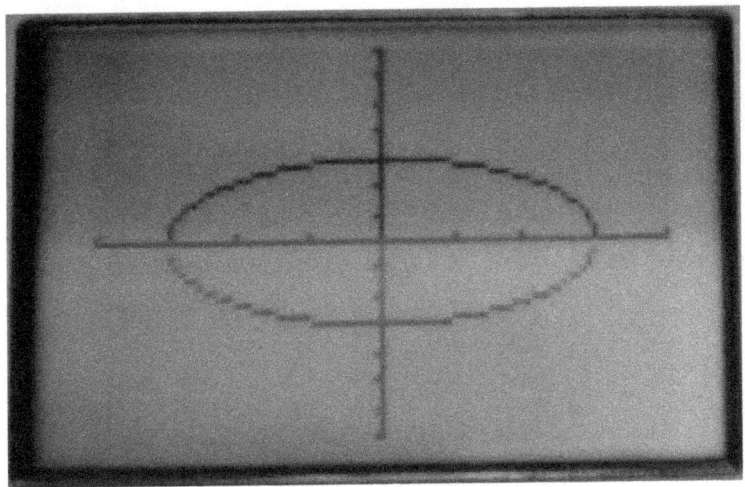

Figure 4.14: Illustration showing that a graphing calculator distorts *all* graphs if the correct zoom mode has not been selected (see §4.4.2). The function that is plotted is that of a circle, but the graphing calculator shows a squashed, elliptical shape. Notice the pixelation effect that makes the rendition even worse.

each axis will be *stretched* to fit the display in order to utilize all of the display in both horizontal and vertical directions. In the "standard" zoom mode, correct proportions are not preserved, and this means that *all graphs rendered by the graphing calculator will be distorted.* In the case of a circle, the distortion is easy to assess visually, "at a glance," because we know what the simple familiar shape *should* be. However, in general, it may not be at all obvious that the calculator has distorted a graph.

The graphing calculator will have a zoom mode that compensates for the aspect ratio of the physical display. A student may be unaware that a special mode has to be selected in order to correct for the aspect ratio of the display device because he/she may not have been paying attention in class just at the time it was mentioned, and because he/she is likely not to have studied the manual carefully. Consult the manual for your graphing calculator to find out how to select this mode. It is usually an option in the zoom menu and it will be called something like "ZSquare" or "Zsq." I

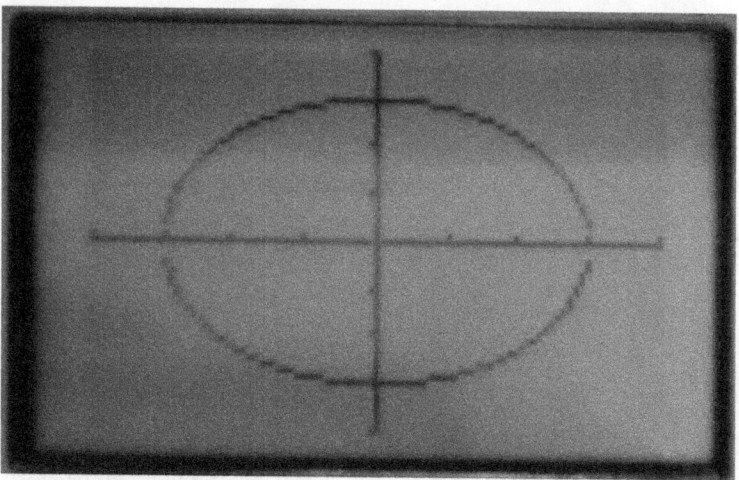

Figure 4.15: Illustration showing that a graphing calculator distorts *all* graphs if the correct zoom mode has not been selected (see §4.4.2). The function that is plotted is that of a circle, but the graphing calculator shows a squashed, elliptical shape. Compared to figure 4.14, the horizontal and vertical axes minimum and maximum values have been set to be equal to each other in an attempt to recover the true shape of the circle but it has failed.

have made another plot of the same circle that was plotted in figure 4.14 and figure 4.15. This time the correct zoom mode has been selected. The result is shown in figure 4.16. It can be seen that now the plot does show something that looks like a circle. Notice also that the calculator shows gaps in the perimeter of the circle. This is a further consequence of the finite pixel resolution. You can see that the rendition of a circle by the graphing calculator is really quite abysmal, even when everything is set correctly.

4.4.3 Strategy

The pitfalls with the graphing calculator may well have been discussed in class, but even a brief lapse in attention could mean that the student misses some vital information. Then, when the student goes home and attempts some problems, he/she may be horrified to see that a graph looks nothing

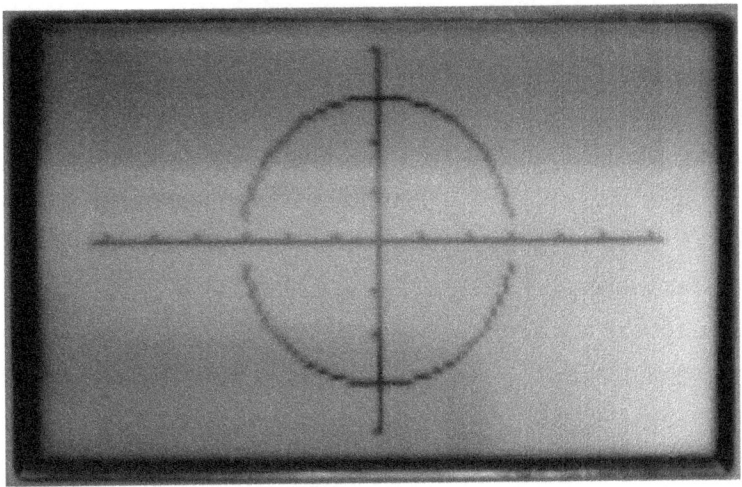

Figure 4.16: Illustration showing how a graphing calculator can plot a circle that is not distorted (see §4.4.2). The function that is plotted is that of the *same* circle as in figure 4.14 and figure 4.15 but this time a zoom mode has been selected that does not tie the horizontal and vertical ranges of the axes to the aspect ratio of the physical display. Notice also that the calculator has still left gaps in the circumference of the circle due to the finite pixel resolution, so the rendition of the graph is still compromised.

like it "should," or to realize that something is terribly wrong.

So, here is what I suggest. The goal is to build intuition: eventually when the student has sufficient experience, he/she *will know* when something is wrong and what is wrong, and/or which parts of a graph on a graphing calculator are likely to be artifacts and which parts are sufficiently accurate. However, in order to build that intuition, the student must construct any graph in a graphing calculator problem twice: once with the graphing calculator, and once with an independent, more accurate method. Ideally, the latter method would be to draw the graph manually. However, this is very time-consuming. If the student really does not have time to do that, then there are free computer-based graphing calculator tools that are available. Use of these is a better option than not using any noncalculator method at all. Some of these are online graphing calculator applications, whilst others are stand-alone applications. There are some links to help with this on the website http://www.helpyourchildwithmath.com. It is important to bear in mind, however, that even some of the computer-based tools may suffer from the same problems that the graphing calculator does! Along with the links to the tools on the website http://www.helpyourchildwithmath.com, I have given a brief description of each tool, along with any relevant caveats and things to watch out for. Remember, as I mentioned earlier, although it is rare for a student to have difficulty in learning how to actually *operate* the graphing calculator, pointers for memory joggers and other aids can be found on the website http://www.helpyourchildwithmath.com. If your child is still really stuck and having difficulty, this would be one of the situations that would benefit from short-term tutoring (see chapter 5). Short-term tutoring would also be helpful in providing guidance on the problems and caveats for the graphing calculator that I have discussed in this chapter. If you have a limited budget for tutoring, training in handgraphing, graphing intuition, and the use of a graphing calculator would be an excellent use of funds because the benefits are long lasting, and because the leveraging factor is very high. A full discussion of this and other high-impact uses of what I call "targeted tutoring" can be found in chapter 5 ($\S 5.5$).

Chapter 5

Tutoring Options and How to Optimize the Return on Limited Funds

5.1 I Wish I Could Afford Private Tutoring

No matter how extraordinary your child's regular teacher at school is, the fact is that he/she will never be able to spend one-on-one time with your child, working on individual needs and weaknesses, as much as a private tutor would be able to. Clearly, your child could potentially make enormous progress, and a significant improvement in performance and grades in math, with the attention and training that a tutor could provide. Most people dismiss private tutoring as a viable option on the grounds that it is unaffordable. In this chapter I would like to demonstrate that such a dismissal may be misguided.

There are two basic reasons why private tutoring may not be beyond your reach, and you and your child may in fact be able to benefit significantly from private tutoring. The first is that getting just a few private lessons from a tutor *at the right time, targeting very specific and carefully thought-out goals*, can provide significant leveraging of funds, and it can have a large payoff. I will discuss exactly what kind of circumstances and targeted goals are appropriate, and what you and your child should do to get the most out of such an endeavor. The second reason is that there is an enormous range in the cost per lesson for private tutoring. I will discuss why there is such a large price range, and I will show you that the lower end of the price range does not necessarily mean that you will get lower quality tutoring compared to the most expensive lessons. There certainly are differences in what you get according to what you pay for, but I will explain what to expect in various scenarios.

I will also show you how you can get the tutoring that you need from a tutor that is not so experienced (and therefore less expensive), by having the tutor utilize available tools and *your* help. You may realize that you might after all be able to afford private lessons on a regular basis. The frequency will obviously depend on your budget, and I will describe what benefits you could expect from getting weekly, biweekly, or less frequent lessons. There are things that you and your child should do in between lessons in order to get the most value from them, and I will discuss those too.

5.2 Independent Tutor versus Tutoring Agency

So how much does private, one-on-one tutoring cost? At the lower end of the range you can expect to pay something of the order of $15 to $60 per lesson for a tutor who is a college student, working independently (of an agency), but the cost really depends on the experience level of the individual tutor. You will get a better idea of what to expect, and how to negotiate, as we proceed with the discussion. At the upper end, you might pay as much as $80 per lesson, *or even more*, for a tutor who is working with an agency. Tutoring agencies vary a great deal in what they charge but you are unlikely to find one that charges less than $50 per lesson. In general, the cost of the lesson covers the time for the tutor to travel to and from your home (or wherever the lesson is to take place). That cost is also supposed to cover time that the tutor spends preparing the lesson and grading work that the tutor requested to be done since the previous lesson. However, if a significant amount of time has to be spent by the tutor beyond this, compensation is negotiable and should be discussed by you and the tutor in advance. An example might be a situation in which the tutor prepares a special diagnostic exam, delivers or mails it to the student, and then grades it. You should be aware that the length of a lesson set by tutoring agencies is usually less than an hour (typically 40 to 50 minutes), whereas the length of a lesson set by a tutor working independently is more likely to be a full hour. You should firmly establish the length of each lesson in order to make proper comparisons of the cost amongst various choices.

Typically, a tutoring agency takes a commission from the cost of the lesson that may be as much as 50%. Thus, the tutor gets paid less than the amount you pay for a lesson, and at a commission rate of 50% it is *a lot* less. The commission is intended to cover the expenses of the agency in terms of staff salaries, advertising expenses, and other administrative and running expenses. You may wonder why a tutor would join an agency rather than work independently, since the tutor would then earn twice as much money for doing exactly the same amount of work. The reason is quite simple: unless the tutor already has candidate students, the tutor would have to risk upfront costs of advertising in order to find clients, and even then he/she may have trouble establishing a contract. This is because the independent tutor may not have the perceived credibility that is provided by a tutoring agency, especially an agency that has been around for a long time.

A significant part of the agency's business is to find and match tutors and students, and they are generally very good at this. A new tutor working with an agency can quickly acquire enough students to fill his/her schedule. The perceived credibility of the agency gives parents, who are the ones ultimately paying, the perception of confidence that their money is being well spent. Therefore, in reality the tutor may in fact earn less money if he/she did not join an agency, simply because of the lack of clients and because of advertising costs. However, if the tutor were able to establish enough clients himself or herself (perhaps through recommendations and word of mouth), the tutor would obviously be better off working independently. In order to prevent tutors "running off" with clients that were found by an agency, the agency typically requires the tutor to sign a contract, effectively promising that he/she will not "run off with students," even after a period of one to two years after leaving the agency.

In my time, I have worked with many agencies, and I have also worked independently. Even though agencies take a significant commission, whenever I moved to a new town (which I did frequently in my younger days), going with an agency was the best option. The agency could very quickly provide me with suitable students and it could *maintain* the supply of students that I needed. Advertising my services in a regular newspaper generally did not produce enough results if I was new to the area. Although the better tutoring agencies screen and interview tutors in person before hiring them, tutors with only one or two years of experience may be hired if the agency judges them to qualify under their criteria. Thus, it is possible that if you work with a tutor through an agency you could pay the same amount of money for somebody with only one or two years of experience and somebody with decades of experience. In contrast, if you hire a tutor independently, you will be in a position to negotiate the price, depending on the tutor's experience. However, you do have the option of specifying a minimum level of experience if you work with an agency, although the agency may not be able to comply with your request. On the other hand, a tutor with limited experience may still actually be very good. If you had found the same tutor (or he/she found you) independently of an agency, you might have been paying less for the same quality of tuition.

It is also important to bear in mind that an experienced tutor working independently of an agency is entitled to charge as much as an agency, according to the market value of the service that he/she provides. What you have to establish is whether you want to (or whether you can afford to) work with a tutor with a lot of experience, or whether are you willing to work with someone less experienced. You should be aware that agencies in the medium price range do not usually provide any special training to the tutors: you get the same service as you would if the same tutor were working independently. The more expensive agencies will have developed their own tools, methods and training. However, there are other considerations. One benefit of working with an agency is that you will be matched with a tutor in a short time, since the agency's business is to build and maintain a pool of tutors. It will take longer for you to find one yourself (remember that you will probably have to interview several people and get references).

Another benefit of working with an agency is that if the tutor you hire seems unsuitable, or otherwise unsatisfactory after a lesson or two, you have the option of asking the agency for another one, and they will again be able to oblige in a short time. If you did this by yourself you will waste more time, losing continuity. Time is already very limited and critical during the school semester, and if you are only getting lessons once every two weeks or so, this kind of messing around will be counterproductive and a waste of money. On the other hand, if you do decide to go with a less experienced tutor, there is a section on the website http://www.helpyourchildwithmath.com that is aimed at providing less experienced tutors with some guidance and advice, providing the benefits of my experience that extends over a period of more than 25 years. Thus, you can potentially get higher quality tutoring for a more affordable cost.

5.3 Cost-Effective Tutoring Options

So, you have some decisions to make which basically come down to two things: how much you can afford, and the level of experience that you desire from a tutor. You could argue that there really is only one factor, money, because if money were not an issue then you would obviously want to get the most experienced tutor, as frequently as you need. Of course, the best option would be to get a tutor with many years of experience because the extra cost will definitely have a higher payoff. However, if that is beyond your means, you will still benefit enormously if you find a suitable (but less experienced) tutor, and if you and your child are willing to do what is necessary to get the most out of the investment. I will discuss this further shortly, but first you must consider some important questions that I list below.

For the purpose of cost estimation I will assume a nominal figure of $20 per lesson for a tutor with limited experience (such as a college student), working independently of an agency, and $60 per lesson for an experienced independent tutor, or a tutor working with an agency (who may or may not have as many years of experience). This is intended only as a rough guide. When considering the following questions you should also bear in mind that for kids in 8th grade and below, the number of years of experience that your tutor has may not be the most important factor to look for. Enthusiasm, a passion for teaching and mentoring, and a talent for working with kids of the appropriate age, is likely to be more important for success and value for money than the number of years of experience. A tutor who cannot invoke a rapport with the student is unlikely to spark inspiration and get results, no matter how experienced the tutor is. So here is the checklist that you need to consider. The various options may seem rather complicated but the information is presented in the form of a worksheet in §5.3.1. There is also a spreadsheet on the website http://www.helpyourchildwithmath.com that greatly simplifies the calculations for the different options.

1. Decide how much you want to (or are able to) spend on private tutoring in the school year, or in a semester if you only want to try it for one semester. As a baseline guide we can estimate how much it would cost to get one lesson every week for an entire school year, assuming 40 weeks in the school year. Using our nominal rates of $20 per lesson for a college student and $60 per lesson for an experienced tutor, this translates into a "ceiling" of $800 and $2,400 per year respectively. The actual amount might be less because it is possible that you could get a tax deduction. The exact amount obviously depends on your income and on what tax rules are in effect at the time, but as a rough "guesstimate" you could assume a 20% discount, which would then mean a cost ceiling of $640 to $1920 per year. As a concrete example, in the following steps, let's suppose that you can afford $500 per semester. With a 20% tax adjustment that means you can effectively spend approximately $600 (that is, $625 rounded to the nearest $100).

2. Having set your budget per semester, next decide whether your child needs regular and frequent tutoring, or whether he/she could benefit from selective, occasional tutoring (for example, just before major exams, or on specific topics that are particularly weak areas, or on particular topics that can benefit most from targeted tutoring). If you are not sure, read the section on selective, targeted tutoring later in this chapter (§5.5) and come back here.

(a) If your child needs regular, frequent tutoring, divide your total semester budget by 60 (dollars). Then divide this number by 20 (weeks). There are several possible outcomes, and these are listed below.

(i) If the above number was more than 1.00 then you can afford a lesson once every week at the more expensive rate. Since you are paying at the high end, you may as well get the benefits of working with a tutor through an agency, unless you already know of someone, perhaps from a recommendation.

If your calculation gave you a number less than 1.00 but greater than 0.50, then you can afford a lesson approximately every two weeks or so.

If your calculation gave you a number less than 0.5 then you cannot afford regular, frequent tutoring at the high-end price. In that case follow steps (ii) through (iv) below to see what your options are. Note that lessons that are less frequent than once every two weeks are *not* regular. If your child has lessons less frequently than once every two weeks you will be wasting your money. In my experience, the lack of continuity becomes a major factor. This also means that if you are going to spend money on only a few, targeted lessons, such lessons should also *not* be spread out over too long a time period.

In our example of a one-semester budget of $600, we got exactly 0.5 for the "critical number," or one lesson every two weeks. This is borderline because it leaves no room for extra lessons just before exams, and in such cases you should consider option (ii) below.

(ii) If the result of the calculation in (a) was less than, equal to, or close to 0.5, then you need to consider getting a less experienced tutor. First, multiply the number you got in (a) by 3.0. This gives you the average number of lessons per week that you could buy with your budget at the low-end price. Using our example budget we get an average of 1.5 lessons per week for the semester. This works out well at one lesson per week, plus some extra for specials such as exam preparation, and/or focused sessions on troublesome topics.

(iii) On the other hand, if the number you got in (ii) was less than 1.00 but greater than 0.5 then you can afford the lower-priced lessons approximately once every two weeks with some extra for exam preparation, and/or focused sessions on troublesome topics.

(iv) If the number you got in (ii) was around 0.5 or less, it means that regular lessons even in the lower price range are not a viable option, and you are better off spending your money only on highly-targeted blocks of sessions, as described in (b) below.

(b) If your child doesn't need regular, frequent tutoring, or if you followed (a)(i) through (iv) above and found that your budget constraints do not allow for regular, frequent tutoring, then the best way that you can spend your money is to focus on a block or more of a few carefully designed sessions. I will discuss later in the chapter how you can work with the tutor and your child to figure out what material and topics such sessions should cover, and how to set the goals according to what needs to be achieved.

Finally, I point out again that if you really cannot afford even the lowest end of the price range, then consider exchanging the services of a young college-student tutor for food. As I mentioned earlier, college students are always hungry and trying to save money and, being away from home, will appreciate some good home-cooked food. In my graduate student days I did this on occasion myself. The student will also appreciate it if you are able to recommend him/her to someone you know who *can* pay for the tutoring.

You may also be wondering if you could pool together with another parent, and have a tutor teach two kids at once. In my experience this is generally a bad idea, unless the two kids have very similar needs and issues with the math, and this is rarely the case (I am assuming of course that the two kids will be covering the same material in school, at the same level). The divided attention may be a problem. Having said that, it *can* work, and I have been in a situation myself where it has worked, teaching two brothers together. You can try it out for one or two lessons to see if it will work in your case.

5.3.1 Tutoring Worksheet

Here is a worksheet that captures all of the criteria above to help you decide exactly what kind of tutoring is appropriate for your needs and budget.

1. Write down your total budget for tutoring *per semester*: ....

2. Does your child need regular (weekly or biweekly) tutoring, or a few targeted sessions to address particular needs or topics? Circle whichever is appropriate:

(a) regular

(b) targeted

If you selected (a) go to item 3 below, but if you selected (b) go to item 4 below.

3. Regular tutoring

Divide your budget dollars in item 1 above by 60. *Is the answer greater than 20?*

If YES: You can afford *weekly* tutoring by an experienced tutor, either from a tutoring agency or independent of an agency. However, if you use a less experienced (and independent) tutor you could get two to three times as many lessons. Using the guidelines in this chapter, decide whether it will be more beneficial to your child to get more lessons with a less experienced tutor, or a smaller number of lessons with a more experienced tutor. Decide whether you want to use an agency or not, using the guidelines discussed in this chapter. Remember that even if you use an agency (paying for the associated higher cost), you may still end up with a less experienced tutor, unless you specify your requirement for a tutor with a minimum amount of experience. *You are now done with this worksheet.*

If NO: Is the answer to item 3 above (budget dollars divided by 60) greater than 10?

◇ *If YES* : You can afford *biweekly* tutoring by an experienced tutor, or *weekly* tutoring by a less experienced tutor (plus some extra for exam preparation or other targeted topics). Decide which of the two options is best for your child using the guidelines given in this chapter. If you go with an agency, you can only afford *biweekly* lessons for the semester, and bear in mind that you may still end up with a relatively inexperienced tutor, unless you specify your requirement for a tutor with a minimum amount of experience. Again, decide what is best for your child using the guidelines in this chapter. *You are done with this worksheet.*

◇ *If NO*: If you get here it means that your answer to item 3 above (budget dollars divided by 60) is less than or equal to 10. Now, instead of dividing the budget dollars by 60, start again and divide your semester budget dollars by 20. Is the answer greater than 20?

    o *If YES*: You can afford regular *weekly* tutoring with a less experienced tutor.

    o *If NO*: Is your answer to "budget dollars divided by 20" greater than 10?

        ⋆ *If YES*: You can afford *biweekly* tutoring with a less experienced tutor.

        ⋆ *If NO*: You cannot afford *weekly* or *biweekly* tutoring, and it would be more effective to spend your money on targeted tutoring (with a less experienced tutor). Using the guidelines in this chapter, decide what kind of targeted tutoring would best benefit your child, and then calculate how many lessons you can afford.

4. Targeted Tutoring

If your budget only allows for a block, or blocks, of targeted tutoring, or if you know that your child needs some targeted tutoring, then you need to figure out what is feasible. Using the guidelines in this chapter, work out a rough plan of what you would like to achieve and roughly how many lessons you will need to reach those goals. If you are not sure, read the rest of the chapter first (in particular §5.5) and come back here.

(a) Write down the number of lessons desired here: ………

(b) Divide your semester budget by 60. Is this number greater than that in 4(a)?

    ◇ *If YES*: You can afford to work with an experienced tutor with a tutoring agency, or independent of an agency. Using the guidelines in this chapter, decide which is best for your child's needs, remembering that you may still end up with a less experienced tutor from an agency, unless you specify a certain minimum experience level.

    ◇ *If NO*: You will need to find a lower cost (and therefore relatively less experienced) tutor. Using the guidelines in this chapter, decide whether this option would still benefit your child. This will depend on your exact goals, and the actual cost of the tutoring.

5.4 How to Find a Suitable Tutor

If you have now decided how much, and what kind of private tutoring you can afford that is suitable for your child, you may be wondering how you would go about finding a good tutor. If you have decided to go with a tutoring agency, the task is much easier and I will discuss this case first.

5.4.1 Using an Agency

Using local directories and/or the internet, get contact information for at least five agencies, more if you can. Call each one to establish some critical information in order to directly compare the different agencies. Remember that cost is not the only factor. You should start judging the agency as soon as you call, even if you only speak to an administrative person who is not going to be doing the actual work of matching a tutor to your needs. The general attitude of anyone who works for the agency will tell you something about how much the agency cares about its customers, or potential customers. If the agency employs people who do not reflect the general posture of the agency (even if it is someone who just answers the telephone), then you do not want to deal with them: move on to the next agency. Try to speak to someone as high up in the agency as you can. Do not be put off if you find that the agency actually consists of only one or two people: such agencies may give you a more personal and genuine service than a large one, and that service and the associated tutors may be just as good, or better, than those that you would get from a large agency. In addition, a small operation will have less overhead, and it may be taking less commission from the tutors. Following is a minimal list of critical information that you should try to glean about each agency.

1. Obviously, cost per lesson, but just as important, the actual time duration of each lesson.

2. Does the cost include the tutor's travel time and any time spent preparing lessons and grading, outside of the actual lesson time? It should do, but it is worth checking.

3. Is there a discount scheme if you buy a certain number of lessons in advance? What is the refund policy on advance purchases?

4. What is the policy for cancellation of a lesson? For example, a lesson may have to be cancelled due to a child being sick. Usually the agency will require notice of cancellation in advance, but the time period for that is decided by the agency. How much do you have to pay if you miss that deadline? The amount may be some fraction of the price of the lesson, or it may even be the full cost.

5. Ask for some details about how the tutors that work for the agency are screened. What are the minimum qualifications required of a tutor? Are the tutors interviewed? If so, are the tutors interviewed in person by the agency, or are they just interviewed by telephone? Obviously the former is better, but the latter is also acceptable. How many references were provided by the tutor to the agency? Three is good, two may be acceptable. Are you, as the client, provided any information about what the references said?

6. Are you allowed to specify a minimum number of years of experience that a tutor who is selected to work with you should have?

7. What are the procedures in the case that you are not satisfied with the services of a tutor who is assigned to you?

8. How much does the agency involve itself in training its tutors? No training is not necessarily a bad thing, and may in fact be more desirable in terms of a tutor not having to stick to "one-size-fits-all" type of techniques. Your purpose with this question is mainly to establish for your own information what procedures that a tutor associated with a particular agency is required to comply with.

9. Try to establish how much of the cost per lesson actually goes to the tutor (i.e., cost of the lesson minus the commission rate that the agency charges). The agency may not give you this information, however. The reason for you to have that information is that a tutor who has to pay the agency less commission will generally be happier, and more likely to give you a higher return for your money.

10. Try to establish whether the agency spends significant amounts of money on advertising. This constitutes overhead for the agency, which will ultimately come from your pocket, and the higher cost will not necessarily give you a higher quality of tuition. You can get just as good quality of tuition from an agency with lower overheads, since the best tutors do not preferentially join agencies that have large overheads. Certainly, a larger, or "big-name," agency may have more rigorous screening criteria, but you must establish this yourself because it is not necessarily true.

5.4.2 Finding and Interviewing an Independent Tutor

Finding a suitable independent tutor is going to require considerably more effort on your part than finding a tutor through an agency. First of all, you must clearly define what you need. Using the guidelines in previous sections above, decide what experience level of tutor you can afford, and whether you want tutoring on a regular basis, or in block sessions for highly-targeted purposes. Next, you should find suitable candidates and then screen them. There are several options for finding suitable candidates, and these are listed below.

1. Word of mouth.

2. Local newspapers or internet listings of candidates looking for work.

3. Proactive advertising at local college notice boards (if it is allowed), internet blogs, or local notice boards at other establishments that allow it.

4. A variation on method 3 above, in which you place an advertisement in local newspapers, college campus newspapers, or internet listings. This is the most expensive and risky method but it could turn up more possible candidates.

As I have mentioned before, if you can only afford a tutor with limited experience, it may well be adequate for your purpose, depending on your specific goals. In particular, the following are good examples of specific goals that could be achieved by using a tutor with limited experience, yet the return in terms of your child's improved performance could be significant.

1. Having the tutor obtain or make *timed* diagnostic and/or practice tests, then having your child do the tests in his/her own time. The tutor grades the tests and then comes to go over and work through a test with your child, identifying and improving weak areas, and retesting if necessary.

2. Targeted sessions to improve proficiency and competence with a graphing calculator.

3. Focus sessions to improve competence in specific topics and/or administer oral drills if you are unable to do them yourself.

4. As mentioned previously, if the student is in 8th grade or below, and if the tutor has a particular talent for teaching kids and working with kids, the tutor may be able to competently handle any math topic. In other words, the number of years of experience is not as important as being able to communicate and work well with your child, in order to get results.

It is worth pointing out that parents who do look for tutoring help from a local college student, often make the mistake of getting in touch only with the mathematics department of a college. Parents tend to forget that physics and engineering students have to routinely deal with advanced math topics in their studies, and students taking *any* science courses have usually had to demonstrate competence in math in order for them to be doing those courses. I would go further and say that you should not dismiss the possibility of finding a college student who is *not* a science or math major, if you are looking for a tutor to help with math at the 8th- or lower-grade level.

In order to teach 9th-grade students and above (for example, geometry, algebra II, precalculus, and calculus), the less experienced tutor will have to put in considerably more effort into lesson preparation. Even if the tutor is a college student who is taking advanced math or science courses, it is quite possible that he/she will have forgotten some of the more basic material. The college student may not even realize how much material he/she has forgotten since leaving school. For example, "geometric proofs" are commonly forgotten, as they are the kind of topics that most people, even math majors, are able to recall only for a limited time after learning them. On the other hand, calculus problems have a much longer retention period and a college math major should not have to put in as much time for lesson preparation for calculus. Overall, a less experienced, less costly tutor may be good enough for your purpose, even for 9th- to 12th-grade subjects, if the tutor is prepared to put in the extra time outside lessons, and if he/she is otherwise satisfactory. One reason why the less experienced tutor may be willing to put in the extra time is that for the tutor it is as an investment for gaining experience, so that *eventually* he/she will be able to command a higher income. All of these issues be can discussed with your prospective tutor.

Once you have identified suitable candidate tutors, you need to screen them. Meeting the candidates in person for an informal interview is by far better than just speaking on the phone. However, if speaking on the phone is the only option due to unavoidable circumstances, then it is better than not speaking to the candidates at all. From what I have said so far, you may already have a good idea of what questions to ask the candidates, but I will summarize the minimum list of items that you need to cover. You could either invite the candidate to your home to conduct the interview, or you could meet him/her at a bookshop, library, coffee shop, or other suitable establishment, whatever is most convenient for both of you. If the candidate is coming to your home, you could introduce him/her to your child if you like, although it is not necessary. If you do, it should be done after the interview. If you meet the candidate outside your home, it is probably not a good idea to take your child with you.

1. Call the candidates to make appointments and ask them to bring an updated resumé to the interview, or if there is enough time, request that the resumé is mailed to you in advance if possible.

2. Obviously, the first thing is to establish what experience the candidate has, particularly with respect to the broad subject areas I have described (for 8th grade and below, and in the major 9th- to 12th-grade subjects). At this stage you don't need to specify the specific topics that you require to be covered for your child. Ask the candidate what he/she does for a living in order to place things in context, and if he/she is a college student, ask what subjects he/she is studying. Ask the candidate to talk about any other relevant experience, especially in connection to working with children in any capacity, particularly if the candidate has no direct tutoring experience. For example, baby-sitting work, or work at a summer camp would be useful for providing character references from adults who have worked with the candidate.

3. Now explain what you require for your child and any particular topics your child has difficulty with. Try to establish, preferably subtly, reasons why the candidate is interested in tutoring, not only at this point in time, but in general. An indirect way of doing this would be, for example, to ask if tutoring is something that the candidate has aspired to doing for some time. Now, even though a primary motivation is very likely to be to earn money, you will find that it is quite easy to recognize a person who genuinely wants to help others learn. These people get personal satisfaction from helping others achieve their goals, and that is the kind of person who you should be looking for. So, for example, a college student who needs to earn extra money would have several options for how to go about doing it. Of such students who choose tutoring, some will be making that choice because it is something that they would like to be doing even if they didn't need to earn extra money. You may think that tutoring is quite lucrative, but when you factor in the travel time and the lesson preparation time, the earnings are really not disproportionately high.

4. Next, you should negotiate the price, having established the experience level of the candidate. Clarify the exact length of each lesson and make sure it is understood that the price of the lesson includes travel time and lesson preparation time. Clarify and agree on possible exceptions to this, such as customized test preparation and grading. At this stage you would also begin the discussion of whether you want regular lessons, or targeted blocks of lessons. If the tutor is not so experienced, you should make sure he/she fully understands the necessary commitments. Also establish where the lessons would take place (usually it would be in your home, but other arrangements in public places are possible).

5. As the interview draws to a close you should ask for the names and telephone numbers of three people who can provide a character reference. The three people should not be relatives of the candidate. They could be previous employers, previous or current teachers, advisers, mentors, or other professional contacts. They need not live in your town. If the candidate has trouble coming up with more than two people you could expand the criterion to include friends, but you will have to use your judgment to assess the objectiveness of the information that you get from such references. If you have not eliminated a candidate during the interview, follow up the references. You should be looking for qualities such as accountability, reliability, trustworthiness, verification of relevant statements on the resumé, and competence to carry out the proposed tutoring.

Since the candidate will be working with minors, you should especially establish the candidate's suitability in this respect. A previous employer, mentor or supervisor at a place that involved working with children, such as a summer camp, would be an excellent source of information in this respect. If you cannot get such information then it is better to be on the safe side and move on to another candidate. If a candidate claims to be good with children and fit for the job, and if it is hard to find somebody who could verify it, then that in itself is not a good sign. In general, even if a tutor has glowing references, you should not leave a tutor alone with your child. Plan for an adult to be at home for the duration of the tutorial. The same applies for a tutorial in a public place, unless you know your tutor well enough to have established trust.

6. After each interview is over be sure to write down critical notes from the interview, including your impressions and specific lists of items that you thought were strong and weak points of the candidate. It is important to do this, and to do it as soon as possible, because when it comes to comparing the candidates, you will be surprised by how much you can forget, especially as the interviews may be spread over a period of a week or more. If you like, you can make up a semiformal checklist grid that you can fill out (with room for actual comments), so that your assessment of the candidates is more uniform. You can even make up a point system for various criteria.

7. When you have completed all the interviews, review your notes and rank the candidates. Call the top candidate after you have made your decision. It is a courtesy to let the others know of your decision so that they may move on. It is not pleasant to have to tell the candidates who were not selected, but be honest and say that the person you chose better suited your needs. This is much better than saying that the candidate you selected was better qualified, because that is ambiguous, since there are many factors that affect your decision. Arrange an appointment with the selected candidate, allowing extra time for the first lesson (about 15 to 30 minutes), so that you can discuss your child's particular needs, strengths and weaknesses, and the general plan for the lessons. Be sure to pay the tutor for the extra time. If he/she feels cheated, bad feelings may adversely affect the quality of tutoring that you get.

5.5 Targeted Tutoring

I have said that if you decide not to go for regular, frequent tutoring, your child may still benefit from a limited set of targeted lessons with specific goals in mind. This option may be chosen either because you cannot afford more frequent tutoring, or because it is more appropriate for your child's needs. In this section I will discuss the particular situations that could benefit from targeted tutoring. However, first of all it is important to understand and appreciate two things.

1. It is absolutely critical that you have a clear plan of what you hope to achieve from the limited number of lessons. You must have very specific goals. Without a crystal-clear agenda and set of goals, you will be wasting your money: you may as well throw your money onto a log fire. You should allocate time with the tutor for you to come up with a plan together for the targeted lessons. Before the first lesson you should then discuss the plan and specific goals with your child, and ensure that he/she fully understands what is expected of him/her, especially if it involves doing particular assignments or timed tests in between the lessons.

2. The targeted lessons should not be spread over too long a time period. Again, you will be wasting your money if the lessons are spread over too long a period in time. For example, do not arrange for four to five lessons spread over an entire semester, unless each lesson is self-contained and attacks only one specific "issue." The targeted lessons will usually be more effective if they are done in a relatively short amount of time. Once or twice a week will be appropriate in most situations. Unless the agenda involves reviewing material for an exam, arranging for tutorials more frequently than twice a week is not recommended as time should be given to "digest" what was covered in the lessons.

Now I will list the specific situations that targeted tutoring would be appropriate for, and that would most likely produce results, with a good return on your investment. For each situation I will give some advice on how to plan the sessions and set goals.

5.5.1 Resolving Issues with Problematic Topics

The most obvious situation is to address specific topics that your child is having difficulty with, or to strengthen skills and proficiency in particular areas that may be weaker than others. There will likely be more topics to cover than you have the resources for, so you must decide what those topics are going to be, by means of discussions with both your child and the tutor. Having decided on the topics, discuss with your tutor how much time should be spent on each topic, and what the particular difficulties might be. Discuss whether these difficulties can be traced to a lack of proficiency in more fundamental topics, in which case the tutor must go back to strengthen those. Remember my calculus student who was in trouble because she had forgotten her multiplication tables? Another example may be a student having trouble with precalculus or calculus because he/she may have lost proficiency in basic geometry and/or trigonometry. Yet another example might be a student having trouble with logarithms because he/she may have got rusty on the rules of exponents.

You get the idea. Your child will almost certainly need one diagnostic lesson before such problems are identified so the plan and the goals need to be somewhat elastic. Discussion with the tutor after each lesson will be critical. It is important not to try to cover too many different topics with limited resources. You will get a higher return from targeting one or two topics, identifying the foundational topics that are causing the problems, and then following up with strengthening those. You may be surprised by how many "branches" that will need following up, just by attacking one topic.

The tutor should give appropriate exercises or problems for your child to do in between each lesson. The actual material should depend on the results of the tutorial, so you may need to give the tutor a day or so after the lesson to come up with the appropriate exercises. Having said that, the tutor should consider giving, as part of the homework, the *same* exercises or problems that were done during the tutorial, *but* this time the tutor would ask your child to try to do as much as possible without looking at the solutions. Then the student looks at the solutions, puts them away, and tries again to go as far as possible. This is repeated until entire problems can be done without looking at the solutions. You will be surprised by how much can be forgotten in a short time, and by how effective it is to do the *same* problem over and over until it can be done without looking at the solution. I use this technique very successfully all the time and it was a critical factor for myself, when I was at school, to attain top grades. For every topic I would find as many worked examples as I could get my hands on, and I would then repeat doing them until I could do them without looking at the solutions a single time. After that, doing a new problem on the same topic was a breeze because *the process of repetition had highlighted which parts of the problem I was having difficulty understanding*, and completion of the process had then improved that understanding. The point here is that *forgetting particular steps in solving a problem happens because those steps were not properly understood in the first place*. Once something is *truly* understood it is far less likely to be forgotten.

One way to structure and formalize the process described above is to go through a complete worked problem and write down a set of very brief memory joggers, or *prompts*, at critical steps in the problem. Then, the student puts away the worked solution and uses the prompts (which may consist of only one to a few words) to solve the problem. On the next attempt the student tries to do the problem "cold," with no prompts. If that proves to be too difficult, the student makes a new set of prompts that are even briefer than the first set (and the new set most likely will consist of a smaller number of prompts).

It is common to think that doing the same problem over and over again is of limited value because after a while some of the solution is simply recalled from memory without thinking. It is wrong to conclude this, because, on the contrary, repeating the same problem over and over pinpoints precisely where the difficulties are. The student will get stuck at the same places over and over, but the number of hurdles will get less and less, until eventually there are only one or two, and those will finally get resolved too. The student and the tutor should pay attention to which particular points are the last to get resolved. A pattern may emerge even from different types of problems because there may be something in common with the issues that are the last to get resolved. I will also add that I have often given my students a practice exam that is the *same* exam that they have already done, perhaps even only a few days earlier. It is extremely rare for a student to get 100% on a repeat exam that he/she has done before. Obviously, the score needs to be adjusted for the fact that the student has done the problems recently. The reason why I give the same exam again is that it really narrows down where the biggest problems are, which then tells me how I can most effectively and efficiently help the student.

In terms of a tutor helping with targeted topics, as I have described in this section, you will generally get what you pay for. A more experienced tutor is desirable, but if you cannot afford that, you can still get a good return for your money with a less experienced and less expensive tutor. If this is the case, then since the less experienced tutor may not have a ready reservoir of resources at hand, you can get a better return on your investment if you offer to spend a little extra on an additional book or two that has worked problems in the topics that are going to be covered. The books may or may not be exclusively on those topics. You could also offer to pay a little extra for the tutor to research such additional materials, or you could offer to spend the time doing that research yourself. Either way, compared to the total cost of the tutoring, the little extra money and/or time invested will greatly leverage what you are already spending, thereby increasing the benefit to your child. To help you and the tutor with this, there are some pointers on the website associated with this book (http://www.helpyourchildwithmath.com) that may be useful for the tutor.

5.5.2 Diagnostic Testing

Another situation that is suitable for targeted tutoring is one in which your child could benefit from diagnostic testing. Such testing may be appropriate under a variety of circumstances. The most common of these circumstances occurs when a student is experiencing general difficulty and/or underachievement in math, but the origin, or root, of the problem is not known or understood. Careful diagnostic testing can identify where the problem areas are in order that they can be tackled. School teachers generally do not have the time or resources to administer and analyze such diagnostics at a level of detail that a tutor working with you and your child can. On the other hand, the results and information from the diagnostic testing can be relayed to your child's teacher(s). I have actually been in a situation myself where a student's parents and teacher arranged to meet with me at the school in order to discuss the specifics of the student's problem areas in math. Even without an actual meeting with a student's teacher, information from diagnostic testing is invaluable to both the student's parents and his/her teachers because it enables the help that parents and teachers provide to be more focused, relevant, and efficient. The information is also invaluable to the tutor for the same reasons. I myself (as a tutor) use diagnostic testing frequently as a powerful tool, usually with every new student, and whenever a situation requires it. For example, a common situation is one in which the student will be doing a major exam that is to cover material that the student may not have been exposed to for some time.

An experienced tutor will already have the materials ready to be able to put together diagnostic tests that are appropriate for a given student, and he/she may even tailor the tests as necessary. On the other hand, a less experienced tutor may not have such resources, and it will serve you well to work with the tutor to research materials that are available already, either in books or online, and help put together appropriate tests. Remember that your involvement here is due to the fact that you will be paying a lot less for the less experienced tutor. You are effectively paying the difference with your time. You may also offer to pay for any books that need to be purchased (for example, books containing practice tests or problems). There is now a lot of material also available online, and the website http://www.helpmychildwithmath.com has some useful, carefully selected links for this purpose.

Note that more than one diagnostic test may be necessary. The tests should be done outside the regular tutorial time, under your supervision. You should enforce strict examination conditions and strict timing. The duration of each test will have been agreed upon between you and the tutor. It is important to remember that the length of time given for the diagnostic test is a critical factor for the purpose of the test. The tutor needs to know where *all* the student's problem areas lie in terms of knowledge, skills, accuracy, and *speed*. The student may know all the material well, but if the test cannot be completed in sufficient time, the knowledge and skill is useless. Before taking the tests (or actually, any kind of test or exam), I suggest reading part 2 of this book (study skills and exam success techniques), discussing it with your child, and making sure he/she understands how exam performance can be improved.

Even if the student is more advanced and reads part 2 of this book himself/herself, it is still a good idea for you *both* to read the material and discuss it. I recommend an initial meeting with the tutor (without your child present) to discuss the particulars of the diagnostic tests in the context of your child's needs, and to set a schedule for taking the tests, as well as for the follow-up tutorials. The tutor could then mail or deliver the tests to you after the meeting. The completed tests could then be mailed back to the tutor (or he/she could pick them up), before the first tutorial. Ensure that there is enough time for the tutor to thoroughly go over and grade the tests, and to come up with a plan for the tutorials. You should come to an agreement before the tests are taken on how much you are going to pay the tutor for preparation of the materials, grading, and assessment.

5.5.3 Exam or Test Preparation

Another situation that would benefit from targeted tutoring is of course exam or test preparation. The exams could either be regular school tests, or standardized tests. Many of the points above, under "diagnostic testing" (§5.5.2) apply here, including meeting with the tutor to draw up a plan before beginning the tutoring sessions. The plan should, if possible, include having your child do timed practice tests in between the lessons under your supervision, if necessary. This will be important for maximizing the effectiveness of the tutoring because the tutor can then better tailor the lessons to the student's particular needs. It may even be helpful to set a timed diagnostic test before the first lesson. Also, as described earlier, it is important for you, as a parent, to read part 2 of this book, on exam techniques, and discuss it with your child, making sure he/she understands the methods and implements them. Again, if you are working with a less experienced tutor it will benefit you if you help with researching and securing materials such as practice tests. There are some pointers on the website http://www.helpyourchildwithmath.com that will be helpful for this purpose. As you know already, for practice tests designed for standardized exams, there is especially a lot of material available from a variety of sources that is "ready to go," in books, as well as online.

As part of the plan for lessons geared towards exam preparation, you and the tutor should discuss what is going to be covered, according to the number of lessons that you plan to arrange. The important thing is not to try to cover too much because, in the worst case, nothing will be covered in sufficient depth, possibly making the lessons a waste of time and money. Another way that you can maximize the benefits of the tutoring is for you and your child to come up with a list of specific math problems that he/she may be stuck on or does not understand. It is not very efficient to spend tutorial time waiting for the student to find the problems, or to try to remember them. So make sure everything is ready beforehand. On a related note, the tutorial should not be consumed on just one or two problems: this can easily happen, and is again a waste of time of and money. In your preparatory discussion with the tutor you should make it clear that if a problem is taking too long (perhaps because the student continues to have trouble with it), the best thing to do is to move on to the next problem. However, the tutor should also ask the student to try to make progress again after the lesson, to think about it some more, and to be prepared to discuss it again in the next lesson.

The most effective use of time during tutorials is for the tutor to go over the solution of carefully selected problems (in addition to the problems that the student has specifically mentioned that he/she is having trouble with). Then the student should do the same (or similar) problem by himself/herself, with prompting as necessary, especially if too much time is being consumed. There will likely not be enough time for the tutor to go over every problem that was not correct. Rather, the tutor should go over only the most troublesome issues, and just give pointers for the rest, requesting that the student try them again before the next lesson.

In chapter 9, I mention that there are certain techniques and skills for spotting quick and short ways to solve certain types of multiple-choice problems. These short cuts are very often missed by students, and this is not helped by the fact that the "big-name" companies with big, thick books on test-taking strategies don't always tell students about them either (see §9.2 for a more detailed discussion). Training in these methods is an excellent use of targeted tutoring. For the less experienced tutor I have put some tips and advice on the website `http://www.helpyourchildwithmath.com`.

For standardized tests there are many courses available for specific purposes, such as the *PSAT/NMSQT*[1], *SAT*[2], and *ACT*[3] exams. A common question that parents have is whether such courses are worth the cost, and whether they are effective for significantly increasing a student's score. The courses are generally very expensive, but the offerors have a lot of experience behind them and a track record. However, it is also important to remember that the factors that affect whether or not your child's score will increase are not only a function of the experienced instruction. The results also depend of course on whether your child does certain necessary tasks himself/herself. In other words, it is possible to pay a lot of money for a course and not see the results that you hope for, if your child does not do his/her part (see part 2 of this book, on exam preparation techniques). On the other hand, you will have more control in getting real results with an experienced private tutor, and this may cost less. So the answer is that if you can afford one of the "big-name" expensive courses, the chances are good for helping to raise your child's score, *if* he/she does his/her part. If the price tag is too high however, you can get similar increases in performance and score *if* you can find the right tutor. In other words, more effort is required on your part, in return for the lower cost. Of course, with the private tutoring option the student must still do the necessary work himself/herself in between the lessons, but you will have more control in fine-tuning the plan, in terms of working with the tutor, and possibly changing tutors if it is not working out.

How frequent targeted lessons should be for exam preparation really depends on your child's particular situation. I find that lessons for exam preparation benefit from "doubles" (two lessons back to back), as opposed to several separate lessons in a week. For very important exams, I usually

---

[1] PSAT/NMSQT is a registered trademark of the College Board and National Merit Scholarship Corporation, which were not involved in the production of, and do not endorse, the work in this book.

[2] SAT is a registered trademark of the College Board, which was not involved in the production of, and does not endorse, the work in this book.

[3] ACT is a registered trademark of ACT, Inc., which was not involved in the production of, and does not endorse, the work in this book.

find that the students need somewhere between two to four lessons a week for two to three weeks. Obviously, if you cannot afford that many lessons, a smaller number will still benefit your child, but you must plan carefully exactly what is to be covered in the lessons.

Another question parents (and students) often have, pertains to how quickly can one expect to see an increase in the score in exams, and by how much. It is common to find that a significant increase occurs after the first few lessons, but then the improvements are slower thereafter. This makes sense when you consider that the student begins to implement methods that he/she may have been unaware of, compensating for previously achieving far less than his/her potential. So whether you go for a course, or for private tutoring, if your child is doing exactly what is asked of him/her, you can usually expect to see real results very quickly. For example, I have worked with a student who increased her *SAT* math score by well over a hundred in just two weeks. However in the month that followed the score hovered around the same level, eventually increasing only by another 20 or so.

5.5.4 Graphing and the Graphing Calculator

The graphing calculator plays an important role in algebra II and beyond, and is something that students commonly fall into several traps with, resulting in underperformance. This is because of the lack of training, especially with respect to some subtle issues that I have discussed in detail in chapter 4. These issues may well have been discussed by the child's regular teacher at school, but are easily missed, usually because of lapses in paying attention on the part of the student. It is common for students to assume that there is nothing particularly difficult with the graphing calculator so there is a tendency to "switch off." Therefore, increasing proficiency with the graphing calculator is something that can be an excellent use of targeted tutoring. A lesson or two with the graphing calculator can result in a significant difference in skill level. The details warrant an extended discussion, and the reader is referred to chapter 4 for this. A related topic is that of graphing curves manually, and this is another area in which students unnecessarily underperform because of lack of training and knowledge. Manual graphing goes hand in hand with using the graphing calculator, so the two topics should be addressed together. Again, details were discussed in chapter 4.

As a parent, you should remember that your child will naturally claim that he/she is perfectly well-acquainted and competent with the graphing calculator and/or manual graphing. Consequently, he/she may strongly resist the proposed tutoring sessions. As you know, the gap between a child's perception of his/her ability to handle a particular topic, and his/her *actual* ability may be large. As I have mentioned before, this is not just a problem with grade-school students: I have seen severe cases of it all the way up to Ph.D. level. Although the kind of resistance I am talking about is common with respect to any subject or topic, in my experience it is particularly acute with respect to graphing, and the graphing calculator. This is partly because these topics *seem* like they are easy ("no-brainers"), but they are in fact not so easy. Fundamental mistakes are very common, and misunderstanding is common. Yet, the student may not even realize that he/she has misunderstood something, or that he/she is making mistakes that in most cases don't necessarily lead to the wrong answer, but in some situations those mistakes could make a lot of difference. Proficiency in graphing, and using the graphing calculator is critical, not just for topics that explicitly make use of such skills, but for 9th grade and above, there are things that the student should be learning that bleed into, and benefit, many other areas of the student's math skills. So, if you can afford it, or if you can provide such training yourself, you must find a way to persuade your child to agree to at least a couple of training sessions in handgraphing and using the graphing calculator.

5.5.5 Interpretation of Key Phrases in Questions

A significant and common factor that results in underperformance in math problems and exams is the incorrect interpretation of questions. If a student misunderstands a question and provides a solution to a fictitious question, the result is a large and unnecessary loss of points. Yet, there are certain standard phrases and frameworks that are used over and over again in math questions, so it is possible with the correct training to avoid falling into common traps. A related issue is the "translation" of so-called "word problems" in math into the correct equations. It is common for students to have difficulty in setting up the correct equations, even though they might find it easy to actually solve the equations (if the math problem began with the equations already given).

In many applied math problems setting up a diagram is also critical to solving a problem and it is also common for students to have difficulty in setting up the diagram correctly. Again, with the correct training it is possible for a student to rapidly improve his/her ability to translate word problems into equations, and a diagram if it is appropriate, for a given problem. Therefore, if a tutor can put together a set of carefully selected example problems, then training in the interpretation of key phrases, and in translating word problems into equations and diagrams is an excellent use of targeted tutoring. By reducing the chances of misinterpreting math problems, just a few lessons can result in a significant gain in exam (and homework) performance.

5.5.6 Customized Oral Drills

Earlier in the book I discussed the power of oral drills (§2.7 and §3.6), and some important examples of key oral drills are given in appendix A. I have also mentioned that if you are unable to administer the drills yourself, having someone help in this area is a very good use of paid tutoring. Some instructions on administering the drills are also given in appendix A, and these may be useful for a tutor who is not so experienced. More specific oral drills can be designed and tailored to address specific difficulties that your child may be experiencing. Constructing and administering such "customized drills" is something that even a less experienced tutor can come up with, because the material will be drawn from exercises that will already have been done by your child as part of diagnostic testing, other tests or exams, or regular assignments.

5.6 Case Study: The Student Who Dropped From a Grade B to a Grade C

I will now tell you a true story that is an illustrative warning of how paying for tutoring *could* be ineffective and a waste of money, if you and your child do not do what is required to actually benefit from the tutoring. The story concerns the very unusual case of a student I once tutored, whose grade actually went *down* after I tutored her for over a year. For the sake of anonymity, I will refer to the student as Sally. I have never before, or since, had a student whose grade went *down* after I had worked with him/her. There are cases I have had in which the students grade did not go up, but Sally is the only one whose grade went down. Sally's case is interesting to examine because it demonstrates very dramatically that benefiting from tutoring is not guaranteed. Although Sally's case is unusually extreme, we may hope to learn something from it, in terms of ensuring that you and your child are maximizing the benefits from tutoring in every way possible.

Now, Sally was a very bright student, and she was actually very enthusiastic about the math, and genuinely interested in virtually every topic. She was keen and quick to learn and understand new material. When I first started tutoring Sally (in algebra II) she was consistently getting "B" grades or higher at school, in homework, tests, and exams. The goal of Sally and her parents was to raise her performance level in order to achieve consistent "A" grades, with the help of tutoring. After some diagnostic testing and a couple of tutorials, I confirmed her B-grade performance, but I could already tell from working with her that she had A-grade potential. I was convinced that in a couple of months I could help Sally combat the underachievement, and bump her up to get consistent "A" grades. I enjoy such a challenge because it can have a tangible result in improving a person's life in far-reaching ways. For example, if Sally was able to get the consistent "A" grade in math that she wanted, it would open the doors to the career choices that she desired. I came up with a detailed plan that included frequent test-based monitoring to give myself, Sally, and her parents the feedback necessary to know whether the desired results were being achieved.

Well, two months passed and my own testing, as well as school work, showed that Sally was still at a "B." Everyone including myself was of course disappointed, but I was extremely puzzled because during the tutorials Sally was picking up things very quickly, and was able to do well with problems on *new* topics that I gave her during tutorials. She was able to do the problems while I observed, without too much prompting or too many hints from me. What was going wrong? I tried to trace back and analyze how all the tutorials and the overall plan had been going so far, in order to try to figure out what the problem was. From the analysis I could only come up with one hunch.

I tested out my hunch, giving Sally some targeted, custom-made exercises to do under timed conditions in between tutorials. I made a point to speak to her parents, requesting that they ensure that Sally did the exercises that I gave her. After a couple of times of doing this my hunch was confirmed. *Sally did not do the exercises that I had set her.* In my analysis in which I tried to figure out what was going wrong, I had realized that Sally almost *never* did the exercises that I had asked her to do in between tutorials. The reason why this had "slipped through the cracks" was that she always had an excuse that usually went along the lines that she *did* do some relevant work in between the tutorials, it was just that it was not the work I had asked her to do. Sally would even show me the work she had done, instead of the work I had asked her to do. Although I did tell her every time that she should really have done the work that I had asked her to do, I was hesitant to reprimand her too much because she was making an effort, and she was not lazy. I would ask Sally why she did the other work, and not what I had asked her to do, and her response was usually one of two reasons. Either she got interested and diverted by something she saw in a book or elsewhere, or she decided herself that it would benefit her more if she did the work that she did, instead of what I had asked her to do.

I had tried to explain to Sally and her parents several times that even if two exercises are on the same topic in math, the outcome of doing the different exercises may be completely different in terms of developing or improving a particular skill. It is analogous to somebody saying that he/she wants to tone and strengthen his/her biceps, but instead of following tried and trusted techniques, the person decides to lift two bags of potatoes thirty times every day.

So, when Sally's grade had not improved in two months, and I had confirmed that she was still not doing the exercises that I had asked her to do, I explained again to her and her parents that ignoring that advice was the single most likely reason that Sally was still underachieving. Each time, Sally would promise that she would do the work that *I* had set. Sometimes she did do it, but most of the time she did not. Her parents were too busy to make sure that she did what she was supposed to, and ultimately they could not enforce my requests. This went on for over a year, and Sally still consistently achieved mostly "B" grades, interspersed with the occasional "A." Then the unthinkable happened. One day Sally dropped to a "C." As you can imagine, this was devastating and deeply disappointing for everyone, including myself. Sally was very bright, and perfectly capable of obtaining consistent "A" grades, but she never reached her full potential. Understandably, Sally's parents discontinued the tutoring.

The lesson to be learned from Sally's case is that tutoring may be ineffective if the student is not willing to do his/her part, and if the parents are unable to enforce the tutor's requests. If the tutor is experienced, the student must take the advice that is offered, and do *precisely the work that is requested in between tutorials*. If the tutor is not so experienced, you must work with the tutor to figure out what your child needs to do in between tutorials. It is easy for a student to get sidetracked and do things other than those requested by the tutor. I have seen this phenomenon all the way up to the Ph.D. level.

5.7 How to Get the Most Out of Tutoring

In this section I will summarize the key factors that will help you to get the most out of tutoring, from the point of view of maximizing the effectiveness of the tutoring for your child. Aside from getting the best results, it will leverage your money (as well as your time and effort). Some of the points have already been discussed, but it is worthwhile collecting everything together.

1. You and your child must *first* achieve the goals discussed in chapter 1 and chapter 2. Specifically, your child must be as receptive as possible to learning math, and he/she must already have started implementing the day-to-day techniques described in chapter 3. Ideally you will also have already discussed the study techniques and exam preparations skills described in part 2 of this book.

2. You must have a definite plan for the frequency and purpose of the tutoring, as described in this chapter. Formulate a plan with the tutor before any lessons begin.

3. Discuss progress with the tutor regularly, as the plan may need to be dynamic. It may need to be modified as necessary. The discussions with the tutor can be brief, but if you need a more in-depth discussion, allocate a time in advance, and pay the tutor for his/her extra time.

4. If you only have a limited budget, don't use tutoring *only* for homework help because the long-term benefits will be limited. It provides little leveraging of your money, and it will not necessarily improve your child's performance in tests and exams. You should ensure that your child does as much of the homework as possible *before* tutorials, and only bring up those parts of the homework in tutorials that presented difficulty. In fact, as a matter of routine, I usually ask the student at the beginning of the tutorial what he/she has been doing at school since the previous tutorial, and if there are any specific issues with the homework that need to be discussed. Parents and tutors should note that it is very common for a student to report that everything is fine and that there were no problems with work covered in class, when in fact at some later point it becomes clear that everything was not "fine." So I usually throw out some "friendly feeler" questions as spot checks while I am browsing through the student's class notes and/or homework.

5. Make sure that you and your child do exactly what is requested by the tutor in between tutorials. If you (or your child) have a different opinion as to what needs to be done, discuss it with the tutor first.

Chapter 6

Ingredients for Exam Success

6.1 Maximizing Exam and Test Performance

This chapter through to chapter 10 constitutes part 2 of the book and is specifically about how students can strive to achieve their full potential for performance in exams and tests. The discussions necessarily cover preparation and study techniques, in addition to strategies to employ whilst actually taking exams and tests. This part of the book is written in the second person, aimed at the student. This is because it is intended to be read by your child if he/she is in or above 9th grade or so, as well as by you, the parent. If you both read this part of the book, you should both discuss what you have read, because some things may have been missed. If your child is not going to be reading this part of the book, then you should read part 2 of the book in its entirety yourself, and teach your child what you learn, in stages.

Exams are designed to enable a person of average intelligence and ability to not only pass but in fact to do fairly well. Yet an alarmingly large number of perfectly capable people continue to be disappointed by failure, or by not achieving the grades that they are capable of attaining. Why is it that some people do very well in exams whilst others do not? Obviously there is some connection with intrinsic ability, but this is far from the whole story. It is a fact that people are simply not taught how to do well in exams. In other words, how to best utilize and recall acquired knowledge, and how to apply that acquired knowledge under the time and psychological pressure imposed by the exam itself. Unfortunately, there is not enough focus in the classroom on successful exam preparation and exam-taking techniques. This is particularly disappointing when you consider the fact that from a very early age a person's life can be affected in a significant way by their success (or otherwise) in exams.

Really, there are *no* secrets. The techniques described here are not new. They are just not sufficiently well-known. All of the techniques can be used by absolutely everyone to increase their exam performance. That could mean the difference between passing or failing, or between "C" and "A" grades, or even between failing and getting "straight A's." Improvement in performance depends on *you*, and how much *you* are willing to apply these techniques. Many people make mistakes in their study techniques. If you follow the advice in this book, you will be able to avoid unnecessarily wasting time. You will also learn what to do on the night before an exam, depending on your particular circumstances. You will learn what to do during the exam itself. You will be also be able to better handle "blackouts," those horrifying periods when your mind becomes completely blank. You panic and your whole body is mesmerized, and you could be left completely helpless.

Remember that the key to success in *anything* is to have a positive attitude. Without this, anything you attempt to do will not be as good as it could be. You must go into an exam or test *believing* that you will exceed your expectations in performance. If you aim for anything less, that is very likely what you will achieve, or worse. If you do all the things in this book to help you, you should notice a very substantial improvement in your exam performance.

6.2 Concentration and Distractions

The mind generally works in bursts of concentration lasting in general from 15 to 30 minutes. Obviously this varies a lot and depends on many factors (like how much sleep you've had, for example). The point is that there will be natural breaks in your concentration. That's fine. However, to make the most of those periods of concentration, you must be totally focused. If your desk is facing a window you may waste large amounts of time gazing out of the window, and your concentration will never get geared up to its peak capability. You must use your time wisely. Have your desk facing a wall if you need to. If you can't move it, cover the window. The point is that you should have *no visual distractions while you are studying*. That includes television! No TV.

With respect to listening to music while you are studying, everyone is different, and in fact, once you have learned to build up concentration levels sufficiently, it may not be such a problem. Listening to music while studying is generally not as bad as being exposed to visual distractions. In fact, in some cases it can even help to start off an intense period of concentration. Once your mind is racing it will automatically shut out the music, no matter how loud it is. On the other hand, for some people music may be as distracting as visual interference. Find what works best for you (but be honest with yourself). At all times during study, try to avoid listening to radio stations which have a lot of talking and/or commercials as this can be extremely distracting. Also, if you are trying to simulate examination conditions (see chapter 8), you should *not* listen to anything.

6.3 Maintain Accessibility to Topics That You Already Covered

It is important, for each subject area in math that you study (for example, geometry, algebra I, algebra II, etc.), to form an ongoing mental map of what you have learned and a "bird's eye view" of how the different subtopics that you have learned relate to each other. For younger students this is something parents can help with. It is helpful to have a full list of subtopics that you are going to study for the entire subject area, and it is important to regularly examine the list in the context of what you have learned.

It is common for students to forget about a subtopic as soon as they move on to the next one. There are deep relationships between various subtopics in math, and maintaining a "mind map" helps the brain to organize and recall information. In practice, what does this mean you have to do? You don't have to do much. Something as simple as browsing back through your textbook every now and then, just quickly scanning over pages in the textbook that you have already covered, may be sufficient. This "browsing" may seem like it wouldn't do much, but it is a very powerful start to maintaining a mind map, and it alerts the brain to the fact that the information is not to be stored in a part of memory that is not readily accessed. In other words, *regular browsing will make the information more accessible when it comes to exam time later.* This is actually a very powerful and "deep" fact that is highly underappreciated. You may not be aware of it, but you will remember more than you think you might, in the process of browsing. This semiregular and "gentle" recall of information prevents the brain from filing away stuff to the "back of the drawer," because the brain gets the message that you're going to need that stuff. Even just regularly browsing the "contents" pages of a textbook can be very powerful.

At the next level, you can do more than just browse. The way this works is that when you browse the textbook you may see a keyword and think, "Yes, I remember doing that in class, but *I can't remember a single thing about it!*" If this happens (and it will happen often), you should immediately look up your notes on that particular topic and slowly, even after just skimming your notes, a lot of it will come back to your memory automatically. Then go back and continue browsing. Keep looking up your notes when you need to. Ideally this should be done once a week or so, but in practice this may not be possible. Try to do it as often as you can.

6.4 Don't Spend Too Much Time on Your Favorite Areas

When you are reviewing for exams you should not spend too much time on your most favorite topics This is because it is likely that you are already competent in these areas and it may be more useful for you to spend some of that time on your *least* favorite topics. In fact you may subconsciously devote virtually no time to topics that you do not like, and this will adversely affect your performance in exams.

Success in anything (and exams are no exception), involves doing things that are not pleasant. You *must* spend time on topics that you dislike. Inevitably, you will also be reviewing and preparing for exams on subjects aside from math, and you must apply the same principle to your overall studies too. If math is one of your least favorite subjects, make sure that you organize your review schedule for each week in a way that does not allocate a disproportionately small amount of time to math.

6.5 The Wall Sheet: a Powerful Memory Aid

Here I will describe a very powerful technique to commit difficult topics to your long-term memory. In the course of your studies you will find certain specific items (usually definitions, rules, or equations), that you always have trouble recalling. Start constructing a "wall sheet." Take a piece of paper that has dimensions of 8.5 inches by 11 inches (or approximately 22 cm by 28 cm). As you come across the specific items that are difficult to recall, write a little memory jogger on the sheet, using small neat handwriting. Avoid using complete sentences. Try to use diagrams or symbols as much as possible, keeping words to an absolute minimum. Stick this sheet up on the wall in front of your desk. If you cannot stick it on the wall, prop it up on your desk using a stand made from card. Then, when you get natural lapses in your concentration, you will look up, and the wall sheet will be there. Even if you look at it for only a few seconds each time, that information will be going straight to your brain. Long-term memory will be in the process of being carved out.

A word about mnemonics, which are a combination of letters designed to jog your memory into recalling a long sentence, group of words, a mathematical rule, or some collection of facts. Personally, I find that mnemonics do not work for me because I often cannot remember what the mnemonic itself means (I have always had a terrible memory!). However, everybody is different, and you have to find out what works best for you. I have taught students for whom mnemonics were useful to some extent, but remember that mnemonics are not effective for everyone. What works for *me* better than a mnemonic is to actually visualize a formula, for example, and to put the *use* of a rule or formula *into practice* enough times that it becomes committed to memory, *through improved understanding*.

Understanding *why* a formula or equation is what it is, rather than just taking it as given, automatically commits it to memory in a very powerful way. If you do utilize mnemonics, *use them sparingly*. The more of them that you utilize, the less will be their collective effectiveness. What is even more important is to understand that every time you make use of a mnemonic, it takes you one step further away from building intuition. This is because the mnemonic detaches you from the core meaning, or subject matter, of what you are trying to commit to memory. Anything that hinders the development and nurturing of intuition will ultimately have a detrimental effect.

Now, back to that wall sheet. At first, you will resist looking at the wall sheet after you have put it up. That's normal. After a while your brain will get used to the idea, and will not resist as much. Then you will not mind looking at it. Eventually you will find that you do not need some of the things on the wall sheet as they will have become ingrained into your memory after being exposed to it day after day. You may then replace some of the items with new ones when you think it is safe. It is better to make a new one, rather than make the old one messy.

You should restrict the material that you put on your wall sheet to things that you have *a lot* of difficulty with. This is because if there is too much information on the wall sheet, the purpose will be defeated because the brain will refuse to digest too much information at once, and it will simply become "blind" to the wall sheet. You may have a separate wall sheet for different subject areas, but do not put more than two up at any one time. If you have several wall sheets, rotate them around on a regular basis.

Chapter 7

Reviewing for Exams

7.1 Set Goals and Get Focused at Every Study Session

It is well known that the mind will achieve far more when there is a *definite* and *specific* objective, as opposed to simply a vague idea or plan. This is because the mind has a natural tendency to meander, wander off on a tangent, or procrastinate. You will be in a constant battle with this tendency, and if you don't take control of it you could easily waste hours and hours, while being fooled into thinking that you have done a lot of studying. You may as well have been doing something else far more enjoyable.

You need to get focused. How can you do that? Sit down at every study session with a *definite purpose*. Decide on an *exact* time for the duration of your study session. This is very important as it immediately helps to focus your mind. Then write down exactly what you hope to achieve in that session. Set your goals slightly higher than you think is realistic. If you set them too low, you will underachieve and possibly waste time. If you set them too high and don't achieve them all, that's fine because you can carry them over to the next session. Setting your goals high also helps to focus your mind.

You don't need to make a detailed plan. For example, it could be something as simple as, "In the next two hours review solving quadratic equations and do problems 1 to 15 on the review sheet." The main point is that you should set a *length of time* and *specific objectives* for your study sessions.

7.2 Nurture Your Active Memory

What you are about to learn in this section will help you avoid what is probably one of the most important mistakes people make in their study techniques.

7.2.1 Passive and Active Memory

Your memory can be thought of as operating in two modes: *passive* and *active*. To understand the difference, imagine looking at a word in a foreign language and then having to think of the equivalent word in your own language. That's passive memory. Now imagine looking at a word in your own language and then having to think of the equivalent in a foreign language. That's much harder, right? That's *active* memory. Another example of *passive* memory is a multiple-choice question, in which you are given several alternative answers to a question, out of which only one answer is correct. A corresponding example for *active* memory would consist of having to answer the same question, but without being given the multiple answer choices.

7.2.2 Active Memory Can Be Trained

Much like muscles that are never used, the powers and capabilities of active memory diminish through lack of use. Unfortunately, the manner in which most people study discourages the growth of active memory. Typically, we make notes from class or textbooks, read our notes several times, and complete exercises set in textbooks or by teachers, usually with the permission to look things up in textbooks and notes. All this makes use mostly of passive memory. This is highly unfortunate because, apart from multiple-choice questions, exams largely test your *active* memory. This is probably the single most important reason why people underachieve in exams.

In the same way that everyone can promote muscle growth by appropriate training of muscles that have been underused, every single person can train their active memory to become more powerful. It can be learned. How? It is so easy, yet most people simply do not do it. It takes more time than passive studying, but *active* studying is far more effective, so that in the end it will actually save you time.

The techniques for training active memory differ somewhat from subject to subject, but the essence of it is the same in every case. In math, what you have to do is to try to *iteratively repeat* solving a problem that is typical of its type, without *eventually* looking up anything. I have already talked about this in §3.4 and §5.5.1, but I will repeat some of it here because it is so important. A homework problem that you have done before is ideal for trying this out, but it could be any problem that you want to master. Write out the problem (or a brief version of it) on a blank piece of paper and put all of your notes, papers, and books aside and try to do the problem. You can look at your notes and textbook as much as you like immediately prior to attempting the problem, but once you start, you must try to go as far as you can. Then when you get stuck, take a *quick* look at your notes and/or text for a clue, but then put the notes and books aside again. You must really try hard before reaching the point of having to look things up. After doing so, continue trying to solve the problem. When you get stuck again, repeat the quick-look procedure. Continue until the problem is done.

Next, get another blank sheet of paper, put the first attempt aside, and then *do the problem again*. This time you will be able to get further before you get stuck. When you do get stuck, do the quick lookup again. Repeat the entire process until you can do the problem from start to finish without looking anything up. To make the process even more powerful, try doing *the same problem* again a couple of days later.

As I mentioned in §5.5.1, one way to structure and formalize the process described above is to go through the complete worked problem and write down a set of very brief memory joggers, or *prompts*, at critical steps in the problem. Then, you put away the worked solution and use the prompts (which may consist of only one to a few words), to solve the problem. On the next occasion you attempt to do the problem "cold," with no prompts. If that proves to be too difficult, you should then make a new set of prompts that are even briefer than the first set. The number of prompts in the second set will most likely be less than the number of prompts in the first set.

It is a mistake to think that doing the *same* problem over and over is not useful on the grounds that you will begin to recall some of it from memory without thinking. On the contrary, repeating the same problem over and over again pinpoints *precisely* where the difficulties are. You will get stuck at some of the *same* places over and over again, but the number of times that this happens will get less and less, until eventually there are only one or two hurdles, and those will finally get resolved too. You should pay attention to which particular points are the last to get resolved. A pattern may emerge even from different types of problems because there may be something in common with the issues that are the last to get resolved. You will be able to narrow down where the problems are, and that will help you to use your time most effectively and efficiently, and most importantly, it will help you to understand what you didn't understand before.

The process described above is rigorous training for your active memory. You may be surprised by how quickly that you begin to see substantial results. You may also be surprised that *you are better able to solve other, completely unrelated problems*, because certain mental processes have been activated or enhanced, and this will have a very beneficial carry-over effect on *everything* that you study. However, you must make it a habit. That's the difficult part. The natural tendency for the mind is to be lazy. Training active memory is challenging, but the benefits are absolutely enormous.

You will find that people who perform well in exams have very likely already figured out the power of *active* study techniques. It is not difficult to figure this out for yourself because the line of reasoning goes something like the following. In the exam you are going to have to answer questions without the benefit of being able to look things up. Therefore, it makes sense to try to simulate this situation before the exam, by trying to answer questions without looking things up, and then check your performance afterwards. The process could be repeated over and over again until the results are satisfactory. The difficult part, however, is actually *doing it* (as opposed to just thinking about it).

7.3 Don't Just Think It! Write It!

The actual process of *using your muscles to write* something is a powerful long-term memory aid. The more that you write out things (and in different ways), the more your long-term memory will be etched out. It is not good enough simply to read and think (although this is important for reviewing large amounts of material shortly before taking an exam, *but only if* you have done the long-term ground work). Writing out full solutions to problems in math is especially important compared to other subjects, whether it is part of reviewing for exams or whether you are learning new material.

Writing things out can also help you to *understand* difficult problems. For example, if you see a fully worked solution to a problem in a textbook, but don't understand one or more of the steps, try simply writing out the solution yourself. You may be surprised that while you are doing that, you suddenly understand something that you didn't before. Sometimes the brain has a strange way of working. Despite its enormous capacity, the brain can really benefit from an external "scratch pad." When you come across something that you don't understand, sometimes just writing out the steps in a brief form can make a great deal of difference.

7.4 Discipline and Motivation

It's all very well having these study techniques at your disposal but how do you get yourself to sit down at that desk in the first place? All the techniques I have discussed are useless if you don't sit down at the desk. You may find every possible excuse not to do so and that's natural. We will naturally do everything we can to avoid pain and unpleasantness. You must discipline yourself and keep yourself motivated.

First, you must keep focused on *why* you are doing this studying and *why* you want to do well in the exams. Always think of the long term, and how success in exams will improve your life. Doing well in the exams will give you more choices for college, and for later on in life in many tangible ways. Every day, visualize doing well in the exams and how it will benefit you. The more specific you can be, the better. Imagine yourself actually doing the things that you desire, that will be made possible by doing well in the exams. Imagine how it would *feel*. It could mean going into a particular career or doing something that you have always dreamed about. It could mean a real and substantial difference in your potential salary. Think about what your life would be like if you did not do well in the exams. Tell yourself of all these desires and benefits day in and day out. This is sometimes called "autosuggestion" to your subconscious mind, and it is extremely powerful for providing motivation and discipline.

The more emotion that you can put into the "visualizations," the better. Imagine yourself actually coming out of the exam room, elated, having performed brilliantly in the exams. Parents can play a vital role in the motivational aspects of achieving your full potential in tests and exams, and it is important to heed their advice and suggestions.

7.5 Active Memory for Proofs and Derivations

This section is especially important for students studying geometry because there are a lot of *proofs* that must be learned and recalled for exams and tests. These proofs (and other derivations of certain key results in several subtopics) often involve steps that are not obvious, and it is easy to get stuck. You should learn proofs and derivations using active memory, and use temporary wall sheets to help. In general, for any topic in math, make sure that you understand, if at all possible, the relations between different equations and formulas because this will vastly reduce the amount you have to remember.

Make sure that you know the *fundamental* equations and formulas, from which everything else can be derived. For example, certain equations in calculus can be very tricky to derive, and you simply have to know them. Use wall sheets. After a while, many types of derivations will become second nature, and you will never forget them. You must also make sure that you know what formulas and information will be *given* to you as part of an exam. On the other hand, just because certain information or formulas will be given, don't think that it is a reason not to learn to recall the formulas (or other information) that will be given. It is easy to misuse the information that is given to you for an exam, and I have found that this often trips up the unwary student.

When solving applied math problems, always draw a diagram first, before you do anything else. This helps to crystallize and focus your mind on the problem. The diagrams should be large and clear. Setting up a diagram correctly can actually be critical for solving a problem correctly. Practice with setting up diagrams for applied math problems is something for which targeted tutoring is an excellent use of because it greatly leverages a limited budget (see §5.5.5).

Chapter 8

Simulated Exams and Tests

8.1 The Vital Importance of Simulated Exams

By now, you should be in no doubt as to the importance of training your active memory. Taking this one step further leads you to what is a critical factor for significantly enhancing your performance in exams, and striving towards your full potential. That additional step is to impose a time limit, in order to simulate exam conditions as perfectly as possible. This additional step brings in a whole new dimension because it simulates, to some extent, the psychological pressure that you will experience during a real exam.

Even though you know that if you fail or do not do well in the simulated exam, believe me, if you are not cheating yourself, you will be sweating. This is because you know that if the real exam is not very far away, if you underperform in a simulated exam, you will very likely underperform in the real exam. If you get a "C" in the simulated exam, you know that you have a considerable amount of work to do if you want an "A" in the real exam. The adrenalin will also be pumping because of the natural human fear of failure. Even though you know very well you are doing a simulated exam, you also know the implications of the results.

8.2 Set Yourself TIMED Exams

An airline pilot would not go and fly an aeroplane simply after only learning the theory, and without having been in a simulator. So why would anyone go into an exam without having been through simulated exams? You *must* set yourself *timed* exams *regularly* (this is something your parents can help you with). The timing must be strict. You may have to do simulated exams without someone in the room supervising, but remember, if you cheat, you will be cheating yourself. There is then little value in doing simulated exams.

Making up a simulated exam can be done by selecting relevant questions from a textbook, review materials, or exams from previous years if they are available. There are also a lot of books that are available, containing plenty of questions. An often underappreciated fact is that *it does not matter much whether you have seen the questions before, or even done the entire paper before* (unless of course you got a score of 100%). I have often given simulated exams to students that contain questions that they have done before, and I can tell you, even the Ph.D. students rarely get 100% *even though they had seen and done the questions before*. No, the importance of the simulation is to get yourself accustomed to the psychological pressure, to fine-tune your timekeeping discipline, to improve your speed and accuracy, and to identify your problem areas early, so that you can begin to address them. Simulated exams will also help you to assess how well your active memory is doing. Your parents can help you with the entire process of preparing, administering, and assessing the results of simulated exams.

If your performance in a simulated exam is not satisfactory, you should not object to repeating the *same exam paper*, again under simulated exam conditions (after further study in the areas that were problematic). As I have mentioned in §5.5.1 and §7.2.2, repeating the same problems and simulated exams is a powerful way of narrowing down the hurdles in your understanding, and iteratively conquering those hurdles in a hierarchical fashion until all the issues are resolved. Obviously, if you are repeating the same problems or exam, you will need to realistically adjust your score to compensate, but the principal purpose is to systematically eliminate difficulties.

8.3 How Often Should You Do Simulated Exams?

How often would an airline pilot practice in a simulator before flying a plane? Basically, pilots will not fly a real plane until they have absolute confidence that they will have a safe flight, no matter what the flying conditions. Similarly, you must repeat doing simulated exams until you can walk into the exam *knowing* that you will get the grade that you desire. When you do the real exam, one of the ultimate goals is that you should not have to be surprised by anything that you see on the exam paper. Doing simulated exams will help avoid any surprises.

8.4 Do Multiple-Choice Exams Even If They Are Not Required

Even if there is no multiple-choice component in your exams, it will help you immensely if at least some parts of your simulated exams include multiple-choice questions. Ideally you should aim for roughly equal amounts of time on multiple-choice questions and on free-form questions. I will discuss strategies for answering multiple-choice math questions further in chapter 9, but here I just want to point out that the particular advantage of multiple-choice questions is that they are an excellent way of broadly reviewing a subject area and very *efficiently* finding your weak points. Multiple-choice questions lend themselves perfectly to making simulated exams, and if you are short on time for making simulated exams, they are convenient. There are many books and web resources available that have "ready-to-go" multiple-choice questions.

If you *are* required to take multiple-choice exams, you should *never* take them lightly. For some reason, many people are under the false impression that they are easy, and in particular, easier than free-form exams. This is a mistake, because they are not necessarily easier.

8.5 Mental Preparation

Do not neglect the importance of mentally preparing yourself for exams. It is not unlike the mental preparation people go through before a sporting or athletic event. These people can also verify how critically important it is. It is well known that autosuggestion, in other words, self-talk, is a powerful stimulus for the subconscious mind. If you convince your subconscious by autosuggestion that you believe that you will achieve what you want, your subconscious will take care of the rest and make it a reality.

As to the question of whether or not you should "cram" the night before an exam, strictly speaking you should not, as it goes without saying that your mind should be as fresh and as rested as possible in the morning. However, in practice, as you may be only too aware, especially at the higher grade levels, when it comes to the night before the exam, you realize that you may not have done enough. In this situation you should decide to do a little bit and then "call it a day."

Don't do any *new* math problems at the last minute because you might get stuck on something, get frustrated, and end up spending too much time on it. It can totally destroy your confidence. No matter how good you are on a particular topic, it is always possible to come across a question that appears to be impossible to solve. Getting thrown off like this could affect your performance on the entire paper, as a result of attacking your confidence and spreading a fire of doubt in your mind. Stick to reviewing problems that you have done before. Then tell yourself that you have done as much as is reasonably possible. You know that you cannot possibly know everything, and whatever eventually shows up on the paper may work in your favor.

8.6 Is It Worth Paying for Exam Preparation Courses?

There are many companies that offer courses to prepare for standardized exams, such as the *PSAT/NMSQT*, *SAT*, *ACT* exams, and others. These courses are often very expensive. The question parents usually have is whether it is worth paying thousands of dollars for an exam preparation course in relation to the likely benefit, in terms of enhanced exam performance. The "big-name" companies (you know who they are), do claim a high success rate, but at the same time, nothing can be guaranteed. Since it is still risky, parents want to know whether it is worth the risk, or whether they could get the same benefits for a lower cost, in a different way. I don't want to tread on the toes of the companies that offer exam preparation courses, but I will give parents the following advice (see also comments in §9.2). If you are even thinking of spending that much money on an exam preparation course, why not spend a small fraction of that money, say $50 to $100, on paying somebody to come and assess the likely benefits that your child might get from an exam preparation course, in relation to the cost. I discussed how to find a short-term tutor in §5.4. In fact, you may then also assess (together with the tutor and your child), whether the tutor could do the exam preparation for a similar or lower cost than the larger company, taking into account the experience level of the tutor. I refer you also to the discussion in §5.5.3.

Chapter 9

Multiple-Choice Exams

In multiple-choice exams you must typically choose a correct answer from three to five possible answers. Don't take these types of exams lightly. They can be *hard*. What makes them hard is that you are given barely enough time to finish the paper, and there are often deliberate answer choices thrown in to trick you, in order to really test how well you know and understand the material. You have to think *fast*, and *accurately*. The questions are designed so that there is usually not enough time to *derive* the correct solution, or to work backwards from each possible answer. You may be able to do this for some questions but not *every* question.

9.1 Three Key Tips for Multiple-Choice Exams

The three most important things that you can do for multiple-choice papers are the following.

1. Learn the techniques of *eliminating* at least one or two answer choices. If you know what to look for, you can usually eliminate at least one answer choice very quickly, and this can *significantly* increase your chances of getting the answer right. If you do this consistently for the whole paper, it can result in a significant increase in the score for the paper.

2. *Force yourself to move on when you get stuck.* This is absolutely critical for multiple-choice exams, much more so than for free-form exams. Many students fall into the trap of thinking that a little more time spent on a question on which he/she is "nearly there," is worth sacrificing. This is a big mistake because in a multiple-choice exam, *you get NO points for trying very hard or for getting an answer nearly right.* Your work leading up to the solution *gets no credit*, and is irrelevant for a multiple-choice exam. Even if the answer is right, the extra time is *robbed from another question.* You only get one point per question, so *you lose, whether or not you get the question that you spent extra time on right or wrong.*

For example, if you have to answer 40 questions in 60 minutes, do not spend more than the average allocation of 1.5 minutes on any question, even if you think you are close. *You must move on and finish the paper.* This is true even if you think you have almost got the answer. I will emphasize this again, since it is so critically important: *in a multiple-choice exam you are given NO credit for effort or trying extra hard.* All that counts is that you get the answer right. You get no credit for the buckets of sweat produced in getting to the answer. It is actually much worse than that. *If you spend 6 minutes on a question on which you should have spent only 1.5 minutes, you effectively lose 3 points by trying too hard on that question, because you have used up the time for 3 other questions.* Moreover, if you got that answer wrong after spending the extra time, *you will lose 4 points.* Do not give away points like that.

3. *Make sure that you don't throw away points by filling the "grid-ins" incorrectly.* In many cases, especially with standardized tests, such as *PSAT/NMSQT, SAT, ACT* exams, etc., students are required to fill out a grid by marking an appropriate spot for the correct answer choice, in a very particular way. For a given exam you will have access to detailed instructions on how to fill out the grid. For example, for the standardized exams mentioned above, there are many exam practice books available which also have a section explaining the "grid-in" instructions. The problem is that it is very easy to make a mistake and fill out the wrong spot on the answer grid, corresponding to the wrong answer, even if you worked through the entire problem correctly. It is of course senseless to throw away points in this way, but it is easily done. Make sure that you are not a victim of this. Doing realistic simulated exams is an excellent way of reducing the possibility of making such fatal mistakes.

9.1.1 The Techniques for Elimination

In general, you can usually eliminate at least one or two of the answer choices straight away because they are clearly absurd, implausible, or otherwise easily deduced to be wrong. If you are forced to guess answers and have not yet started to run out of time, don't do it completely blindly: make sure that you don't choose the ones that are obviously absurd. Beyond the one or two answers that are easily identified as being incorrect, there are "tricks" and techniques for eliminating additional answers, often very quickly. In the spirit of the title of this book I will talk about the techniques that don't require too much technical detail, and I will give a couple of realistic examples in §9.2 that can easily be followed, simply using common sense and hardly any math.

One of the critical skills that you should learn, that is extremely useful for eliminating multiple-choice answers, is how to read and interpret certain features of equations quickly, "at a glance," without plugging in numbers. For example, under what circumstances does the output of the equation increase when the input is increased, and when the input is decreased? Under what circumstances does the output decrease? What is the behavior of the function when the input is very large and when it is very small? Can you utilize the fact that a *real* (see crib sheet) "squared" quantity (numeric or algebraic) must be positive? Also, evaluating an equation for an input value of 0 and/or 1 is very quick and easy to do so you should ask yourself whether doing so would tell you something useful. Again, I will illustrate some of the techniques in a couple of examples in §9.2.

A "trick" that is useful if the question involves units of a physical quantity (for example, feet, pounds, miles etc.), is that some of the answers may have the wrong units, and these answer choices can be eliminated quickly. The "units" in each answer choice, if relevant, are one of the first things that you should check in the answer choices. For example, if you are asked for the correct formula for the maximum height of a ball thrown into the air, you may find that one of the answers has units of time and not distance. Without doing a detailed calculation, you can eliminate that answer straight away. What many people don't realize, however, is that this basic principle has many ramifications, beyond the questions that are obvious candidates. *Even if the units are not explicitly given, the algebraic expression must be composed of the correct combination of variables so that if it did have units, it would be correct.*

In other words, an algebraic expression with no explicit units given *must* resolve to, for example, a distance if you are told that the formula is for a distance. Or, as another example, it must resolve to a velocity, if it is supposed to be a velocity, and so on. Some "jiggery-pokery" may be required to test some of the answer choices to see if they resolve correctly. This is called "dimensional analysis," but the student may not yet have formally heard it called by this name. However, he/she will certainly be familiar with the concept by the time he/she is in 7th grade or so.

Usually, calculators are not allowed in multiple-choice exams in math. You should take this as a big clue. In general, for grade-school multiple-choice exams, you should never have to do lengthy, tedious calculations or unreasonably long algebraic manipulations. The questions are usually designed to only require straightforward and easy calculations, estimations, or manipulations. If you find that you are in the midst of a horribly long calculation or if algebraic expressions are just not leading to a resolution, you should take that as a clue that you have very likely done something wrong. Instead of struggling and forging ahead, go back and carefully check your method, your assumptions, and look for mistakes. For questions that require numerical calculation without a calculator, it is obviously important to have developed, practiced, and cultivated your skills in estimation (see §2.6).

In numerical problems, round off all the numbers, and make a ball-park estimate before even considering the possible answers. You may find that only one or two of the answers are compatible with your ball-park estimate. Even if you only eliminate one answer choice in this way, it puts you in a much better position than if you did not eliminate one answer choice. If you are left with more than one choice, try to see if there is any other information or knowledge that you can use to eliminate further answer choices. Then, if there is still more than one choice, go to the next level of refinement and accuracy in estimation, and repeat this to see if you can be left with only one answer choice. Usually, you will never need to do more than three iterations.

I will now give you another rule of thumb, but be careful, it does not always apply, so you must be cautious. You should use it only when you really have no idea what the answer might be (or even what the question means). When the answer choices are statements that you have to determine the truth of, *a correct answer will generally require a statement with more words in it.* This is because *a true statement, or a correct definition, requires many qualifying clauses or conditions*, but false statements or incorrect definitions need not be rigorous at all, and therefore they will generally use less words. Actually, this applies to both technical, and non-technical subjects.

Following on from what I have just said is something that is a bit more reliable, but the principle should still only be used as a guide when you are forced to guess. That is, true statements can very rarely be unconditional. In other words, true statements cannot usually be associated with words such as *never*, *every*, *all*, or *always*. On the other hand, expressions such as *may be*, *some*, *sometimes*, *usually*, *typically*, are more likely to be associated with true statements. In fact, did you see, that sentence you just read is an example, where I used the expression *"more likely"* to cover cases that don't agree with the rule, making the overall sentence a true statement. It is much easier to make a false statement and throw in words like *never*, *all*, or *always*, because no exceptions have to be accounted for if the statement is false anyway. In fact people who make up the multiple-choice questions try to avoid "giveaways" like this, but they don't always succeed. You should always be on the look out for such cases.

There are a host of other, more specific techniques for elimination in multiple-choice math questions that are dependent on the type of math content in the question, but unfortunately it is beyond the scope of this book to go into more details. There are plenty of books out there that can help the student with this, and the techniques mentioned above. Learning and enhancing all of these skills is something that is highly suited for getting short-term help from a tutor (what I call "targeted tutoring"), especially if you are on a limited budget (see discussion in §5.5). Also check the website http://www.helpyourchildwithmath.com for links to suitable resources.

9.1.2 The Mechanics of Guessing

In some multiple-choice exams you do not get any penalties for giving incorrect answers, but in some types of exam you are penalized with negative points for wrong answers. In the latter case the penalty is generally a negative fraction of the allocated points. If you do not get penalized for incorrect answers then you can get a minimum nonzero score *just by guessing the answers to all of the questions.* For example, if there is a choice of five answers for every question, then on average you would score 20% if you just guessed all the answers blindly. That's another reason why multiple-choice exam papers are designed with critical timing in mind. That's why, if you don't finish the paper, you *must* allocate at least a minute to guess all the ones that you did not, or could not, answer. However, before guessing, make sure that you did your very best to eliminate as many of the answer choices as you could. As you go through the paper and come across questions that you cannot do, you should make a note of all the answers choices that you think are clearly incorrect. Otherwise you will waste time trying to remember what you deduced, when you come back to the questions that were not completed.

In the case of exams that give a negative score for an incorrect answer, you *must* find out before the exam what fraction of a point is taken off your score for every incorrect answer. You must also understand the circumstances under which it is wise to guess with these kinds of exams. Let's take an example, in which you get a score of negative one-quarter $(-1/4)$ for every incorrect answer. Let's also assume that every question has five answer choices. Now suppose that a particular multiple-choice exam has 100 such questions, and that you guess all of them *blindly*. On average you would get 20 answers correct and 80 incorrect. That would give you a total score of zero, because $20 + [80 \times (-1/4)] = 0$. This is the way these kind of multiple-choice exams are usually designed: you get *exactly* zero for blind guessing, on average.

However, many people do not realize the horrific implication of what I have described above. That is, if you did not know the answer to any of the 100 questions but you tried to figure them out, *you could get a score that is worse than blind guessing!* You could get a score as low as -25! That is a profoundly important fact. Now suppose that for every one of the 100 questions, you are able to eliminate one answer choice (this is usually easy), and further suppose that you guess blindly amongst the other four choices. If you eliminated one answer choice correctly for every question, you would get, on average, 25 correct answers and 75 incorrect. Your average score would then be 6.25, because $25 + [75 \times (-1/4)] = 6.25$. *This is better than zero.*

The bottom line is this: *if there is a penalty for incorrect answers, you must eliminate at least one answer choice for every question before you guess*, and this is usually very easy to do. Thus, **for any question that has a penalty, if you really cannot eliminate at least one answer choice, you must leave that question blank**. Having said that, remember, *if there is no penalty, never leave a question blank, and instead, select an answer for every question, even if it is done by blind guessing*. For multiple-choice exams that do not carry penalties for incorrect answers, it is unforgivable to burn points by not guessing the answers to questions that you did not have time to finish. If you know this is going to happen, force yourself to stop a minute before the end of the exam to blindly fill in the guessed answer choices. You may also want to consider leaving all of the guessing until the end (if you do not have to do too much of it), because you may have an inspiration, or sudden memory recall, before the end of the exam.

9.2 The "Big-Name" Advisers' Strategy

The "big-name" companies, or test-preparation advisers (you know who they are), have lots of big, thick books on strategies for tackling multiple-choice questions on standardized tests such as the *PSAT/NMSQT*, *SAT*, and *ACT* exams. However, the strategy that they recommend for an overwhelming proportion of the questions (covering a wide range of topics), is simply to "pick a number," or some variation on that. In other words what they recommend for most questions that have algebraic expressions as the answer choices, is to simply choose a number (or numbers) and plug that number (or numbers) into every single answer choice and evaluate the expression in the context of the question, and thereby choose the answer that is appropriate. Sometimes this strategy produces two possible answer choices instead of one, so you then have to pick another number in order to eliminate the incorrect answer choice.

I happen to think that the strategy described above has three severe problems that can directly impair a student's performance in an exam. The first is that it is extremely *time-consuming*. Most of the questions are actually not designed to be done in this way, and the student could easily run out of time. Second, it involves a lot of steps, and *the more steps that there are, the higher is the chance of making a mistake*. I have come across countless multiple-choice questions that could be answered literally in seconds using different methods, instead of the long-winded, plug-and-grind method. To do the former however, requires the student to have a good (as opposed to superficial) understanding of the topic, and to know how to very quickly eliminate incorrect answers. I will show you a couple of examples shortly. Yet the "big names" insist on the "pick-a-number" method for those very same questions. The third problem is that the "pick-a-number" method literally throws away any hope of developing intuition. I discussed the importance of developing intuition at length in chapter 2, as well as the importance of learning how to spot mistakes. If a student practices for standardized tests with excessive use of the "pick-a-number" method for a particular topic, he/she *will not develop an intuitive understanding of the topic*. The student will therefore be *more prone to making mistakes*, and his/her general ability to spot mistakes will be severely compromised.

The alternative strategy is to eliminate two to three answer choices using the methods described in §9.1.1, and use your *understanding of the topic, combined with logical reasoning*, to select the correct answer choice. A "hybrid" approach is also possible, plugging in numbers, but only after being left with two or so answer choices. If you do end up using the "pick-a-number" method for all of the answer choices, you should make sure that you have done enough timed practice work to ensure that your speed *and accuracy* is good enough to achieve your desired score for a particular exam. But you will be heavily squeezed for time. Again, training in how to spot the quickest and easiest ways to tackle particular types of multiple-choice questions would be a good use of targeted tutoring (see also §5.5).

I will now illustrate what I have been talking about with two examples. If you are reading this as a parent who hasn't looked at an equation for years, don't be put off. My point is that I can show you how to get the right answer despite that (mostly making use of common sense).

Example 1. If the outermost perimeter of a wheel on a vehicle has a radius of r meters, what is the number of revolutions made by the wheel if the vehicle travels a distance of d kilometers, if the wheel does not slip?

(A) $\dfrac{d}{500\pi r}$

(B) $\dfrac{500}{\pi r d}$

(C) $\dfrac{500d}{\pi r}$

(D) $\dfrac{\pi r}{500d}$

(E) $\dfrac{1000}{\pi r}$

Now, the "big-name" advisers would recommend that you pick numbers for which you can easily work out what the answer should be, and plug those into each answer choice to see which one gives your expected answer. As I mentioned before, this can consume unnecessary time (robbing time from other questions) and the method is prone to mistakes creeping in. I will show you how to do this question in *seconds*. Here goes. Scan the answers. You see that one answer choice (E) does not have the distance traveled (d) in it. That can't be right: there must be more revolutions if the vehicle travels further. Eliminate that answer choice. Then you see that answer choice (B) has *both* the size of the wheel and the distance traveled on the bottom (denominator): that must be wrong because the number of revolutions will be larger if the distance traveled is larger and/or if the wheel size is *smaller* (an "opposite" dependence). You're already way ahead by having eliminated two answer choices (which could be done in about 2 to 3 seconds). Answer choice (D) can be eliminated because the distance traveled is on the bottom, but the number of revolutions has to increase if the distance traveled increases. That leaves just (A) or (C), which means that you have to decide whether the "500" goes on the top or on the bottom. The equation has to give you an answer that is a "pure number" that has no units (number of revolutions), but d is in kilometers and r is in meters so it is d that must be made bigger to match the units of r, so the "500" goes on top. Thus, if you have the right training, the correct answer choice of (C) could be obtained in 5 to 10 seconds, many times faster than the "pick-a-number" method. The regular average time allocation for this question would be 90 seconds. Now let's do another one.

Example 2. Two points on land are x miles apart, but on a particular map drawn to scale, the same two points are y inches apart. If two other points on land are $x + 3$ miles apart from each other, what is the corresponding distance, in inches, on the map?

(A) $\dfrac{y(x+3)}{x}$

(B) $\dfrac{x}{y(x+3)}$

(C) $\dfrac{(x+3)}{y}$

(D) $\dfrac{y}{(x+3)}$

(E) $\dfrac{x}{y}$

Again, the "big-name" advisers would have you pick numbers and tediously plug them into each answer choice, doing it a second time if that still left you with more than one possible answer. However, you can do this problem in 2 to 3 seconds, stupendously faster than the "pick-a-number" method. You see, the answer has to be a distance. So it cannot be (E) because that has no units, it is a pure ratio (it is a "distance divided by a distance"). But (C) and (D) also have no units: there is a distance on top (numerator) and a distance on the bottom (denominator). Furthermore, answer choice (B) does not have units of distance either because there is a "distance squared" on the bottom and a distance on the top (giving a net result of a reciprocal distance). That leaves only answer choice (A), which is actually the only answer choice that has units of distance. This question is similar to an actual question that appeared on a standardized test. The amazing thing about it is that to get the correct answer in 2 to 3 seconds, *doing it in your head*, you don't even have to read the question properly! In fact you don't even have to fully *understand* the question! All you have to know is that x and y are distances and that the answer has to have units of distance. The original average time allocation for this question was 90 seconds. By being properly trained you buy yourself an entire 87 seconds that can be used for other questions. The testers appear to have slipped up and made the question too easy (for the properly trained student) without realizing it. If I were making an exam with a question like this, I would have put in at least two other answer choices that had units of distance.

What I find additionally puzzling is that the "big-name" advisers frequently recommend the "pick-a-number" method in preference to working out the solution using actual mathematical and physical principles, which would be quicker (but not as quick as methods such as those in the preceding examples). You may also be wondering why the "big-name" advisers would universally recommend a strategy that robs the student of valuable time, is prone to error, and that also robs the student of developing intuition. I don't know, but one thing is for sure. You don't have to have much experience to teach the "pick-a-number" strategy, which, at face value can be marketed as "foolproof." In fact you don't even have to be a math teacher to teach that method. Thus, the "big names" can hire people with little or no experience to teach the method. On the other hand, it takes a certain amount of skill and experience to teach students how to do certain questions in *seconds* without writing down a single thing.

Chapter 10

Strategies During Exams

10.1 Read the Paper Slowly, Comprehend Each Question

The time that you invest initially to scan over the *entire paper*, and the time that you spend carefully reading the questions, is very critical. If you don't do this you could easily misinterpret a question and waste a huge amount of time getting no score. Don't worry if you see somebody madly scribbling away as soon as he/she gets the paper. You should not care how anyone else is going to perform in the exam. Your only concern should be *you*. There will always be people who start writing almost immediately, and you should *ignore them*. Ignore anyone who starts writing before you do, or who seems to be writing more, and/or faster than you.

There will also be people who finish the exam well before time, put their pen down, and then proceed to sit with a smug smile. They may even be allowed to leave the room and go home. Ignore these people too. For all you know, they could have totally messed up the exam, despite the big grins. To put it simply, *ignore everybody*.

10.2 Decide on the Order of Attack

So many people lose out by forgetting or neglecting a simple fact: you do not (usually) have to answer questions in the order that they are presented in the paper. This can make a *big* difference. This is mainly because if you attempt a hard question early on, you may get stuck and end up spending a lot of time on it, and get nowhere. You may feel that you have to spend even more time on it, because you might think that you've invested so much time on it, and you might not be able to let go of it. Yet, you could be spending that time picking up many more points on easier questions. Remember, for every minute that you are stuck, you are literally *throwing away and burning up points* that you would be getting from doing easier questions. *Do the easiest questions first*. Therefore, after reading the paper, decide on the best order in which to attempt the questions.

10.3 Know and Understand the Critical Keywords in Questions

So many people flush away good grades too often by misinterpreting or not understanding a question. They answer a completely different question to that which is asked. A lot of time can be wasted getting no score. This is another reason why doing simulated exams is so important, because you will quickly learn from your mistakes.

Watch out for critical words in a question that can be missed, or misinterpreted if a question is read too fast. For example, *not, except, sometimes, always*, and some other small words can completely change the meaning of a question. With enough practice you will be able to understand precisely what is required of you for each question, and there should be no surprises in the exam.

10.4 Pay Attention to the Points Scheme and Stick to Time

Usually an exam paper will state how many points are allocated to each question or to parts of questions. Knowing the total duration of the exam and the total number of points (which may not be 100), you can work out roughly the number of minutes you should be spending for every point.

If you exceed this limit the warning bells should start ringing. Don't forget to subtract (from the total duration), the time required for reading the paper. For example, for a three-hour (180-minute) exam having a total of 85 points, if you allocate 10 minutes for reading the paper, the time you should be spending for every point is 2 minutes per point, because $(180 - 10)/85 = 2$. Thus, for example, if a question carries 6 points, say, you should aim to spend no more than 12 minutes on that question. **Every minute that you spend on a question that is over the time limit translates into points that you are potentially throwing away from the remaining questions.** In particular, if you are stuck on a certain question, you could be doing it wrong, so you really will be throwing away points at the expense of the remaining questions.

If the exam paper does not show you the points allocations for the questions or parts of questions, you should make reasonable estimates based on the content.

On the other hand you should also not rush through the questions too fast for the obvious reason that you will increase your chances of making mistakes. If you have been doing simulated exams as described in chapter 8, then you will have a better idea of how to pace yourself, and how to approach the trade-off between *speed and accuracy* that is required.

10.5 Force Yourself Out of Being Stuck

The subject of this section is somewhat related to the previous section, but it is important enough to warrant its own section. When you get stuck on a question, even after you have spent far too much time on it, the natural tendency is not to be defeated, but rather to keep attempting to complete it. At some point you must force yourself to drop it and move on. You must weigh up how many points you are losing by not answering other questions that you could be doing, versus how many points you would lose by dropping the question that you're stuck on. This is easier said than done.

You have to develop a habit for being able to drop questions when you need to. Simulated exams are a good way of developing such a habit.

Suppose that you have a two-hour exam, and that you must answer four out of eight possible 30-minute questions. Further suppose that on one of the questions you spend 15 minutes, but get stuck and do not write anything at all. If you decide to abandon that question, what is the best thing for you to do for the remaining 15 minutes? If you use it on the other three questions, then even if you get a perfect score on those three questions, you will have lost 25%, which is a lot. Therefore you should keep to the 30 minutes for the other questions, and then try to pick up *some* points on one of the *other* four questions that you have not yet tried.

10.6 Graphs

It is important to remember that you can usually pick up relatively easy points for questions that require you to draw a graph. I talked in detail about drawing graphs in §4.1, so here I will just recap with a brief summary.

- Always use a pencil, and not a pen, unless you are explicitly asked not to use a pencil.

- Always use a *sharp* pencil and ensure that the entire graph, and its annotation, is *neat*, and not too small.

- Always use a ruler for drawing the axes (and any other lines that should be straight).

- Make sure that all of the axes are clearly labeled with the names of the quantities being plotted, and their associated units if applicable.

- Choose a sensible scaling for the numbers to be marked on each axis. It is critical that your initial calculation of the scale for each axis is correct. Watch out for things that look "obviously wrong."

- Clearly write the "tick-mark" numbers just below the horizontal axis, and just to the left of the vertical axis.

- Give each graph a title explaining what the graph is supposed to show, including something about each of the two quantities that are plotted against each other.

- For the data points use a symbol that leaves no ambiguity as to the numerical values that the data points correspond to. For example, use crosses or single points enclosed by circles. Do not use filled circles.

- If you are required to join the data points, make sure that the curve is smooth. If the data points are from measurements of some sort, remember that the curve does not have to go through all, or indeed any, of the data points.

These are minimal requirements for a graph. Refer to chapter 4 for a much more thorough discussion. In particular, for questions involving a graphing calculator, refer to the advice in §4.2 to §4.4.

10.7 Don't Blow It on Neatness

Remember that the person who will eventually assess your paper is human too. He or she will have the tedious task of getting through a stack of papers, and moreover, may be tired and/or may not be in a good mood. A manuscript that is difficult or impossible to read, because it looks like it was written in hieroglyphics, is not going to be very welcome. At worst, if an answer is actually impossible to read, you will get no score for what may otherwise be a perfectly good answer. At best, if some of the writing has to be deciphered, you may not be given the benefit of the doubt. In either case, you owe it to yourself to write neatly. Be honest and assess the legibility of your writing. If it is bad, time invested practicing writing neatly will result in a big payoff.

The importance of neatness applies equally well to diagrams, drawings, equations, formulas, tables and graphs.

In addition, by "neatness," I include the *orderly layout* for the solution of a math problem. All too often, a student will start off with large writing, not anticipating the number of steps required for the solution, and then he/she may quickly run short of space on the page. The student will then jump from one side of the page to the other, and possibly back again, trying to squeeze everything into tiny spaces. This sort of thing inevitably leads to muddled thinking, mistakes, and incorrect solutions, because it is difficult to maintain continuity in thinking from one erratic step to the next. It is also very difficult to spot mistakes, while the solution is being written out, and also while tracing back afterwards. The student should lay out each step logically, from left to right, top to bottom, without jumping back and forth from one place on the paper to another.

10.8 Write Down SOMETHING

In an exam you will be chasing after every single point that you can get your hands on. For every second that you spend doing nothing, you will be throwing away and burning up points. Even if you spend some time thinking, that time will be wasted unless you write something down. So, in an exam, always write down *something* because it may just be right. Many students end up writing *nothing* for a question, even after spending time on it. Sometimes they are afraid of writing something that is wrong, or something that is nonsense. At other times, it may just be a case of "freezing up." It sounds obvious, but students frequently forget a simple fact: it is impossible to get credit for something that is not written down.

10.9 Dealing with Blackouts

It can happen that during the exam you could be doing quite well, but then suddenly, for no reason, your mind goes totally blank, and you find yourself freezing up and panicking. The harder you try to concentrate, the worse it seems to get. It's a horrifying experience, as you feel totally powerless. It can happen with a question that you might "normally" be very good at, for which you know the material very well. You may even have done very well with similar questions in simulated exams. Yet it can still happen. Even when you get your concentration back, you may find yourself going around in circles, or getting stuck. A blackout can easily affect the outcome of the entire paper, if you let it.

When you experience a blackout, the best thing to try first is to attempt a different question completely, and then try to come back to the one that you blanked out on. If you find that you are "completely blank" on every question that you attempt, then it is better to stop completely and put everything down. Losing 5 to 10 minutes in this way is better than losing a much larger amount of time that would result from driving yourself deeper into an abyss. Tell yourself that this is "normal," it happens, and that it will be over soon. Meanwhile, think of something pleasant. Forget for a moment that you are doing an exam. After a while, try starting again with a different question, because you may not be able to go back immediately (or at all) to the one that you left.

Remember that if you go "blank" in a multiple-choice exam, there are powerful techniques available to you for still getting some correct answers for certain types of questions, even if you don't remember how to do a problem. These methods were discussed in chapter 9.

10.10 The Nightmare Calculation

It can happen that you start out a question on what, from your previous experience, seems likely to be a fairly straightforward analytical calculation. You know this because you have solved similar problems before.

However, at some point, instead of the expressions and equations gradually reducing to simplified forms (as they should), they become more and more complicated. Before you know it, the whole thing becomes a mess, and the calculation becomes cumbersome and neverending, or else you get stuck. When things don't begin to simplify, and/or the algebra seems to be taking up way too many lines and way too much time, you can be pretty sure that you have made a mistake. As soon as you begin to suspect that this has happened, don't waste any more time, go back right to the beginning to see where you went wrong. First read the question carefully again in order to make sure that you understood it correctly. Then wade slowly through each line, looking for "dropped" or missing items, or items that were carried over incorrectly from a previous line. Remember that questions in grade-school exams (and for many other levels, in fact), are rarely designed to be long-winded.

10.11 Show Every Step

You should *always* show all intermediate steps in calculations, derivations, proofs, or any other type of problem-solving question. This may sound obvious, but all too often this advice is ignored. *If you do not show your working then you simply cannot get any credit for something that is not written down.* Even if your final answer is incorrect, you could potentially get credit for your intermediate steps, but not if you don't write them down. At important and key points in the problem, briefly explain what you are doing and why, *even if it seems obvious.* You do not lose points for stating the obvious! It could actually gain points for you by enhancing clarity.

If you think that you made a mistake and need to cross out some parts of the working, make sure that the parts that you cross out are still readable. The examiner will be able to follow your reasoning better, especially if the part that you crossed out *happened to be correct after all*.

Remember the discussion about developing intuition (chapter 2), learning to look out for the signs of mistakes having been made, and "sanity-checking" your answers. Get into the habit of checking the units, dimensions, and the order of magnitude of your answers by quick estimation. All of this will help you to quickly spot mistakes. If you have to solve an equation, and have a little time to spare, put the answer back into the equation (or apply the inverse process), to see if it fits. In addition, use clear, annotated diagrams wherever they will help, *even if a diagram was not requested in the question*. Sometimes, you can pick up a point or two simply by drawing a correct diagram, even before you attempt to answer the question.

Chapter 11

The Parental Crib Sheet

Throughout this book I have emphasized the importance of *engaging* your child with meaningful conversation about what he/she has been studying in math (for example, see discussions in §1.2 and §3.3). Although this alone will go a long way, you will find that as you do this, with the help of this chapter, you may be able to help with some of the homework yourself, or at least answer some important questions that your child may have. In the following pages is the "parental crib sheet" that will help to empower you to be able to begin that process and gain a quick and basic, but *functional*, understanding of what your child will be doing in math from 1st grade all the way up to 12th grade. You will *not* have to solve any math problems if you don't want to. No prerequisite knowledge is assumed. You most likely don't have the need to understand *how* to do the math, you might just want to understand *what something means*, in simple terms. The crib sheet will give you a basic understanding of what your child may be talking about, and/or enable you to to decipher his/her homework.

Sometimes all you might need is a quick memory jogger, and the crib sheet should help to serve that purpose. Perhaps your memory may be jogged enough for you to be able to even help your child yourself with a complete homework problem, or problem set, without any further effort. You may surprise yourself by just how much you are able to recall after reading some of the crib sheet entries. Then, if you want to take it further using that foundation, there are plenty of books available. You can also go to the website http://www.helpyourchildwithmath.com to find some resources to get more detailed and technical information online if you need it. There are already a lot of resources available for *students* who need a reference for quick memory joggers, with full technical details. Some of these have also been carefully selected and collected on the website http://www.helpyourchildwithmath.com.

The words or phrases in the crib sheet are the most common that might come up for elementary-school through to high-school level, and the explanations are designed to be *nontechnical and practical, and in the exact context that you need them.* This will hopefully facilitate at least some rudimentary, relevant, and meaningful conversation with your child. For this, you don't need rigorous definitions, but just enough detail to clue you in. Great care has been taken, however, to ensure that the definitions and explanations in this crib sheet are *accurate* and reflect the true meanings, but without the gobbeldygook. You will also notice that some definitions in the crib sheet are more detailed than others. The longer definitions will usually correspond to items that might be encountered in "real life" (for example, see the entry for *triangulate*). I have also included some applied math/physics terms in the crib sheet because they can often come up in math problems.

If you were to search on the internet for some of the items in this crib sheet, you may get a huge number of results that you have to sift through, and many of them will be out of context, or overly technical (and consequently much of the information may not be useful for what you need). There is no uniform academic level or quality for information on the internet. In contrast, the explanations for each item given here have precisely the right context that you need, at the right level (because you only need to understand enough to help your child, not to do the work for them). Thus, the crib sheet is designed to save you a lot of time. The index to this book is very comprehensive. Although the entries in the crib sheet are arranged alphabetically, the quickest way to locate a word or phrase in the crib sheet is to consult the index in this book.

Finally, I have tried as much as possible to avoid sending you around in circles by minimizing the cross-referencing of different entries in the crib sheet. However, this is very difficult to avoid completely, because some concepts naturally require some knowledge of other concepts and/or terms. I have tried to make such cases easier for you by pointing out at the very beginning of an entry in the crib sheet which item or items that you may need to look up first, before continuing. Any word or phrase in italics in the crib sheet specifically means that the italicized word or phrase has its own entry (at the appropriate alphabetical position) in the crib sheet.

– A –

AAA

In *geometrical proofs*, "AAA" is an acronym for "angle-angle-angle," referring to the fact that if all three corresponding pairs of angles of two triangles are equal, then one triangle can be transformed into the other by simple scaling (i.e., they are *similar triangles*). Note that "AAA" cannot be used to prove that two triangles are equivalent (*congruent*) because more information is needed.

AAS

In *geometrical proofs*, "AAS" is an acronym for "angle-angle-side," referring to the fact that if you can prove that two adjacent angles and a nonincluded side of a triangle are equal to the corresponding quantities for another triangle, then the two triangles are equivalent (*congruent*).

abelian

First look up *commutative property* if you need to. The term *abelian* is usually used in the context of *abelian group*, which has the same meaning as *commutative* group. In plain English, a *group* is a bunch of items (for example, numbers), together with some *operations* (for example, addition), that can be applied to two or more of the *group* members. The group is *abelian* if the order of the members for the *operation* does not matter. For example, $1+2$ is equal to $2+1$, but $1 \div 2$ is not equal to $2 \div 1$ (i.e. *division* is not *commutative*).

abscissa (plural: abscissae)

A fancy word for the value of a point on a regular two-dimensional graph that is plotted on the horizontal *axis* (often referred to as x). Note, however, that in some disciplines the term *abscissa* is used synonymously for the entire horizontal *axis*.

absolute value

In grade-school math, there are three common meanings. In the simplest context it means ignore the negative sign on a number if there is one. For example, the absolute value of -24 is 24. More generally, it could mean ignoring the negative sign on an entire *expression*. Physically, the *absolute value* might correspond to the length of something, regardless of its orientation. For example, I could say that the tip of my hand is resting -24 inches from the top of my shoulders, but the length of my arm is always 24 inches, not -24 inches.

Symbolically, the *absolute value* is represented by two vertical bars placed at either side of the mathematical expression. For example, $|x - 2|$ means "the absolute value of (whatever $x - 2$ is)."

For the second context, first look up *complex number* and *vector* if you need to. Both *complex numbers* and *vectors* must be represented in a space with more than one *dimension*. The term *absolute value* in this context is the actual length of either entity in that space. Another word that is synonymous with this meaning of *absolute value* is *magnitude* (of a *complex number* or *vector*).

In the third context, the term *absolute value* is used to distinguish the nature of a numerical quantity from a *relative* value of that quantity. The latter is a value *relative* to some reference that would normally be given in the context. For example, if I place an object in water, it will float if the *absolute value* of its density is less than approximately one gram per cubic *centimeter*. Or, equivalently, I could say that if I place an object in water, it will float if its density *relative* to water is smaller.

acceleration

In the simplest context, the actual number tells you how quickly or slowly the *speed* of something is changing. For example, if I drop something near the surface of the Earth, after 1, 2, and 3 seconds its *speed* will be approximately 32 feet per second, 64 feet per second, and 96 feet per second respectively. Its *acceleration* is 32 feet per second per second. In a more advanced context, *acceleration* also covers change in direction, even if the *speed* doesn't change (as in circular motion at constant *speed*, for example). In that case, *acceleration* tells you how tightly curved the path of an object is (e.g., compared to a straight line on a flat surface).

accuracy

There is a common misconception of the meaning of *accuracy* versus *precision*. The misconception and confusion results in the two words being used interchangeably. However, their meanings are very different. The term *accuracy* refers to the the size of the uncertainty in a numerical quantity. The term *precision* refers to the representation of a number. The two terms have nothing to do with each other because *accuracy* depends on the capabilities of the measuring device.

For example, suppose the odometer on a car is such that the smallest change in distance that it can measure is 1 mile. Suppose that over the period of a week, you drive 1000 miles, and you want to find the *average* daily mileage. You find that your calculator tells you $1000 \div 7 = 142.857$ miles. The *precision* of this answer is greater than the *accuracy* of the odometer because the number 142.857 has six *significant figures*. But the last three digits have no meaning, because your original measurements only had an accuracy of 1 mile. There is no way that you can achieve an *accuracy* that is higher than 1 mile. So the *average* mileage is really 143 ± 1.0 miles per day. See also *precision*.

acute angle

An angle that is less than 90 degrees.

acute triangle

A *triangle* in which all three angles are less than 90 degrees (i.e., *acute*).

addend

A number that is taking part in an addition *operation*.

addition formulas

This usually refers to *trigonometric addition formulas*–see crib sheet entry for this.

additive identity

See also *identity*, and *multiplicative identity*. The *additive identity* is something that you would add to a mathematical item that has absolutely no effect on that item. The item need not be a number. It could, for example, be a *matrix*. For a regular number, the *additive identity* is obviously zero.

additive inverse

See also *inverse*, *multiplicative inverse*. The *additive inverse* is something that you would add to a mathematical item that gives a result of zero. The item need not be a number. It could, for example, be a *matrix*. For a regular number, the *additive inverse* is the negative of that number.

adjacent angles

Angles that share a common line and *vertex* (the point at which the second line defining an angle meets the first line).

adjacent side

First look up *right-angled triangle* if you need to. The usual context refers to one of the sides in a *right-angled triangle*. However, one of the *acute angles* in the *triangle* must be identified for the term to mean anything. The *adjacent side* is the one that, together with the *hypotenuse* (longest side), encloses the chosen angle. See also *opposite side*.

AEA

See *alternate exterior angles*.

AIA

See *alternate interior angles*.

algebra

There are a variety of contexts for the use of the term *algebra*, but in the most basic contexts, *algebra* covers: elementary *operations* involving numbers and/or *variables*; *simplifying* and/or manipulating *expressions* involving numbers and/or *variables*; solving equations for an *unknown variable* or *variables*. See also *linear algebra*.

algebraic expression

A string of letters and/or symbols that might represent a mathematical or physical quantity, or quantities.

algebraic number

First look up *rational number*, *polynomial*, and *polynomial coefficient* if you need to. For the purpose of grade-school math, an *algebraic number* can be thought of as a number that can be expressed as a function of *rational numbers* using a number of terms that is *finite*. A more formal definition is that an *algebraic number* is one that is the solution of any *polynomial equation* with *rational coefficients*.

alternate exterior angles (AEA)

In *geometry*, when a straight line (here known as a *transversal*) cuts two lines, there are four angles formed "outside" the space enclosed by those two lines. The two pairs of diagonally-opposed angles are the *alternate exterior angles*. See also *alternate interior angles* and *corresponding angles*.

alternate interior angles (AIA)

In *geometry*, when a straight line (here known as a *transversal*) cuts two lines, there are four angles formed "inside" the space enclosed by those two lines. The two pairs of diagonally-opposed angles are the *alternate interior angles*. See also *alternate exterior angles* and *corresponding angles*.

altitude

There are two common contexts. One (in applied math or physics) is the vertical distance (height) above some reference level. The other context is in *geometry*, in which the *altitude* is the height of a *triangle*, when one of the sides is horizontal. In other words it is the (length of a) straight line that originates at a *vertex* of the *triangle*, and that meets the opposite side of the *triangle* at 90 degrees (i.e., it is *perpendicular* to the opposing side).

analytic, analytical

In the context of phrases such as *analytic calculation*, *analytic manipulation*, *analytic solution*, the meaning is usually that no numerical aids such as a computer or calculator program are required to proceed. All of the work is done using appropriate mathematical rules and methods.

analytic geometry

Synonymous with *coordinate geometry*.

angle bisector

A line that lies between two lines, and that cuts the angle between those two lines exactly in half.

angle measure

See *measure (of an angle)*.

Angstrom (Å)

A unit of length equal to 10 billionths of a *meter* (10^{-10} m, or 10 *nanometers*). X-ray wavelengths and the size of atoms are of this order.

angular momentum

First look up *momentum* if you need to. The term *angular momentum* refers to curved motion of an object and it is a measure of how much *turning force* would need to be applied over a given amount of time in order to bring the object to rest. It is a law of physics that if the *angular momentum* of a system changes, an external *force* (strictly speaking a *torque* or, turning *force*), must be involved.

angular speed

A measure of the *rate* of rotation, in units of the angle rotated per given unit of time. The angular measure is usually in *radians*. Thus, a revolution rate of 1 revolution per second corresponds to an *angular speed* of 360 degrees per second, or 6.28 radians per second, because by definition, 360 degrees is equal to $2 \times \pi$ *radians*.

antecedent

In the field of *logic*, the *antecedent* is the part of an "if...then..." *conditional statement* that comes straight after the "if" (i.e., it is the condition). For example, in the statement "If your car has run out of gas it will stop," the part that is the *antecedent* is "your car has run out of gas."

antilogarithm

First look up *logarithm* if you need to. The term *antilogarithm* is synonymous with *inverse logarithm*, sometimes abbreviated to just *antilog*. The *antilogarithm*, or *inverse logarithm*, is the reverse process of forming the *logarithm* of a number.

aphelion

In applied math or physics, *aphelion* is the farthest distance of an object from the sun in the object's orbital trajectory around the sun.

apothem

First look up *regular polygon* if you need to. *Apothem* refers to the *radius* of a circle drawn inside a *regular polygon*, such that the circle touches every side of the *regular polygon*. Another way of saying this is that the *apothem* is the *inradius* of an *inscribed circle* for a *regular polygon*.

arc

Usually this means a partial *perimeter* of a circle. However, it could mean part of the *perimeter* of a different curved, two-dimensional geometrical object.

arccos, arccosine (Also known as "inverse cosine.")

First look up *cosine* if you need to. The *function arccos* is the reverse *operation* (or *inverse*), of the *trigonometric function* known as *cosine*. The resulting number is an angle. Note: *cosine* is pronounced as in "co-sign."

arccosec, arccosecant (Also known as "inverse cosecant.")

First look up *cosecant* if you need to. The *function arccosecant* is the reverse *operation* (or *inverse*), of the *trigonometric function* known as *cosecant*. The resulting number is an angle.

arccot, arccotangent (Also known as "inverse cotangent.")

First look up *cotangent* if you need to. The *function* arccotangent is the reverse *operation* (or *inverse*), of the *trigonometric function* known as *cotangent*. The resulting number is an angle.

Archimedes

Famous Greek guy who operated in the third century B.C., and made some amazing advances and discoveries in mathematics and science. There is way too much information to do him justice here, so you had best look him up.

arcminute

A measure of angles that is equal to one-sixtieth of a degree.

arcsec, arcsecant (Also known as "inverse secant.")

The result of the reverse *operation* (or *inverse*), of the *trigonometric function* known as *secant*. The resulting number is an angle.

arcsec, arcsecond

A measure of angles that is equal to one-sixtieth of an arcminute, or equivalently, one degree divided by 3,600.

arcsin, arcsine (Also known as "inverse sine.")

The *function arcsine* is the reverse *operation* (or *inverse*), of the *trigonometric function* known as *sine*. The resulting number is an angle. Note: *sine* is pronounced like "sign."

arctan, arctangent (Also known as "inverse tan.")

The *function arctan* is the reverse *operation* (or *inverse*), of the *trigonometric function* known as *tangent*. The resulting number is an angle.

area

You will usually find formulas for the *area* of some common geometrical shapes summarized in the back or front of your kid's textbook. In the spirit of the title of this book, I won't list them here.

Arg, arg

See *argument*, definition number (3).

Argand diagram

First look up *real number*, *complex number*, and *imaginary number* if you need to. An *Argand diagram* is a graphical representation of a *complex number* in the form of a standard graph that has horizontal and vertical *axes*. The horizontal *axis* corresponds to the *real* part of the *complex number* and the vertical *axis* corresponds to the *"imaginary"* part of the *complex number*. Sometimes a *complex number* in this graphical representation is specified by the *coordinates* along the horizontal and vertical *axes*. However, it can also be specified by the length of a line joining the point representing the *complex number*, to the *intersection* of the *axes*, and the angle made by that line with the horizontal *axis*. The length of the connecting line is called the *modulus*, and the angle is referred to as *Arg* (of the *complex number*).

argument
First look up the following that you need to, if any: *hypothesis*, *logic*, *deductive reasoning*, *inductive reasoning*, *function*, and *complex numbers*. The term *argument* can have several contexts, and I will give you the three that are likely to be most relevant to you.
(1) A series of statements starting with a *hypothesis*, *premise*, or observational facts, leading to support of the truth (or otherwise) of a conclusion. Application in the subject of *logic* is usually much more rigid than in science. See also *deductive reasoning* and *inductive reasoning*.
(2) Something that you insert into a *function* as an input, or into some other mathematical procedure, in order to obtain a new item or items (which may or may not be numbers).
(3) Mathematical entities called *complex numbers* are composed of two regular numbers, and in a certain notation, one of them is called the *argument* (shortened to *Arg*), and it is essentially an angle, so it has units of an angle. However, the *argument* has an infinite number values. As well as the first (or principal) value, additional values can be obtained by adding multiples of 360 degrees. The principal value is written with a capital "A," as in *Arg*. See also *Argand diagram*.

arithmetic mean
A fancy name for the regular *average* of a set of numbers. Just add up the numbers and divide by the number of numbers.

arithmetic progression
Another name for *arithmetic series*.

arithmetic series or arithmetic sequence

A *series* or *sequence* of numbers in which any two adjacent numbers in the sequence always give the same number when you subtract one from the other (the difference is called the *common difference*).

ASA

In *geometrical proofs*, "ASA" is an acronym for "angle-side-angle," referring to the fact that if you can prove that two angles and the included side of a *triangle* are equal to the corresponding quantities for another *triangle*, then the two *triangles* are equivalent (*congruent*).

aspect ratio

The *ratio* of the width of a rectangle to its height. It can expressed as a proportion, for example, 4:3, or as a single number, for example, approximately 1.33 (equivalent to a proportion of 1.33:1).

ASS

See SSA.

associative property

This refers to the property of a mathematical *operation* applied to three items (first on one pair and then applied to that result and the third item). The *operation* is *associative* if the final answer does not depend on which pair of numbers you apply the *operation* to first.

asymptote

Some mathematical *functions* "blow up" to *infinity* for certain inputs to the *function*. A *vertical asymptote* is the vertical line on a graph of the *function* that marks the input values for which the *function* "blows up" to *infinity*. Some mathematical *functions* seem to slowly try to reach a certain value when you make the input very large (negative or positive), but never get there. A *horizontal asymptote* is a horizontal line on a graph of the *function* that marks the value that the *function* tries to achieve on the extreme left and/or right sides of the graph, but never does. It is also possible for the graph of a *function* to have *slant asymptotes*, which are neither horizontal nor vertical. The idea is the same however: the *function* tries to approach the *asymptotes*, getting closer and closer to them as higher and higher input values are included, but the graph never touches, or reaches, any of the *asymptotes*.

attitude

In applied math or physics, *attitude* usually means a pointing direction (for which you need to specify three angles in three dimensions).

augmented matrix

First look up *matrix*, *linear equations*, and *simultaneous equations* if you need to. An *augmented matrix* is usually a temporary combination of two *matrices* that are manipulated according to predetermined rules to end up with the new, *augmented matrix*. The purpose of doing this is usually to solve a *matrix equation*. This usually corresponds to solving a set of *simultaneous linear equations*.

average

If there is no qualifier on the word *average*, then it usually just means the simple *average* (i.e., the total of all values of a quantity divided by the number of values). This is also known as the *arithmetic mean*. See also *weighted mean* (equivalent to the *weighted average*), and *geometric mean*.

axes

See *axis*.

axiom

A starting point of an *argument* or theory that cannot be proved (or is to be accepted as true without *proof*). *Geometry* has lots of them. For example, the statement "The whole is greater than a part," is an axiom.

axis (plural: axes)

Usually refers to some kind of reference line (there is more than one context). See also: *coordinate axes*, *axis of symmetry*.

axis of symmetry (plural: axes of symmetry)

In two dimensions it is a line that divides an object or figure into two parts that are exact mirror images of each other. In three dimensions it could mean that if an object is rotated around its *axis of symmetry*, it would be impossible to tell what angle it had turned through, because the object does not look any different when it is rotated around that axis. Alternatively, there may be a definite number of values of rotation angle for which the object appears to be unchanged. See also *rotational symmetry*.

– B –

bar graph
A graph consisting of vertical or horizontal rectangles (bars), whose lengths represent numerical attributes of quantities that are labeled for each bar. The numerical attribute that is commonly plotted for a bar is the number, *frequency* (of occurrence), or percentage of the quantity that is represented by the bar. See also *histogram*. The main difference between a *bar graph* and a *histogram* is that the bars in a *bar graph* may represent items that are separate categories of data, but the bars in a *histogram* generally represent *continuous* ranges in data drawn from a single category or item. Usually, adjacent bars in a *bar graph* do not touch each other, but this is not a requirement. However, adjacent bars in a *histogram* always touch. As an example to illustrate the difference between a *bar graph* and a *histogram*, we could have a *bar graph* in which the bars represent hair color, and we could have a *histogram* for the same *sample* of people, in which the bars represent ranges in hair length, regardless of hair color. In this application, hair color is a *discrete* quantity, and not *continuous*. On the other hand, hair length is a *continuous* quantity in this application.

base
There are two main contexts that are probably relevant for you.
(1) If one side of a *triangle* is drawn or placed horizontally, that side is referred to as the *base*.
(2) First look up *power* if you need to. Counting systems have place values that represent *powers* of a base number. The system that we normally use has *base* 10. Computers use *base* 2 (or binary), in which the place value of a digit in a *binary* number that is greater than or equal to 1, is 1, 2, 4, 8, 16, etc.

basis vectors
First look up *vectors* and *mutually perpendicular* if you need to. A set of

basis vectors are *mutually perpendicular* to each other (*orthogonal*), and have the special property that they are the only *vectors* needed to express any other *vector* in the domain of applicability and context that is being considered. None of the *basis vectors* can be expressed in terms of the other *basis vectors*.

bearing

The usual context that is relevant for you is that for which the *bearing* is a set of angles specifying a particular direction in space, *relative* to a reference direction, or directions.

bell curve

An informal name for the shape of a graph representing the statistical *distribution* of a wide range of physical properties in the real world. The graph looks like a bell (hence the name, *bell curve*). For example, the heights of a sample of people drawn at *random* from a population, when plotted as frequency (of a given height) versus height, usually forms a *bell curve*. The correct mathematical *expression* is either a *normal distribution* or *Gaussian distribution*.

best fit

One can attempt to fit data (of various sorts) with a mathematical *model* that is characterized by a set of parameters that have some freedom during the fitting process. The best fit refers to the fit obtained when some predetermined criterion (for "goodness of fit") is obtained, as the *parameters* are varied. The best fit therefore yields an "optimal" set of *parameters*.

bi-

A prefix used in many mathematical terms, that usually means two of something.

biconditional

A condition for something to be true "if and only if..."

binary (number system)

First look up *base* if you need to. The term *binary* usually refers to the *base* 2 number system.

binomial

First look up *polynomial* if you need to. A *binomial* is a *polynomial* that contains only two terms.

binomial coefficients

First look up *polynomial* and *binomial* if you need to. When a *binomial* is multiplied by itself a number of times (or more correctly, when it is *raised to an integer power*), a *multiterm polynomial* results. In each resulting *term*, everything that is not a *power* of the key *variables* is one of the *binomial coefficients*. See also *binomial series*.

binomial probability (distribution)

First look up *probability distribution* if you need to. The *binomial probability distribution* is a means of calculating probabilities of events when the outcome of an event has only two possibilities. Examples are tossing a coin, or the gender of a baby. For example, using the *binomial probability distribution*, we could calculate the probability of a family having three children of the same gender (it is approximately 1/4, or 25%, from $(1/2)^3 + (1/2)^3$). The theoretical *binomial probability distribution* is approached by real data as the number of "realizations" (or *trials*), becomes large.

binomial series

First look up *binomial* and *binomial coefficients* if you need to. A *binomial series* is an expanded *expression* of a *binomial* when one of the *terms* of the *binomial* is 1, and the *binomial* is *raised to a power*, which need not be an *integer*. The series contains several *terms*, and can be *infinite* if the *power* is not a positive *integer*. In grade-school math, a common application of the *binomial series* and *binomial coefficients* is that of calculating *probabilities* of events that have only two possible outcomes (see *binomial probability distribution*).

bisect

A verb describing the act of dividing a line or angle into two equal parts.

bisector

Usually this means a line that divides something (either a length or angle), into two equal parts.

Boolean algebra

See *Boolean logic*.

Boolean logic (after George Boole)

A system of rules defining the truth or falsehood of combinations of other entities that are either true or false. The act of manipulating, and/or *simplifying* complex *expressions* involving *Boolean logic* is called *Boolean algebra*. It is used extensively in digital electronics because a signal can be either "on" or "off," representing "true" or "false."

boundary conditions

Many kinds of mathematical problems yield an entire family of solutions as in intermediate step. The set of solutions for a particular problem requires additional conditions to be imposed on the general set of solutions. Such additional conditions are referred to as the *boundary conditions* because they force selection of only those solutions that match values of physical parameters on some kind of boundary. The boundary could be a line or surface. For example, suppose we solve a set of equations to calculate the temperature inside a star, from the center to the surface. To apply the solutions to the Sun, we impose the *boundary condition* corresponding to the known surface temperature of the Sun, and thereby pick out the solutions appropriate for that problem.

bounded

The usual context relevant to you is that the term *bounded* refers to some restriction on the value of a specified item (for example, a *variable* or a *function*). See also *bounded above* and *bounded below*.

bounded above

A *variable* or *function* (or some other mathematical quantity) whose value cannot exceed a certain value (which may or may not be specified).

bounded below

A *variable* or *function* (or some other mathematical quantity) whose value cannot fall below a certain value (which may or may not be specified).

boundedness

Properties of a *variable* or *function* (or some other mathematical quantity), that describe whether the entity in question is *bounded below*, *bounded above*, or *unbounded*.

box and whisker plot

First look up *quartile* if you need to. The *box and whisker plot* is a powerful and very concise means of displaying various useful pieces of information about a set of data. The data are arranged in numerical order and are divided into four groups (*quartiles*), each containing an equal number of data points. The box is drawn around the middle two *quartiles* (and the *median* is halfway), and the whiskers are drawn to represent the lower and upper *quartiles*.

Boyle's law (after Robert Boyle)

In applied math and physics, *Boyle's law* states that the product of the pressure and volume of an ideal gas is constant, if the temperature is held constant. In other words, if either the pressure or volume change, then the other quantity must change in *inverse proportion* in order to satisfy *Boyle's law*. An ideal gas is specifically defined in physics, and real gases only approximate an ideal gas in restricted regimes.

branches of a graph

Graphs of some *functions* do not always consist of one continuous piece, but instead might be broken up into two or more disjoint pieces. The pieces are sometimes referred to as *branches*.

branches of a hyperbola

First look up *branches of a graph* and *hyperbola* if you need to. A *hyperbola* is an example of a graph that has disjoint *branches*.

– C –

calculus

A branch of mathematics that is concerned with the study of variability, having applications to many areas of science. Students usually study *calculus* in the final year or two of school, and the study is broadly divided into three parts: (1) *differentiation*, which deals with rates of change of *functions*; (2) *integration*, which deals with the reverse process of (1); (3) elementary applications to applied problems in physics, and to a lesser extent, biology, chemistry, and finance. There is much myth surrounding the difficulty of *calculus*. However, ironically, *calculus* is easier than *precalculus* (or the equivalent prerequisite study in your country). Strictly speaking, *precalculus* is not required to understand the concepts of calculus. Rather, the prerequisite knowledge is required to solve a wider range of problems using the application of *calculus*, than would be possible otherwise.

calorie

A unit of energy equal to 4.186 *Joules*. As an intuitive guide, approximately 1000 calories are required (at sea level) to raise the temperature of 1 *kilogram* (2.20 pounds) of water by 1 degree Celsius (or about 0.56 degrees Fahrenheit).

cardinal number

A fancy word that just means a counting number (*integer, natural number*), including zero. Contrast with *ordinal number*.

cardioid curve

In *geometry*, a curve that looks a heart shape, often drawn sideways. It is generated by following a point on the *circumference* of a circle that rolls around the *circumference* of another circle of equal *radius*. It is a special case of a *limaçon* curve.

Cartesian

An adjective indicating that the associated noun has something to do with the work of the French philosopher and mathematician René Descartes (pronounced "Deh-kart)." *Cartesian* is pronounced "Kart-eez-ian."

Cartesian coordinates

A system specifying the position of any *point* in two-dimensional or three-dimensional space, often denoted by x, y, z coordinates. The grid in *Cartesian coordinates* forms a pattern of rectangles, or rectangular blocks, so such *coordinates* are also known as *rectangular coordinates*.

capacity (volume)

For grade-school math, *capacity* usually refers to the *volume* of a three-dimensional container or object. In other words, *capacity* is a measure of the amount of three-dimensional space that is occupied by an object.

center of coordinates

First look up *coordinate system* if you need to. The *center of coordinates* refers to the reference point of a *coordinate system*, which is usually where all the *coordinates* have a value of zero (by definition). The *center of coordinates* is synonymous with the *origin* (of the *coordinate system*).

centimeter (cm)

A measure of length that is equal to one-hundredth of a *meter*, or approximately 0.394 *inches*.

central angle

The angle at the center of a circle formed by two lines extending from the center to points on the *circumference* of the circle.

central limit theorem

First look up *probability distribution*, and *bell curve* if you need to. The term *central limit theorem* is a fancy way of saying that a statistical *probability distribution* that is not a *bell curve* will become more and more like a *bell curve*, as the number of items or data values sampled becomes larger and larger.

centroid

If an object has a composition such that its density is the same everywhere, the *centroid* is the center of gravity point. In other words, if you hung the object from the ceiling by a piece of string (attached to any point on the object), the object will come to rest in such a position that an imaginary line extending along the length of the string would pass through the object's *centroid*. Attaching the string at different points on the object, and hanging it two more times, will give you the exact *centroid* as the *point* of *intersection* of the imaginary lines. In the particular context of two-dimensional geometry, the above is still true, and for the special case of a *triangle*, the *centroid* lies at the *intersection* of three lines drawn from each *vertex* to the *midpoint* of the corresponding opposite side (these lines are called *medians*).

Ceva's theorem (after Giovanni Ceva)
You may need to look up several terms in italics first. In *geometry*, *Ceva's theorem* concerns *triangles* and three lines joining each *vertex* to a point on the opposite side of the *triangle*. *Ceva's theorem* provides a condition that all three such lines should meet inside the triangle at a single *point* (i.e., that the three lines should be *concurrent*). That condition is that each side of the *triangle* shall be split by the appropriate line in such a way that the *ratio* of the long segment to the short segment is equal to the same value of the corresponding *ratio* for the other two sides. See also *Cevian*. The three lines are specific *Cevians* of the *triangle*.

Cevian
In a *triangle*, a *Cevian* is a straight line that joins a *vertex* of the *triangle* to any point on the side of the *triangle* opposite that *vertex*. See *Ceva's theorem* for the condition that the three *Cevians* for the three *vertices* should intersect at a single *point*. The *Cevian triangle* is the *triangle* that is inside the original *triangle* and that is formed by joining the points of intersection of the three *Cevians* with the three sides. The *Cevian circle* is the *circle* that contains the *Cevian triangle* and passes through each *vertex* of the *Cevian triangle*.

chain rule
First look up *calculus* and *derivative* if you need to. The *chain rule* is a

procedure in *calculus* to find the *derivative* of a compound *function* (see also *function of a function*). A compound *function* is made up of a chain of *functions* in which the output of one *function* is fed into the input of another *function*, and the output of that *function* is fed into the input of the next *function*, and so on.

change of base
First look up *base* if you need to. The term *change of base* refers to a process for expressing a number in a different *base*.

change of variable
The usual context refers to a procedure in *calculus*.

characteristic polynomial (of a matrix)
First look up *square matrix*, *eigenvalues*, and *polynomial* if you need to. The *characteristic polynomial* of a *square matrix* is a *function* formed from the *elements* of the *matrix*. The *function* is of *polynomial* type, whose solutions (the *eigenvalues*) are useful for certain kinds of applied math and physics problems.

Charles's law (after Jacques Charles)
In applied math and physics, *Charles's law* states that the volume of an ideal gas is *directly proportional* to its temperature, if the gas pressure is held constant. For example, if the temperature is doubled, then the volume doubles in order to satisfy *Charles's law*. An ideal gas is specifically defined in physics, and real gases only approximate an ideal gas in restricted regimes.

chi-squared, chi-squared distribution
First look up *hypothesis* and *probability distribution* if you need to. The *chi-squared* value is a quantity usually calculated from data in order to test a *hypothesis* because the *probability distribution* of *chi-squared* has particular properties suited for this purpose. The experimental results are compared with the theoretical *probability distribution*, called (naturally), the *chi-squared distribution* to assess the *probability* that the *hypothesis* is supported by the data. The greek notation for *chi-squared* is χ^2.

chord

A straight line drawn from one point on a curve (or graph of a *function*) to another point on the curve. The usual context is a straight line drawn from one point on the *circumference* of a circle to another point on the *circumference*.

circle

The formal definition of a circle is that it is the *locus* of a curve on which every point is *equidistant* (equal distance) from a single fixed point (the center of the *circle*).

circular function

The usual context for this expression is that it is used as another way of referring to the standard *trigonometric functions sine*, and *cosine*, because the circle is the fundamental generator of these *functions*.

circumcenter

First look up *bisect* and *perpendicular* if you need to. In *geometry*, the *circumcenter* is the point of *intersection* of the *perpendicular bisectors* of the three sides of a *triangle*.

circumference

The *perimeter* of a circle.

circumscribed (circle)

First look up *vertex* if you need to. A circle whose *circumference* passes through every *vertex* of a geometrical figure.

closed interval

A *closed interval* is a numerical range of values that is inclusive of the boundary values of the interval.

closed (solution)

This usually refers to the solution of an *equation*, or set of *equations*, that can written as an *algebraic expression* that does not have an *infinite* number of *terms*.

closure property

This refers to whether or not a given *operation* on a predefined set of items gives a result that is part of that predefined set. For example, subtraction is not closed for *natural numbers* because the result could be negative, but negative numbers are not in the class of *natural numbers*.

cm

Abbreviation for *centimeter* (see crib sheet entry for *centimeter*).

coefficient

This can have many different contexts. There are several terms in italics that you may have to look up first. Usually, *coefficient* means a number or *algebraic expression* in front of (to the left of) some other *algebraic expression*. The precise context will usually be apparent in a given situation. The most common usage for your purpose is in the context of *polynomial coefficients*, in which case the term *coefficients* refers to the items in front of the terms consisting of *powers* of the key *variable*, say, x. Another usage is in the context of fitting data with a theoretical *model* or *function*: see *correlation coefficient* and *regression coefficient*.

cofactor

First look up *matrix* if you need to. The usual context for your purpose is that the *cofactor* is a particular construction from the items in a *matrix* that is useful for a variety of calculations.

cofunction

A *function* is a *cofunction* of another *function* if both *functions* have the same value when the inputs applied to the two *functions* add up to 90 degrees (the inputs must be a measure of angle).

collinear

An adjective describing *points* that can all be joined by a single straight line.

columns

Usually refers to the *columns* in an array of *elements* that form a *matrix*. See *matrix* for more details.

combinations, combinatorics

For grade-school math, the most common context refers to the number of ways a *subset* of items can be selected from a larger set of items, taking into account all valid *permutations* of *subsets*. For example, how many ways can I choose a three-letter word from a six-letter word if all six letters are different? There is a particular formula for calculating this for the "simple" cases that appear in grade-school math. The calculation gets more complicated when some of the letters are the same, but it is still within the scope of grade-school math. However, note that the term *combinatorics*, although relevant to some extent here, actually covers a very large field of study in mathematics, most of which is way beyond grade-school math level.

common denominator

An *integer* that can be divided individually by all of the *denominators* of a given group of fractions, without a *remainder* in every case.

common difference

First look up *arithmetic series* if you need to. The usual context refers to the constant increment between adjacent *terms* in an *arithmetic series*, *arithmetic sequence*, or *arithmetic progression*. In other words it is the constant difference between two consecutive *terms* in such a series. For example, the *common difference* in the series 11, 15, 19... is 4.

common logarithm

First look up *base* and *logarithm* if you need to. The term *common logarithm* simply means that the *logarithm* is in *base* 10.

common ratio

First look up *geometric series* if you need to. The usual context refers to the constant *ratio* between adjacent *terms* in a *geometric series*, *geometric sequence*, or *geometric progression*. In other words it is the constant *ratio* between two consecutive terms in such a series. For example, the *common ratio* of the sequence 4, 12, 36... is 3.

commutative, commutative property

A mathematical *operation* on two items is *commutative* if the result (answer) of the *operation* does not depend on which order the items appear in the *operation*. For example, division is NOT *commutative*.

complement

First look up *additive inverse* if you need to. There are many different meanings of *complement* in mathematics, but for grade-school math you will only need to know two. The first meaning is synonymous with the *additive inverse*. The second, although less likely to come up in grade-school math, is in the fields of *set theory*, *logic*, and computer science. In that case, *complement* means "NOT" (i.e., "false" becomes "true," and vice versa). Another use in the field of *logic* is in constructions known as the "*one's complement*" and "*two's complement*," which enable a computer to handle negative numbers.

complementary angle

Given an angle, the *complementary angle* is 90 degrees minus the given angle.

completing the square

A set of manipulations in *algebra* that can help to solve an *equation* that contains an *unknown variable*, its *square*, and a *constant*. It is the basis of the derivation of the *quadratic formula*.

complex conjugate

First look up *complex number*, *imaginary number*, and *matrix* if you need to. The *complex conjugate* of a *complex number* has the *imaginary* part of the *complex number negated*. In other words, a positive sign is turned into a negative one, or vice versa. The *complex conjugate* of a *matrix* has every *element* replaced by its *complex conjugate*. See also *conjugate*.

complex fraction

See *compound fraction*.

complex harmonic motion

See *harmonic motion*.

complex number(s)

In this context, the word complex does not mean "complicated," but rather it means "composite." A *complex number* is a composite number made up of two numbers. These numbers are carried in pairs in many different types of algebraic manipulations, under a specific set of rules. The two numbers are referred to as *real* and *imaginary*. The term *imaginary* is unfortunate because there is a certain degree of unjustified mystery surrounding *complex numbers* that is overplayed in textbooks. *Complex numbers* simply provide a way of performing various *operations* on pairs of numbers at once. The members of the pair of numbers are in some way connected to each other, usually by a physical relationship. The "mystery" originates from the fact that the *imaginary* numbers are multiplied by the *square root* of a negative number, which does not exist in nature. However, humans can invent whatever mathematical concoctions they like, if it is convenient for specific purposes. If *complex numbers* had not been invented, we could still solve the same physical problems by employing some other mathematical device.

complex root(s)

First look up *real number*, *complex number(s)*, and *roots*. The term *complex roots* simply refers to those solutions of *equations* that are *complex numbers*, as opposed to *real numbers*. Graphically, in the former case the graph of the *equation* does not cross the horizontal *axis*, but in the latter case the graph crosses the horizontal *axis* at the values of the *real roots*.

component (of a vector)

See *vector*.

compound fraction

This is a fraction that itself contains a fraction in the *numerator* and/or *denominator*. Also known as a *complex fraction*.

compound function

A compound *function* is made up of a chain of two or more *functions*, in which the output of one *function* is fed into the input of another *function*, and the output of that *function* is fed into the input of the next *function*, and so on. To some extent, the separation into individual component *functions* may be arbitrary in some cases. However, the concept is useful because certain mathematical *operations*, for example, in *calculus*, may be easier to apply to the decomposed *function*, regardless of the exact decomposition.

compound interest
A term referring to the increase or decrease of a balance by a percentage of the value that the balance had on the occasion just after the last increment or decrement was applied. Contrast this with *simple interest*, which refers to the use of the initial balance for calculating every incremental increase or decrease.

concave
An adjective describing a geometrical shape or figure in which it is possible to draw a line between two points on its *perimeter* such that the line lies outside the figure. See also *convex*.

concurrent
Two or more lines are *concurrent* if they intersect at a single *point*.

conditional equation
This just means an *equation* that has *unknown variables* (represented by symbols), as opposed to an equation that just consists of *constants*.

conditional probability
The *probability* that an event occurs, given that some other specified event has already occurred. An example is the *probability* of drawing an ace at *random* from a pack of 51 cards, given that an ace has already been drawn at *random*.

conditional statement
A statement of the type "if...then..."

cone
A three-dimensional figure that is generated by revolving a straight line around an *axis of symmetry*. If the cross section of the base is a *circle* (as opposed to an ellipse), the cone is a *right cone*.

confidence level
In statistics the term *confidence level* is used to describe the *probability* that a particular result was not obtained by chance. In other words it is the *probability* that the result is due to the correctness of the *hypothesis* that

is being tested, and not due to *random fluctuations* giving the same result. The *confidence level* is usually given as a percentage *probability*.

congruence

See *congruent*.

congruent

The usual context is in *geometry*, and it is just a fancy way of saying that two geometrical figures (for example, *triangles*) are in every way identical (aside from their orientation in space). There are specific ways to prove *congruence*.

conic sections

This term refers to certain well-known geometric figures, namely the *circle*, *ellipse*, *parabola*, and *hyperbola*. They are referred to as *conic sections* because they can all be created by slicing a *cone* in various ways. The edge of the flat surface that results after part of the cone is cut off defines the *conic section*. Your kid's textbook will explain exactly how.

conjecture

A statement or *hypothesis* that is about to be proved, or is unproved, or even unprovable (but assumed to be true).

conjugate

First look up *complex number(s)* and *imaginary number* if you need to. The most common context which is most relevant for you is that it is an *operation* on two numbers or *variables* that are combined with a "+" or "−" sign. The *operation* simply changes the sign (positive to negative or vice versa). The result is the *conjugate* of the original *expression*. If one of the items is *imaginary*, then the result is the *complex conjugate* of the original *expression*. The process can also be applied to a *matrix*, whereby every *element* of the *matrix* is replaced by its *complex conjugate*.

conjugate axis of a hyperbola

First look up *hyperbola* if you need to. The *conjugate axis of a hyperbola* is a line of symmetry that is *perpendicular* to the *axis of symmetry* that cuts through the *hyperbola* (the latter *axis* is the *transverse axis*).

consequent

In the field of *logic*, the term *consequent* refers to the result of making a *premise* (the initial proposition). For example, consider the following argument. All giraffes are animals. There are giraffes in the zoo. Therefore there are animals in the zoo. The statement, "All giraffes are animals," is the *premise*. It may or may not be true. The statement, "Therefore there are animals in the zoo," is the *consequent*, or conclusion.

constant

This usually refers to a quantity in an *equation* that is fixed and not allowed to vary. Often it simply refers to a number in an *equation*, but a *constant* can be represented by a symbol.

continuity

The usual context in math refers to the behavior of a *function* or *variable*. Specific conditions must be met for a *function* to be *continuous* at a specified place, and the property of being *continuous* is *continuity*. Usually the conditions for *continuity* are stricter than the conditions for a *function* simply to be unbroken.

continuous

See *continuity* and *discontinuity*.

contrapositive

In the field of *logic*, the *contrapositive* of a statement is formed by *negating* both parts of the statement (the *premise* and the *consequent*). For example, the *contrapositive* of the statement "All coins have at least some monetary value" is, "If something has no monetary value it cannot be a coin." The key property of a *contrapositive* statement is that if the original statement is true, the *contrapositive* statement is always true.

converge

The usual context for your purpose refers to whether the *sum of a series* of numbers, or a *series* of algebraic *terms*, gets closer and closer to some fixed value as you add more and more *terms* to the sum. The alternative is that the *sum* grows without limit (i.e., it *diverges*).

convergence

See *converge*.

converse

The usual context is in the realm of *logic*, whereby the *converse* of a statement in which "B" follows from "A" is that which has the order of "A" and "B" reversed. The truth or otherwise of the *converse* statement is not implied by the truth of the original statement. For example, the *converse* of "Ants are small," is "Something that is small is an ant."

convex

An adjective describing a geometrical shape or figure for which a straight line drawn between any two points on its *perimeter* always lies inside the figure.

coordinate axes

First look up *coordinates* and *coordinate system* if you need to. The *coordinate axes* of a *coordinate system* are the reference lines used to place a given *point* in the system. In the most common usage, in *Cartesian coordinates*, the axes are the usual x, y and z axes. In this system the *axes* are *mutually perpendicular* and the grid system forms rectangles (in two dimensions), or rectangular blocks (in three dimensions).

coordinate geometry

First look up *coordinate system* if you need to. The term *coordinate geometry* is sometimes synonymously referred to as *analytic geometry*. Both terms refer to *geometry* that is analyzed in the context of a *coordinate system*, in which every spatial location is identified by a unique set of numbers (*coordinates*). This contrasts with *geometry* that is free of a *coordinate system*. Both varieties are studied at grade-school level, and each has its appropriate arena of relevance. For example, the statement that the angles in a *triangle* add up to 180 degrees can be proved without the use of a *coordinate system*.

coordinate plane

First look up *coordinate system* and *plane* if you need to. A *coordinate plane* is a *plane* that contains a two-dimensional *coordinate system*.

coordinates

First look up *coordinate system* if you need to. Usually, the term *coordinates* refers to a set of numbers that specifies a unique spatial location, or position in space. In three dimensions (e.g., in the real world), you need three numbers. In addition to knowing the *coordinates*, you must be told what *coordinate system* they are referred to, and where the reference point in that *coordinate system* is, otherwise the *coordinates* mean nothing.

coordinate system

First look up *mutually perpendicular* and *orthogonal* if you need to. A *coordinate system* is a means of assigning a unique set of numbers, or *coordinates*, to the spatial location of *points*. There are many different *coordinate systems* that are used, but the most common is the *Cartesian coordinate* system. In three dimensions, this system has three *mutually perpendicular*, or *orthogonal axes* that locate each of the three *coordinates* (usually referred to as x, y, z).

coplanar

An adjective describing objects that lie in the same *plane*.

corollary

After reaching a conclusion based on a *theorem*, a *corollary* is a further conclusion that is necessarily true if the first conclusion is true.

correlation

If two quantities, or *variables*, exhibit a relationship to each other, it can be said that there is a *correlation* between the two *variables*. There are various ways of mathematically testing the *significance* (or strength) of a correlation. See also *correlation coefficient* and *regression coefficient*.

correlation coefficient

A number that is generated from two groups of measurements, using a prespecified rule that numerically assesses the strength of a *correlation* between two *variables*. When combined with a formal calculation of the *significance* of the *correlation*, one can then say what the *probability* is that the *correlation* is produced by chance. The term *correlation coefficient* is often used synonymously with *regression coefficient*.

corresponding angles

In *geometry*, when a straight line (*transversal*) cuts two other lines, there are four angles formed at each of the two intersections. Each of the four angles at one intersection has a corresponding angle at the other intersection in terms of relative positioning. In other words, *corresponding angles* are on the same side as the *transversal* and on the "same" side of each line. See also *alternate interior angles* and *alternate exterior angles*.

cosecant

First look up *sine* (or *sin*) if you need to. The *cosecant* (pronounced co-seek-ant), is a derived *trigonometric function* (of an angle), that is equal to "one divided by the *sine* (or *sin*) function." In other words, the *cosecant* is the *reciprocal* of the *sine function*.

cosine, cos

One of the two principal *trigonometric functions* of an angle (the other is *sine*, or *sin*). You can visualize this *function* by imagining swinging your arm in a circle, pivoted at your shoulder. If you start with your arm straight up in the air, the vertical distance between the end of one of your fingers and the reference level where your arm is horizontal, traces the *function*. The *function* repeats every 360 degrees. The *cosine function* can also be expressed as a *ratio* of the side of a *right-angled triangle* that is *adjacent* to the angle in question, to the longest side.

cosine rule

A *formula* for calculating the length of the third side of a *triangle* when you know the length of two of the sides, and the angle between those two sides. Alternatively, if you know the lengths of all three sides of a *triangle* you can use the *cosine rule* to calculate the angle between any two sides.

cotangent, cot

First look up *sine* (or *sin*), and *cosine* (or *cos*) if you need to. The *cotangent* (of an angle) is a derived *trigonometric function* that is equal to the "*cosine* (or *cos*) divided by the *sine* (or *sin*) function."

coterminal angle

An angle constructed from another angle by subtracting 360 degrees if the original angle is positive, or adding 360 degrees if the original angle is negative.

Cramer's rule

First look up *simultaneous equations* if you need to. *Cramer's rule* provides a method to solve a set of *simultaneous equations* that are *linear* (i.e., no *variable* appears as "*squared*" or as a higher *power*).

cross product

See *vector product*.

cube, cubed, cubing

In three-dimensional *geometry*, a *cube* is an object with six *square* faces. In *algebra* a *cube* is a number or a *variable* multiplied by itself three times (or equivalently, a *variable raised to the power* of three). Both *cube* and *cubed* can be used as verbs. For example, "If we *cube* x..," or, "We *cubed* x and got.."

cube root

First look up *cube* if you need to. A *cube root* is obtained as a result of reversing the *operation* of *cubing* a number or *variable*. For example, what number, when *cubed* would give you 8? The answer is 2, so the *cube root* of 8 is 2.

cubic

First look up *term*, *function*, and *polynomial* if you need to. The term *cubic* is an adjective that usually describes the nature of a *function* (for example, a *polynomial*). It can also be used as a noun. In a *cubic*, the highest summed *power* in any of the *terms* in the *function* is 3.

curve fitting

The process of fitting a *function* to data, that results in a *formula* that will reproduce the data and points in between the data. The *formula* will only be accurate to some level of *precision*, that should be assessed as part of the *curve-fitting* process (but this is often not done at the level of grade-school work).

cycloid

A curve traced by a point on the *circumference* of a *circle* as it rolls along a straight line without slipping. It looks like a series of road bumps, one after the other.

cylinder

A three-dimensional structure whose surface is formed by all points that have a prespecified *perpendicular* distance from a straight line. If each end of the cylinder terminates in a circle, it is a *right cylinder*. A *cylinder* is basically a tube (but it need not be hollow).

– D –

damped oscillation

First look up *oscillation* if you need to. A *damped oscillation* is a repetitive vibrational motion that gets weaker and weaker ("fizzles out") with time. An example is the suspension system in a car, which applies *damping* if there is too much up and down motion. Without damping, you would be jigging up and down for much longer after, say, riding over a bump in the road. See also *harmonic motion*.

damping

See *damped oscillation*.

decibel (dB)

The decibel is a unit that measures the *relative power*, or *relative* intensity of sound (for example). The decibel is also commonly used to measure the *relative* power in an electronic signal. The decibel is really a *ratio*. It can either tell you the intensity *relative* to a predefined number, or it can tell you by how much the intensity changes in a given situation. The human ear is sensitive to a huge range in sound levels, so the decibel is defined in a way that does not scale proportionately (a bit like the Richter scale for hurricanes). For example, if an airplane is 20 dB louder when you are standing next to it, compared to when it is in the air, it means that the sound is 100 times more powerful on the ground than in the air.

deductive reasoning

A method of coming to a conclusion by starting with a *premise*, and then deducing a series of truths, each truth leading to the next in the series. Contrast this with *inductive reasoning*.

definite integral

First look up *integral* if you need to. A *definite integral* is an *integral* that is evaluated between an interval, in which case the result has no ambiguity. Contrast this with an *indefinite integral* that is not evaluated over a definite interval, in which case the result is only a general *formula* rather, than a single answer.

degenerate

For the purpose of grade-school math, there are two principal contexts. The first (and most common) context refers to a situation in which some of the solutions of an *equation* are identical. Graphically, this usually corresponds to the curve of the *function* just touching an *axis* rather than crossing it. The second context refers to the *equation* of a *conic section* (look this up first if you need to). A *degenerate conic section* refers to a situation in which the *equation* that would normally generate the curve of a *conic section* fails to generate the curve, giving a result that is just a bunch of points or lines. The reason for the failure is that the *equations* have algebraic exceptions for being valid generators.

degree (of a polynomial)

First look up *polynomial* and *monomial* if you need to. Aside from being a measure of the size of an angle, *degree* refers to either the highest summed *powers* of *variables* in a *term* in a *polynomial*, or the sum of all the *powers* appearing on the *variables* in a *monomial*.

degrees of freedom

First look up *hypothesis* and *model* if you need to. The usual context for grade-school math is in *statistics*, when fitting a *model* to test data against a *hypothesis*. The *model* will have some number of adjustable (free) parameters (that are to be found by the fitting process), and there will be a certain number of data values. The number of *degrees of freedom* is equal to the number of data values minus the number of adjustable parameters in the *model*.

De Moivre's theorem

First look up *complex number* if you need to. *De Moivre's theorem* provides a relation that is useful for manipulating *equations* with *complex numbers*, in order to find solutions to those *equations*.

De Morgan's law

In the field of *logic*, *De Morgan's law* describes a transformation that demonstrates the equivalence between two particular combinations of logical *operations* on two *variables*.

denominator

The bottom number (or item) of a fraction.

density

In applied math and physics, *density* normally refers to how much *mass* there is in a predefined unit of *volume*. In pure math, *density* may refer to the *density* of points on a diagram (i.e., how closely packed the points are in a given area).

dependent event

The context is usually in the study of *probability* and *statistics*. A *dependent event* has an outcome that is in some way affected by another event. See also *independent event*. In calculating *probabilities*, it is essential to know whether events are *dependent* or *independent*.

dependent variable

A *function* is a relationship between an output *variable* and one or more input *variables*. The input *variables* are the *independent variables* and the output *variable* is the *dependent variable*.

derivative

First look up *calculus* if you need to. The *derivative* of a *function* is another *function* (that could be just a number, under some circumstances), that tells you how quickly or slowly the original *function* changes with respect to the *variable* that the *derivative* was calculated for. For example, the *derivative* of distance with respect to time is *velocity*. The act of calculating a *derivative* is called *differentiation*.

Descartes' rule of signs (after René Descartes)

First look up *polynomial* and *roots* if you need to. Due to René Descartes (pronounced "Deh-kart"), the rule is a method to determine the number of positive or negative *roots* (solutions) to a *polynomial* equation. The method does not actually give you the solutions, but it tells you how many of each type there are, which can be very useful for finding the solutions.

determinant

First look up *matrix* if you need to. The *determinant* of a *matrix* is a construction from the *elements* of the *matrix*, that is useful for solving *equations* involving that *matrix*. It is also useful for solving *simultaneous equations* if they can be recast as a *matrix equation*.

diagonal (of a matrix)

First look up *matrix* if you need to. The *diagonal* of a *matrix* is the set of its *elements* that are literally on the *diagonal* of the *matrix* when it is written out. The *diagonal* only has a meaning for a *matrix* that has an equal number of *rows* and *columns* (i.e., it must be a *square matrix*). Another way of defining the *diagonal* is that it is the set of *elements* whose position in its *row* is the same as its position in its *column* (starting from the top left of the *matrix*). The term *diagonal* may also be used as an adjective (as in *diagonal matrix*), in which case it means a *matrix* in which all *elements* that are not on the *diagonal* have a value of zero.

diameter (of a circle or sphere)

A straight line that passes through the center of a *circle* or *sphere*.

difference of two squares

This phrase refers to a relation that equates a subtraction of two "*squared*" quantities to the sum and difference of those same quantities (not "*squared*"). The relation is so important that from about 9th grade, all the way to studies of *calculus*, it comes up over and over again in many different forms and disguises. Using the *equation* for the *difference of two squares* can sometimes transform an unsolvable problem to one that can be solved immediately. Very often a question will not hint at, or tell the student that the problem should be solved using the *difference of two squares*. Therefore, the student must be alert at all times, asking himself/herself, "Could this be solved using the *difference of two squares*?" With extensive practice and experience, a student can gain intuition about what kind of problems can utilize the relation for the *difference of two squares*.

difference quotient

A device used in *calculus* to find rates of change of a *function* from first principles. The *difference quotient* is formed by taking the difference of a *function* at two adjacent points, and then dividing by the interval between the two points. Then, letting that interval become arbitrarily small makes the *difference quotient* yield the *rate* of change.

differentiable

First look up the following if you need to: *calculus* and *derivative*. A *function* is said to be *differentiable* if it is at all possible to find a *derivative* for it. Obviously this implies that there are certain *functions* for which it is not possible, for a variety of technical reasons.

differential

When used as an adjective, the term *differential* refers to the different behavior or characteristics of a mathematical or physical quantity, for different input parameters. When used as a noun, the term *differential* may refer to the difference in the two quantities being compared. It can also be used in the context of *calculus* where *differential* refers to an *infinitesimally* small change in a *variable*.

differential equation

Before students study *calculus*, all of the *equations* that they have to solve explicitly do not include any rates of change of the *variables* that are to be solved for. A *differential equation* is one in which rates of change of the key *variables* do appear in the *equation*. Solution of such *equations* requires learning new techniques.

differentiation

See *derivative*.

dihedral angle

In *geometry*, *dihedral angle* is the angle between two *planes*.

dimension, dimensional analysis

The most common context for grade-school math refers to the size of a physical or geometric object in one or more of the three spatial, *mutually perpendicular* (or *mutually orthogonal*), directions.

Dimension also refers to a property of *matrices* (look up *matrices*).

The word *dimension* has a more abstract meaning as well. Certain mathematical objects are multidimensional in the sense that they need more than one number to represent all of their attributes. Each of the attributes can be thought of as a *dimension*.

In applied math and physics, another context refers to the *units* of a physical quantity broken down into three of the fundamental ones: *mass*, *length*, and *time* (there are two more that come up in physics). *Dimensional analysis* is the process of breaking down the derived *units* of something into the more fundamental *units*.

directed distance

The distance between two points on a curve measured *along the curve*, in a specified direction along the curve.

direction angle, direction cosine

First look up *coordinate system, coordinate axes,* and *cosine* if you need to. A *direction angle* is the angle made by a line or line segment, with one of the *coordinate axes* of a *coordinate system*. The *direction cosine* is the value obtained by operating on a *direction angle* with the *trigonometric cosine function*.

directly proportional

See *direct variation*.

directrix

First look up *conic sections* if you need to. A *directrix* is a straight line (or lines) that has/have a particular relationship to a curve that is a *conic section* (for example, a *parabola*). A *directrix* is *perpendicular* to the *axis* of the *conic section*, lies outside the curve and, along with the focal points of the curve (*foci*), is a defining feature of the curve. For the case of the *parabola*, the shortest distance between the *directrix* and the *vertex* of the *parabola* is the same as the distance between the *focus* and the *vertex*.

Consult a textbook for more details and diagrams.

direct variation

This refers to a relationship between two quantities that maintain the same proportion to each other (i.e., one quantity is *directly proportional* to the other). This kind of relationship is *linear* because when the two quantities are plotted against each other on a graph, the result is a straight line.

discontinuity

The usual context refers to a break in a *function* in the sense that the *function* suddenly makes a large jump at one or more positions.

discrete, discrete mathematics

The simplest context of the word *discrete* refers to objects or entities that cannot take on *continuous* values (for example, *integers*, the spatial information on a TV screen, etc.). By this, I mean that a *discrete* quantity cannot be broken down into an arbitrarily large number of intervals or subunits. However, *continuous* quantities are commonly represented by *discrete* quantities in the process of digitizing information. For example, a computer screen uses a *discrete* number of pixels to represent an image that appears to be *continuous*. The term *discrete mathematics* refers to the study of entities that cannot be described as *continuous*, and therefore the field covers a large range of topics. You can browse through the "contents" pages of a *discrete mathematics* textbook to get some idea of what these are.

discriminant

First look up *matrix* and *polynomial* if you need to. There are two principal meanings in the context of grade-school math. One refers to a quantity constructed from the *elements* of a *matrix*. It is useful for a procedure to solve *matrix equations*, for example. The other meaning of *discriminant* is that it is an *algebraic expression* that gives certain information on the possible solutions to a *polynomial equation*. For example, it may indicate whether *real number* solutions exist at all.

dispersion

This has many contexts, but the most common one is in *statistics*, where it refers to a particular measure of the spread in values of a set of data. See also *standard deviation*.

displacement

In the context of grade-school math, *displacement* usually means the change in distance of a moving object over an interval of time.

distance formula

A *formula* to calculate the distance between two points in a two-dimensional or three-dimensional setting, given the *coordinates* of the two points.

distribution

In *statistics*, a *distribution* refers to quantities derived from a sample of data, or theoretical values of a mathematical or physical quantity, sorted into groups or intervals of values. The collective information on the number of items from the sample in each of the groups is then the *distribution* of the values in the sample. See also *probability distribution*.

distributive law, distributive property

When multiplication or division is mixed with addition or subtraction in a set of *operations* on three (or more) items, there is a certain ambiguity in the result arising from the order in which the *operations* are applied. The *distributive law* or *distributive property* is a rule that dictates that the sum of two items multiplied by a third item is equal to the sum of two products (first item times third, and second item times third).

diverge, divergent

Several contexts are possible. The verb is *diverge* and the adjective is *divergent*.

(1) Two curves (for example, straight lines) are *divergent* if their mutual separation increases indefinitely.

(2) A *series* of numbers (or items) whose sum does not *converge*.

(3) A *function* whose value increases indefinitely as the input to the *func-*

tion approaches a certain value.

divergent series

See *diverge, divergent*.

dividend

In a division *operation*, the first item, the *dividend*, is divided by a second item, the *divisor*.

divisor

In a division *operation*, the first item, the *dividend*, is divided by a second item, the *divisor*.

DMS

An acronym for *degrees, minutes, seconds*, which is a system of measuring angles. There are 60 minutes (of arc) in 1 degree and there are 60 seconds (of arc) in 1 minute (of arc).

dodecahedron (plural: dodecahedra)

A regular *polyhedron* that has twelve faces that are all regular *pentagons*, with three *pentagons* meeting at each point (*vertices*). There are thirty edges and twenty *vertices*.

domain

The usual context is the set of input values (or *arguments*) for which a *function* is valid (or which is allowed in a given problem). See also *range*.

dot product

The term *dot product* in relation to *vectors* is synonymous with *scalar product*.

double-angle formulas

First look up *trigonometry* and *trigonometric functions* if you need to. The term *double-angle formulas* usually refers to a set of relations in *trigonometry* that allows you to compute the values of key *trigonometric functions* for an angle in terms of the *trigonometric functions* for exactly half of that angle. In other words, the *formulas* give you the *trigonometric functions* for an angle that is double the value of the angle that you plug into the *double-angle formulas*. The inverted *double-angle formulas* are, naturally, known as the *half-angle formulas* because they give you the values of *trigonometric functions* for half of the angle that you plug into the *equations*.

double valued

This refers to a *function* that has two possible values for a single input (or *argument*) instead of just one value. In grade-school math such a *function* is not actually allowed to be called a *function*, which is potentially confusing. You are supposed to say that if a "set of rules" or a graph produces a *double-valued* (or multivalued) result, then the "set of rules" or graph is not a *function*.

– E –

e
A very special number that has no end to the number of decimal places it can be expressed to. To five decimal places the number is $e = 2.71828$. Sometimes it is called the Euler (pronounced "Oiler") number, or the *exponential number*. There is more than one reason why it is so special, as it shows up in many different areas of mathematics and physics. In particular the *function* formed by raising e to the *power* of a *variable* has a *rate* of change with respect to that *variable* that is equal to the *function* itself.

eccentricity
First look up *ellipse* if you need to. The term *eccentricity* is a property of an *ellipse* that tells you how "squashed" it is compared to a *circle* (for which the *eccentricity* is zero). The maximum value of the *eccentricity* for an *ellipse* is 1.

eigenvalues
First look up *matrix* and *matrix equation* if you need to. The *eigenvalues* values of a *matrix* are a set of numbers (or *variables*) that are the solutions to a certain class of *matrix equations* that come up in applied math and physics problems.

element(s) (of a matrix)
First look up *matrix* if you need to. The usual context for grade-school math pertains to the individual numbers, or entries (which could be entire *expressions*) in a *matrix*, which are called the *elements* of the *matrix*.

elevation
For the purpose of grade-school math, there are two different meanings that are relevant. The first is a synonym for height (or *altitude* above some predefined reference level). The second meaning is an angle that effectively tells you how high up from some reference level an object is. For example, if you stand 1000 feet from a building that is 500 feet tall, the *elevation* of

the top of the building can be said to be approximately 26.6 degrees. This is the angle you would have to swing your arm through (starting parallel to the ground), in order to point directly to the top of the building.

eliminate, elimination (of a variable)

A procedure for solving an *equation* with more than one *unknown* by eliminating one of the *variables* from another *equation* by *substitution*, thereby replacing the *variable* by its equivalent in terms of the other *variable*. The *simultaneous equations* must be related to each other.

ellipse

A squashed *circle*, or oval shape. There is a quantitative definition of it, and a specific *formula* for an *ellipse*. It is also an example of a *conic section* because it is the shape obtained if a *cone* is sliced *obliquely* (the surfaces that result from the cut are *ellipses*). See also *eccentricity*.

ellipsoid

A three-dimensional "egg-shaped" figure, or as a special subclass, a *spheroid* (look this up if you need to).

empirical

Facts that follow directly from observational or experimental data. For example, the Sun rising in the east and setting in the west is an empirical fact.

empty set

A fancy term for a *set* that has no members (and consequently the *empty set* has a size of zero).

end behavior

A term that refers to the properties of the graph of a *function* at the extreme ends of the *domain* of input values. If the graph has a sufficiently wide coverage of input values, the *end behavior* corresponds to the behavior of the graph at the extreme left-hand and right-hand ends. Possible types of *end behavior* that are common are: a tendency to *diverge* to *infinity*; reach a constant value; get closer and closer to a constant value; or behave more and more like a different, simpler *function*.

energy
This is a huge topic for which justice cannot be done here. Energy comes up frequently in applied math and physics problems. There are different kinds of energy but the different forms can be converted from one kind to another (but not necessarily with 100% efficiency). There are specific *formulas* for different kinds of energy. All kinds of energy have equivalent *units*, which are usually *calories* or *Joules*.

equation
Two *algebraic expressions* that are equal to each other. One of the *algebraic expressions* could be a number. There may be one or more *unknown variables* in the *equation*. If there is more than one, it is impossible to solve the *equation* for all of the *variables*. You need at least as many different *equations* as the number of *unknown variables* in order to solve for all the *variables*.

equator
The *circumference* of the largest circle that can be drawn around the surface of a *sphere*. When applied to Earth, it is capitalized (*Equator*), and corresponds to the intersection of the *sphere* with a *plane* that is *perpendicular* to the *axis* of rotation.

equiangular
In *geometry*, *equiangular* is an adjective that refers to a figure or shape that has equal angles at the *vertices*. For example, as in an *equiangular polygon*. An *equiangular triangle* is known as an *equilateral triangle*.

equidistant
Usually refers to things that are located at an equal distance to something. For example, a *point* could be *equidistant* with respect to two lines. Several points could be *equidistant* with respect to neighboring points.

equilateral
In *geometry*, *equilateral* is an adjective that refers to a figure or shape whose sides have equal lengths. In an *equilateral triangle*, if all three sides are equal in length, then all three angles are automatically equal.

equilateral polygon

A *polygon* is a shape made up of straight lines that has more than three sides. An *equilateral polygon* is a *polygon* for which all of the sides have the same length.

equilateral triangle

In an *equilateral triangle* all three sides are equal in length. All three angles are automatically equal.

equilibrium

In applied math and physics this can refer to many different types of situations. In general it means that a system is balanced and stable (in time) in some specified manner. In grade-school math it will usually be in the context of mechanics. For example, a pendulum that ceases to swing is in *equilibrium*.

equivalent fractions

First look up *numerator* and *denominator* if you need to. A set of *fractions* that have the same numerical value are *equivalent fractions*. Their *numerators* are different to each other, and their *denominators* are different to each other, but for each *fraction*, the *ratio* of the *numerator* to the *denominator* is the same as that of all the other *fractions* in the set.

escape velocity

The minimum *velocity* that an object needs to be launched at in order to escape the pull of gravity, and avoid falling back. It does NOT apply to systems that have their own power source (such as rockets).

Euclidean (geometry)

All grade-school geometry is *Euclidean geometry* (pronounced "You-Klid-ian"). It is the appropriate type of geometry that is relevant for the everyday world in which we live. Other types of geometry may not correspond to anything real, or may correspond to situations that we do not encounter on Earth.

Euler angles

"Euler," as in Leonard Euler, is pronounced "Oiler." Three numbers (angles) are required to completely specify the orientation of an object in three-dimensional space. To do so, a reference system and a convention is needed, and the three *Euler angles* provide one particular, widely used means of specifying three-dimensional orientation parameters.

Euler constant

"Euler," as in Leonard Euler, is pronounced "Oiler." The *Euler constant* comes up in advanced mathematics and it is not likely to be encountered in grade-school math, but it is mentioned here for completeness, and to point out that it is not to be confused with the *Euler number*, e (see crib sheet entry for e if you need to).

Euler formula

"Euler," as in Leonard Euler, is pronounced "Oiler." First look up *complex numbers*, *exponential function*, and *trigonometric functions* if you need to. The *Euler formula* is a relation that connects two of the principal *trigonometric functions* to the *exponential function*. The relation involves *complex numbers*.

Euler line

"Euler," as in Leonard Euler, is pronounced "Oiler." In *geometry*, the *Euler line* refers to the line joining three special points inside a *triangle*. These are (look them up if you need to): the *orthocenter*, the *centroid*, and the *circumcenter*.

Euler number

"Euler," as in Leonard Euler, is pronounced "Oiler." *Euler number* is another name for the special number e (see first entry under "E" in the crib sheet). The *Euler number* is not to be confused with the *Euler constant*.

evaluation (of a function)

First look up *function* if you need to. The term *evaluation of a function* refers to the process of plugging an input, or inputs, into the *formula* for a *function*, and calculating the result (which could be a number, or any other type of mathematical entity).

even function

First look up *function* if you need to. An *even function* is one that has the same value if the input is *negated* (positive turned to negative, or vice versa).

excircle

A *circle* that is outside of a two-dimensional geometrical figure and touches one side of the figure.

expectation value

In *statistics* the *expectation value* of a quantity that is distributed with a range of values, is the *average* value that you would get if you sampled the distribution a large number of times. In other words, *expectation value* is a fancy alternative name for the *average* value of a data set.

expected value

Synonymous with *expectation value*.

explicit function

There are two contexts, but they are very similar. The first refers to a *function* in which all of the inputs are specified on the right-hand side of an *equation*, and the output appears on the left-hand side. This is the most usual form of an *equation*. However, for some *equations* this is not true (i.e., the output is not explicitly isolated on one side of the *equation*) and a *function* embedded in such an *equation* is called an *implicit function*, or *implicit equation*.

For the second context, first look up *recursive* if you need to. Whereas a *recursive formula*, or *recursive rule*, gives you the *term* in a *series* based on the previous *term*, an *explicit formula*, or *explicit rule*, allows you to calculate any *term* in a *series*, at any specified position in that *series*, without knowing or having to calculate any other *term*.

exponent

A number, *variable*, or *expression* can be multiplied by itself any number of times, and the number of times need not be an *integer*, and it could even be a *variable*. The number of times that an item is multiplied by itself is called an *exponent*, and is written as a superscript. The *exponent* is also known as a a *power*. The action of applying an *exponent* is also referred to as "*raising to the power of..* (the *exponent*)." Note, the *exponent* or *power* is sometimes referred to as an *index*.

exponential, exponential function
First look up *independent variable*, *exponent*, and *function* if you need to. An *exponential function* is a *function* in which the *independent variable* appears as an *exponent* or *power*. This makes the *function* change much more rapidly compared to the case when the *independent variable* does not appear as an *exponent* in the *function*. In the same context, the term *exponential* can be used as an adjective to describe anything that has an essentially similar functional form. For example, see *growth rate*. Note that THE *exponential function* usually refers to the special number *e raised to the power* of the *independent variable*. See *e*, the first entry under "E."

exponential decay
See discussion under *growth rate*.

exponential growth
See discussion under *growth rate*.

exponential number, the
See *e*.

expression
The usual context is a noun synonymous with *algebraic expression*, which is a string of letters and/or symbols that might represent a mathematical or physical quantity, or quantities.

exterior angle
The angle formed by any one side of a geometrical figure, or shape, and the straight-line extension of the adjacent side.

extraneous solution
In solving applied math and physics problems, there may be more solutions of the relevant *equation*, or *equations*, than are needed. For example, some of the solutions may not have any correspondence to physical reality, and

these are known as *extraneous solutions*, which can usually be discarded.

extrapolate, extrapolation

The verb *extrapolate* refers to the process of extending a line, curve, or *function*, beyond that which is given. The resulting *extrapolation* is usually an estimate or approximation, since the true form of the line, curve, or *function*, may be unknown in the new regime.

– F –

factor

A number or *algebraic expression* that divides exactly into another (given) number or *algebraic expression* without a *remainder*.

factorial

The *factorial* of an *integer* is formed by multiplying itself by all consecutive *integers* that are smaller than itself (down to 1). The *factorial* is symbolically written as "!" For example, $5! = 5 \times 4 \times 3 \times 2 \times 1$.

factoring

A verb describing the act of finding the *factors* of a number or *algebraic expression*.

factorization

First look up *polynomial* if you need to. *Factorization* usually refers to the process of breaking down a *polynomial* into a number of *factors*, each *factor* being a simpler *expression*. The process is the opposite of the FOIL method, which multiplies a number of simple *algebraic expressions* (or *factors*), to give a more complicated *expression* for the *polynomial*. See also *linear factorization theorem*.

Fibonacci number

A number in the *Fibonacci sequence*.

Fibonacci sequence

A sequence of numbers in which each member is the sum of the previous two members (the first two numbers in the sequence are defined as 0 and 1).

finite

This is an adjective attributed to the number of items in a group, or to the value of a *function*. In the former case, *finite* can be attributed to a group of items that is countable in the sense that the number of items is not arbitrarily large (*infinite*). In the second case, *finite* can refer to a *function*

whose output value does not become *infinite* or undefined for any values of the inputs that lie in the allowed *domain*.
finite difference
A term that is usually used in *calculus*. It refers to the difference between the values of a *function* at two different places.
finite sequence
A *sequence* of numbers or *algebraic expressions* that does not continue indefinitely (i.e., there is a last *term*, or last member of the *sequence*). Contrast with *infinite sequence*.
first quartile
See *quartile*.
fitting
See *curve fitting*.
floating point (representation)
First look up *scientific notation* if you need to. The *floating point* representation of numbers does not normally come up in grade-school math, but *scientific notation* does, and the two terms are actually equivalent to each other. The difference is that the term *floating point* is usually used when a number is represented in *scientific notation* in a computer or in software.
focal length
This usually refers to a property of a lens or system of lenses. For a single lens, the *focal length* is the distance (or apparent distance) between the lens and the image of an object if it were "placed at infinity" (i.e., very far away from the system). Shorter *focal lengths* indicate stronger "bending" of light. For several lenses the effective *focal length* is a function of the individual *focal lengths*.
foci
See *focus* (*foci* is the plural of *focus*).
focus (plural: foci)
(1) First look up *conic section* if you need to. In grade-school math the most common context for *focus* is that it is a noun that relates to geometric

figures known as *conic sections*, of which there are four principal types (*circle, ellipse, hyperbola, parabola*). A *focus* is a point that is critical for generating the figures. A *circle* and *parabola* have one *focus*, the others have two. Your child's textbook will show you where they are and what they mean exactly.

(2) In optical physics applications, *focus* is a verb that relates to the "bending" of different light rays to a common point or plane. In the same context, *focus* is also a noun that refers to the point at which a lens brings *parallel* rays of light to meet (*converge*), or it is a point from which *divergent* rays appear to originate from (for a *diverging* lens).

FOIL (method)

The term *FOIL* is a *mnemonic* that is supposed to jog the memory on a method of multiplying out an *algebraic expression* of the form: (something + something else) × (another thing + one more thing). As a parent, you don't really need to know what the letters stand for unless you want to learn how to do it yourself, in which case you should consult a textbook.

force

In applied math and physics, *force* is a derived quantity equal to *mass* times *acceleration*. It has both *magnitude* and direction (i.e., it is a *vector*).

formula

In math, *formula* is usually synonymous with *equation*. However, there is a small distinction in that a *formula* takes input *variables* on the right-hand side to give you a result on the left-hand side, which may not be the case in general for an *equation*. The plural is *formulas* (or *formulae* in British English).

fourth-degree polynomial

First look up *polynomial* and *power* if you need to. A *fourth-degree polynomial* is one in which the highest total *power* of the *variables* in any of the *terms* is four. Also known as a *quartic*.

fractal

A *fractal* is a geometric structure that can be successively broken down into pieces that look identical to the whole structure before it was broken down. In reverse, *fractals* can generally be constructed from simple *recursive* relational rules.

fractional exponent, fractional power

First look up *exponent* and *power* if you need to. A *fractional exponent* or *fractional power* is an *exponent* or *power* that is a *fraction*, or whose *absolute value* is less than 1.

free fall

In math and applied physics, *free fall* refers to the accelerated motion of something that is dropped in an object's gravitational field, in the absence of any other forces of resistance or thrust.

frequency, frequency distribution

In *statistics*, *frequency* refers to the number of occurrences of an event, group of events, or values of a *variable*. The number of occurrences may be expressed as a *fraction* of some quantity. The collection of *frequencies* for different events, groups of events, or ranges of the *variable*, is called the *frequency distribution*. A plot of the *frequency distribution* is a *histogram*. In applied math or physics, *frequency* can refer to the rate of repetitive motion of a mathematical or physical quantity (such as the amplitude of a wave). It is equal to "1 divided by the time duration of each cycle of the repetitive motion."

friction

In applied math and physics, *friction* is a *force* that presents resistance to motion. See also *kinetic friction* and *static friction*.

function

A set of algebraic rules *operating* on one or more inputs. A *function* is usually expressed as an *equation*, *formula*, or graph, but sometimes it is represented by a table, consisting of a number of input values together with the corresponding output values. In grade-school math the set of rules for the *operations* must give one, and only one, unique value for a unique set of input values, in order for the set of rules to be called a *function*.

function of a function

A double procedure that involves using the output from one *function* as the input to another *function*. Sometimes a *function of a function* is called a *composite function*, or *compound function*.

fundamental theorem of algebra

First look up *polynomial* and *complex numbers* if you need to. Loosely speaking, the theorem states that every *polynomial equation* (in one unknown) has a number of solutions that is equal to the highest *power* of the unknown. The solutions may, however, not be *real numbers*, but *complex numbers*, and may include repeats.

– G –

Gaussian

An adjective that describes a statistical property of the *population* from which a given quantity or *variable* is drawn from. Specifically, the term refers to the fact that the *variable* in the *population* has a *distribution* that is the standard *bell curve*. Note that *Gaussian distribution*, and *normal distribution* are both equivalent names for the *distribution* represented by a *bell curve*. The "G" in *Gaussian* is a capital "G" because it is derived from a person's name (Carl Friedrich Gauss).

Gaussian distribution

See *bell curve* and *Gaussian*.

generating function

A *function* that, when expanded by applying elementary mathematical rules, generates a series of *terms*, each of which contains some desired information. A *generating function* is therefore a way of encoding a large amount of information in a compact form.

geometric mean

The *geometric mean* of two numbers is formed by multiplying the two numbers and then taking the *square root* of that result. A *geometric mean* can also be calculated for more than two numbers. In that case all the numbers are multiplied together but the *nth root* of the result is taken (look up *nth root* if you need to).

geometric progression

A *sequence* or *series* of numbers in which each *term* is generated by multiplying the previous term by a fixed number (which is known as the *common ratio*). In other words, the *ratio* of any two adjacent terms in the *series* is constant.

geometric proof

First look up *axiom* if you need to. A *theorem* in *geometry* is often proved by a series of deductions based on the *axioms* and rules of *geometry* (as opposed to a series of algebraic deductions based on the rules of algebra).

geometric series

Synonymous with *geometric progression*.

golden ratio

A special *proportion* that occurs in many examples in nature. It is formed by splitting a length in such a way that the *ratio* of the long piece to the short piece is the same as the *ratio* of the original length to the long piece. The value of the *golden ratio* is 1.61803 (to five decimal places).

gradient (of a function)

For grade-school math, the *gradient* of a *function* is synonymous with the *slope* of a *function* at a particular point (refer to the crib sheet entry for *slope*).

greatest common denominator (GCD)

The largest positive *integer* that divides exactly into two or more denominators, that are *integers*, without a *remainder*. In other words, the *greatest common factor* of two or more denominators is the *greatest common denominator*.

greatest common divisor (GCD)

Synonymous with *greatest common factor*.

greatest common factor (GCF)

The largest positive *integer* that divides exactly into two or more other *integers* without a *remainder*.

grid

Usually refers to a two-dimensional or three-dimensional array of numbers (or other mathematical entities) but the number of *dimensions* may also be one, or more than three, in some applications. Graphically a representation of a numerical *grid* will look like "tiled" rectangles (in two dimensions), or "boxes" in three dimensions if the *coordinate system* is *Cartesian* (look these up if you need to).

group (theory)

An area of mathematics that pertains to the study of *sets* of mathematical entities governed by specific rules. *Group theory* is not studied in any great depth at grade-school level.

growth rate

For this you may need to look up the following: *rate*, *linear*, and *exponential*. The *rate* of increase (or decrease) of a quantity, usually with respect to time, in general might itself change with time. A negative *growth rate* results in a quantity that decreases with increasing time. A zero growth *rate* results in a quantity that does not change with time. A *constant growth rate* results in a quantity that changes in *proportion* with time (i.e., it is a *linear relationship*). An *exponential growth rate* is one whose value is determined by the current value of the quantity itself, resulting in that *rate* changing extremely rapidly with time. Likewise for *exponential decay*, except that in this case the quantity in question decreases with time (for example, the number of atoms remaining as radioactive decay proceeds). Examples of *exponential growth* are *compound interest* on savings or on a loan, and the populations of living organisms that reproduce.

– H –

half-angle formulas

First look up *trigonometry* and *trigonometric functions* if you need to. In *trigonometry*, if you know the values of the *trigonometric functions* for a given angle, the *half-angle formulas* provide a means of calculating the values of the *trigonometric functions* for half of that angle. See also *double-angle formulas*.

half-life

This may come up in applied math and physics problems. Usually, it refers to the time required for an unstable radioactive substance to decay until exactly half of the initial number of atoms of the original species remains. The *half-life* is a property of the sample of atoms themselves and not their initial numbers. The decay time of an individual atom is actually unpredictable because the *half-life* is really the *mean* value of a *Poisson probability distribution*.

half-plane

First look up *plane* if you need to. A *half-plane* is a *plane* that only exists on one side of a straight line and not the other.

harmonic motion

In applied math and physics, *harmonic motion* refers to repetitive motion that involves some kind of *oscillation* or *period*. Simple harmonic motion is *harmonic motion* that has a single *period*. Complex harmonic motion is the superposition (sum) of more than one component of *simple harmonic motion*, each having a different *period*. Damped harmonic motion is *harmonic motion* that dies out (see *damped oscillation*).

helical

First look up *helix* if you need to. *Helical* is an adjective describing something that resembles a *helix*, or has the shape of a *helix*.

helix (plural: helices)
A three-dimensional curve that is formed by the path of point describing a *circle*, whilst simultaneously moving in a straight line *perpendicular* to the circular motion, with a constant *speed*.

hemisphere
Half of a *sphere* formed by dividing a *sphere* into two halves of exactly equal *volume*.

Heron's formula
In *geometry*, *Heron's formula* can be used to calculate the area of a triangle if you know the length of all three sides, and if none of the angles are known.

Hertz (Hz)
A unit of frequency (of a variety of physical quantities). One cycle per second is 1 Hz. For example, human hearing is somewhere in the range 20 Hz to 20 kHz (kHz is an abbreviation for "kiloHertz," or 1000 Hz).

highest common denominator (HCD)
Synonymous with *greatest common denominator*, and closely related to *greatest common divisor*, and *greatest common factor*.

highest common divisor (HCD)
Synonymous with *highest common factor* and *greatest common factor*.

highest common factor (HCF)
Synonymous with *highest common divisor* and *greatest common factor*.

histogram
A graph (actually a particular kind of *bar graph*), that shows the *frequency* of occurrence of a quantity (*variable*) in a *sample* of data, versus the value or interval of values of the *variable*. See *bar graph* for a description of the difference between a *bar graph* and a *histogram*.

Hooke's law (after Robert Hooke)
In applied math and physics, *Hooke's law* refers to a relation between the *force* required to stretch or compress an elastic material (such as a spring) by a given amount. The relation expresses a *direct proportionality* between

the *force* and the extension or compression. For example, doubling the extension requires doubling the *force*. Not all materials obey *Hooke's law* and even those that do only obey the law in a restricted regime.

horizontal-line test
Look up *monotonic function* if you need to, but it is not necessary. The *horizontal-line test* is a procedure for finding out if the graph of a *function* could produce the same output for more than one input. In other words, it is a test to see if every output value has a unique input value, or equivalently, a test to find out if the *function* is *monotonic*. You simply imagine a horizontal line on the graph (*parallel* to the horizontal axis) and move the line up and down (or you could use a ruler for this purpose). If the horizontal line (or ruler) never crosses the *function* at more than one *point*, then the *function* is *monotonic* (i.e., every output has one, and only one, input).

hyperbola
First look up *conic section* if you need to. A *hyperbola* is a particular type of curve in the class of curves called *conic sections*. This particular *function* is broken up into more than one *branch*, or disjoint pieces. It has a specific *formula*, or *equation*. The plural is hyperbolas or hyperbolae.

hyperbolic
First look up *hyperbola* if you need to. The term *hyperbolic* is an adjective used to describe a curve or surface that either has certain characteristics of a *hyperbola*, or is a *hyperbola*. See also *hyperbolic functions*, which can be manipulated to yield *hyperbolic* curves.

hyperbolic functions
First look up *exponential function* if you need to. The *hyperbolic functions* are a specific set of *functions* involving combinations of *exponential functions*. The three principal *hyperbolic functions* are "sinh" (pronounced "shine," or hyperbolic sine), "cosh" (pronounced "coshine," or hyperbolic cosine), and "tanh," (pronounced, hyperbolic tangent). The *hyperbolic functions* can be found on advanced *calculators*. The *hyperbolic functions* are related to *hyperbolas* (see *hyperbola* and *hyperbolic*).

hypotenuse

The longest side of a *triangle* in which one of the angles is a *right angle* (90 degrees). The *hypotenuse* is the side opposite to the *right angle.*

hypothesis

A *hypothesis* is a statement or supposition whose truth is unknown, either because its truth or otherwise is about to be established, or because it cannot be disproved or proved. In the latter case, it is assumed to be true so that the implications of that assumption can be explored. When there are a range of possible outcomes of an experiment, a *probability* can be calculated for rejecting one of the simplest, or default outcomes, as a "baseline" comparison, known as the *null hypothesis*. Since there may in general be more than one possibility for the *null hypothesis*, it must be explicitly and carefully defined.

hypothesis testing

First look up *hypothesis, probability distribution,* and *chi-squared* (χ^2) if you need to. *Hypothesis testing* is the process of testing whether a *hypothesis* is true or false, or it can refer to the process of calculating the *probability* that a *hypothesis* can be rejected. In grade-school math the term usually refers to fitting a set of data with a mathematical *model*. The *model* is usually based on a physical scenario that is being tested and constitutes the *hypothesis*. An appropriate measure of the "goodness of fit" and its *probability distribution* is employed to compare the *model* with the data, and to determine whether the *probability* that such a good fit could be obtained by chance (equivalent to the *probability* that the *hypothesis* could be rejected). For this purpose, the so-called "chi-squared" (or χ^2) *probability distribution* is commonly used. In the case of small samples of data, the "Student's t-distribution" (and corresponding "Student's t-test") may be more appropriate.

hypothesize

A verb that refers to the act of making a *hypothesis*.

– I –

icosahedron (plural: icosahedra)
A three-dimensional geometrical figure that has twenty flat identical faces, each of which is an *equilateral triangle*. There are thirty edges and twelve *vertices*.

identity
The usual context is that if two *expressions* or mathematical entities are trivially equal, an *equation* that expresses that fact is said to be an *identity*. For example, $2 \times 1 = 2$ is an *identity*. See also *additive identity*, *multiplicative identity*, and *identity matrix*.

identity matrix
First look up *matrix* (and related terms) if you need to. The *identity matrix* is a *square matrix* that has all *elements* along the *diagonal* equal to 1, and all other *elements* equal to zero. The *identity matrix* leaves another *matrix* unchanged under the *operation* of *matrix multiplication*. The term *identity matrix* is synonymous with *unit matrix*.

imaginary number
First look up *complex numbers* if you need to. An *imaginary number* is one of the two parts of a *complex number* (the other part is called the *real* part).

implicit differentiation
First look up *derivative*, *differentiation*, *explicit function*, and *implicit function* if you need to. The term *implicit differentiation* refers to a process that allows the calculation of a *derivative* from an *equation* that is not an *explicit function* for the quantity that you want to find the *derivative* of.

implicit function
First look up *function*, *dependent variable*, and *independent variable* if you need to. A regular *function* explicitly has the inputs (*independent variables*) to the *function* isolated on the right-hand side of an *equation*, so that

the output of the *function* (the *dependent variable*) explicitly appears on the left-hand side of the *equation*. However, an *implicit function* function does not isolate the output in such a manner: the output *variable* appears on both sides of an *equation*. Additional work is needed to manipulate the *equation* in order to isolate the output *variable*. However, there are some mathematical processes that can be performed on an *implicit function* without ever having to turn it into an *explicit function*.

improper fraction

A *fraction* in which the *numerator* (top) is larger than the *denominator* (bottom).

incenter

First look up *angle bisector* if you need to. In a *triangle*, the *incenter* is the point where the three *angle bisectors* of the *triangle* cross. The *perpendicular* distance between the *incenter* and any of the three sides is the same for all three sides.

inch

A unit of distance approximately equal to 0.0254 *meters* (2.54 cm) and one-twelfth of a foot.

inclined plane

A *plane* surface that makes an angle to the horizontal so that something placed on it might slide under the *force* of gravity. Very popular in applied math and physics problems.

indefinite integral

First look up *integral* if you need to. An *indefinite integral* is an *integral* that gives only a general *formula*, rather than a single answer. In other words, there is an entire family of possible answers. Graphically, this corresponds to finding the area under a curve without specifying between which two points on the horizontal *axis* that you want to calculate the *area* for. Contrast this with a *definite integral*.

independent

There are many possible contexts, but the two most common are *independent variable*, and *independent events* (look these up below).

independent events

In *probability* theory, *independent events* are those for which the *probability* of one event does not depend on the outcome of the other events. For example, successive rolls of a dice are *independent events*, but the outcomes of drawing from a pack of cards without replacement are not *independent events*.

independent variable

A *function* is a relationship between an output *variable* and one or more input *variables*. The input *variables* are the *independent variables* and the output *variable* is the *dependent variable*. On the other hand, a *function* that is *independent* OF a *variable* means that the value of the *function* is not influenced by the value of that *variable*.

index

The term *index* is most often used in one of two ways. One is as an identifying label for a member of a set of mathematical entities that are in some way related to each other. In the second usage, *index* is synonymous with *exponent* or *power* (look these up if you need to).

induction

See *proof by induction*.

inductive reasoning

A method of reasoning (establishing truths), that involves proposing a new "truth" by generalizing a set of observations or *empirical* relations, with the addition of one or more assumptions (which may or may not be true). For example, starting with the statement, "The Sun has risen everyday since recorded human history," we could deduce by *inductive reasoning* that, "The Sun will rise tomorrow." The additional assumption invoked here is that nothing will prevent the Sun from rising tomorrow. Contrast this with *deductive reasoning*. *Inductive reasoning* is not to be confused with *proof by induction*, which does not involve any uncertain assumptions.

inequality

Whilst *equations* have a left-hand side and a right-hand side connected by an "equals" sign, *inequalities* have a left-hand side and a right-hand side that are connected by an *inequality* sign ("$<$" for "less than," and "$>$" for "greater than"). *Inequalities* can be solved in a similar way to the analogous *equation*, with the help of a couple of additional rules.

inertia, inertial mass

In applied math and physics, *inertia* is the property of an object that resists change in the state of motion (i.e., *forces* are required to overcome the resistance). For straight-line motion it is just the *mass* of the object, but for curved motion it depends on the shape of the object as well. The term *inertial mass* was invoked to distinguish the straight-line resistance to motion from *gravitational mass*, but experiments so far have shown both to be indistinguishable from each other.

infinite, infinity

The term *infinite* is used in a variety of contexts with a similar general meaning, with slight but important variations in different contexts. In grade-school math the meaning is either to convey an uncountable numerical quantity that is arbitrarily large, or to convey the fact that a mathematical *series* or *sequence* has a neverending number of *terms*. The latter covers the case of a number that has a neverending number of digits after the decimal point. The word *infinite* is an adjective, and the noun corresponding to an "uncountably large number" is *infinity*. However, you should be aware of the fact that the exact definition of *infinity* depends on a number of things, including what academic level you are studying mathematics at.

infinite sequence, infinite series

First look up *sequence* or *series* if you need to, An *infinite sequence* or *infinite series* has a neverending number of *terms*.

infinitesimal
An adjective describing something that is immeasurably small.

inflection (or inflexion)
Loosely speaking, an *inflection* is a point on a curve, or the graph of a *function*, that signifies a change in the direction of curvature. In other words, the *function* changes from increasing to decreasing or vice versa. A point of *inflection* is also known as a *stationary point*, a *turning point*, and a *vertex*. The term also includes the case of the curvature instantaneously ceasing to change (the latter is known as a *saddle point*). See also *minima* and *maxima*.

initial value(s)
In applied math and physics, the behavior of a system versus time can be calculated by applying the appropriate *equations*, starting the system off at some specified *initial values* of the relevant *variables*, including the initial (reference) time value.

inner product
The term *inner product* in relation to *vectors* is synonymous with *scalar product*.

inradius
The *radius* of a *circle* that is inside a *triangle*, or other two-dimensional figure, that touches every side of the figure. See also *incenter, inradius, apothem*.

inscribed circle
A *circle* that is inside a *triangle*, or other two-dimensional figure, that touches every side of the figure. See also *incenter, inradius, apothem*.

inscribed triangle
A *triangle* that is inside a *circle*, such that every *vertex*, or point of the *triangle*, touches the inside of the *circle*.

integer
The set of regular counting (whole) numbers and their negative counterparts, with zero included in the set. See also *natural numbers*, which are a

nonnegative *subset* of *integers*.

integrable

First look up *integration* and *integrate* if you need to. In *calculus*, the term *integrable* is an adjective describing whether a *function* is amenable to the mathematical *operation* of *integration* (it may not be for a variety of reasons).

integral

First look up *integration* if you need to. In *calculus*, the term *integral* is a noun describing the result of performing an *operation* known as *integration*.

integral equation

First look up *integration* and *integral*. Before students study *calculus*, all of the *equations* that they have to solve explicitly do not include any rates of change of the *variables*, and they do not include any "cumulative sums" of *functions* involving the *variables* that are to be solved for. An *integral equation* is one in which such "cumulative sums" of *functions* (or *integrals*) involving the key *variables* DO appear in the *equation*, and solution of such *equations* requires learning new techniques.

integrand

First look up *integration* if you need to. In *calculus*, the term *integrand* is a noun describing the thing that is about to have an *operation* called *integration* performed on it.

integrate

First look up *integration* if you need to. In *calculus*, the term *integrate* is a verb describing the act of performing an *operation* known as *integration*.

integration

In *calculus*, the term *integration* is a noun describing an *operation* (or process) on a *function* or curve that is equivalent to finding the area "under the graph of the *function*," or "under the curve". There are many techniques for doing this. The *operation* of *integration* has a special symbol that looks like this: $\int$.

integration by parts

First look up *integration* if you need to. In *calculus*, the term *integration by parts* describes a method of performing an *integration* on a *compound function* that breaks it down into two *integrations*.

integration constant

First look up *integration*, *integral*, and *indefinite integral* if you need to. In *calculus*, the evaluation of an *indefinite integral* results in an answer which is by definition ambiguous (i.e., the solution is really an entire suite of solutions). This ambiguity is in the form of an unknown number that can be added to the stub of the solution, and that unknown number is labeled by a *variable* which is called an *integration constant*.

intercept

First look up *coordinate system*, *x-axis*, *y-axis*, and *z-axis* if you need to. The usual context is in relation to the graph of a *function* crossing another (specified) line or curve. The verb to *intercept* means the act of one curve crossing another curve or line. The noun *intercept* refers to the unique point at which the crossing occurs. For example, the *x-intercept* is the point at which a curve or line crosses the *x-axis* of a graph (the horizontal *axis*). The *y-intercept* is the point at which a curve or line crosses the *y-axis* of a graph (the vertical *axis*). In a three-dimensional graph, the *z-intercept* is the point at which a curve or line crosses the *z*-axis. The concept can be generalized to any *coordinate system*, and the *intercepts* for each *axis* are labeled according to the name of the *axis* in question. Note that although the term *intercept* can also refer to an *intersection* of two curves (i.e., not involving any of the *axes*), it usually refers to crossings with the *axes*.

interest

See *simple interest* and *compound interest*.

interior angle

The angle that is formed by two sides of a geometrical figure that lies inside the figure.

intermediate value theorem

This is a *theorem* concerning the *continuity* of a *function* and its input *variable(s)*, between two points on the *function*. It is really just a formalization of the rather commonsense notion that there always exists an input value that corresponds to any output value that you choose, provided that the function is *continuous* between two points that enclose the chosen point. However, the formalization allows some deductions to be made that follow from this, which may not be so obvious.

interpolate, interpolation

The verb *interpolate* refers to the process of estimating the value of missing data, either from actual observations or experiments, or from evaluations of *functions* that have not been, or cannot be, calculated for the input(s) that you desire. The process of *interpolation* takes the values of data that do exist and uses one of several ways to estimate values where there is no actual data. One method is to fit a curve (or straight line) to the data points, and then use the approximate (fitted) *function* to calculate the points that you need. *Linear interpolation* refers to fitting a straight line, and *polynomial interpolation* refers to fitting a *polynomial function*.

interquartile range

First look up *median*, *percentile*, and *quartile* if you need to. In *statistics*, the *interquartile range* is a measure of the spread of data (or *dispersion*) around the *median value*. The *interquartile range* is equal to the third *quartile* minus the first *quartile*. In other words, it includes data values that are not in the highest 25%, or lowest 25% of the total range.

intersection

The *point* at which two curves or lines meet or cross. However, the term may be used in somewhat wider contexts, but the general meaning should be clear in a given case.

invariant

Something that is fixed and does not change.

inverse

Usually this refers to something, or some process, that is in some sense "opposite" or "reversed." See also *additive inverse, multiplicative inverse, inverse function, inverse matrix*.

inverse function

A *function* that reverses every step of the original *function*. Applying the original *function* to a particular input, and then feeding the output to the *inverse function* would take you back to the original input.

inverse logarithm

First look up *logarithm* if you need to. The *inverse logarithm* is the reverse process of forming the *logarithm* of a number and is synonymous with *antilogarithm*.

inverse matrix

First look up *matrix*, and *square matrix* if you need to. The *inverse matrix* of a *matrix* reverses the action of the original *matrix*. Applying the original *matrix* to an input, and then applying the output of that as input to the *inverse matrix* takes you back to the original input. Only *square matrices* can have an *inverse*. However, not all *square matrices* have an *inverse*, and those that do are called *singular*, and those that don't are called *nonsingular*.

inversely proportional

This refers to a relationship between two quantities such that one quantity increases when the other decreases and, vice versa. The actual functional form depends on the situation but one of the simplest corresponds to the case when one quantity is the *reciprocal* of the other quantity (i.e., the output of the *function* is equal to 1 divided by the input).

invertible

An adjective describing something that can be inverted, or has an *inverse*.

irrational number

First look up *integer* and *real number* if you need to. An *irrational number* is a *real number* that cannot be expressed as a *ratio* of *integers*, or whole numbers. Two examples are pi (π) and the *square root* of 2.

irreducible

In the field of mathematics, *irreducible* has many contextual meanings, but for the purpose of grade-school math it just means that an *algebraic expression* cannot be further *simplified*.

isobar

Lines (contours) that mark *constant* pressure along the line or contour (for example, on a weather map).

isometric projection

A two-dimensional representation of a three-dimensional object.

isometry

An advanced concept in mathematics that is not encountered in grade-school math. It involves abstract geometry.

isosceles trapezoid

First look up *trapezoid* if you need to. An *isosceles trapezoid* is a *trapezoid* (or *trapezium*) with two pairs of sides of equal length (and by implication two pairs of angles are then also equal).

isosceles triangle

A *triangle* in which two of the sides have equal length (and by implication two of the angles are then also equal).

isothermal

Regions or contour lines that have the same temperature (for example, on a weather map).

isotropic

Usually describes a phenomenon that does not depend on the direction or orientation in space.

– J –

Joule (after James Joule)
A *unit* of energy equal to about 0.239 calories. As an intuitive guide, about 330,000 Joules are required to bring 1 kilogram of water to a boiling point (at sea level) when the surrounding temperature is approximately 70 degrees Fahrenheit, or approximately 21.2 degrees Celsius.

– K –

kilogram (kg)
A unit of mass equal to 1000 grams (1000 g). It is approximately equal to the mass of 1 *litre* of water. One *litre* is a little over a quarter (0.264) of a US gallon, and a little under a quarter (0.220) of an imperial gallon.
kilometer
A unit of length equal to 1000 meters (1000 m).
kinetic energy
In applied math and physics, *kinetic energy* is the energy of motion.
kinetic friction
In applied math and physics, this kind of *friction* describes the effective *friction* between two surfaces that are in *relative* motion (contrast with *static friction*).

– L –

latitude

On a *sphere* (for example, on the Earth or another planet), lines of *latitude* are circles parallel to the *equator* that are identified by the angle made between lines joining the center of the *sphere* to the *circumference* of the circle, and the line joining the center of the *sphere* to the *equator*. Angles are measured going away from the *equator*, being positive in the northern *hemisphere*, and negative in the southern *hemisphere*.

lattice multiplication

A pictorial method of multiplying large numbers that is supposed to be easier than the "traditional" method. However, it is actually quite long-winded and not necessarily quicker.

latus rectum

First look up *conic sections* if you need to. The *latus rectum* is a straight line (*chord* in this case) that has a special relationship to the *conic section* curve. It passes through the *focus* and is parallel to another special line called the *directrix*. The *semilatus rectum* is half of the *latus rectum*. Consult a textbook for a diagram showing all these details.

law of large numbers

In *probability* and *statistics* theory, this refers to the fact that in a *sample* of events, as the number of events becomes larger and larger, certain quantities that are properties of the events, become closer and closer to the expected *average*. For example, tossing a coin only a few times may produce unequal numbers of heads and tails, but as the numbers of tosses increases, the number of head and tails will fluctuate away from equality by less and less.

leading coefficient, leading term

In an *algebraic expression*, the *leading term* is usually the one with the highest (summed) *power* of the *unknowns* or key *variables*. The *leading coefficient* is then whatever else is in the *leading term* aside from the *variables* themselves.

leaf-of-stem plot
See *stem-and-leaf plot*.

least common denominator (LCD)
Referring to the *denominators* of two or more *fractions*, the *least common denominator* (LCD) is the smallest whole number that all of the *denominators* will divide into exactly without a *remainder*. In other words, the LCD is the smallest multiple of the *denominators*. The LCD is therefore equivalent to being the *least common multiple* (LCM) of the *denominators*. The term *lowest common denominator* is synonymous with *least common denominator*.

least common multiple (LCM)
The *least common multiple* of two or more numbers is the smallest whole number for which those numbers will divide into exactly without a *remainder*. In other words, the LCM is the smallest multiple of all of the original numbers. The term *least common multiple* is synonymous with *lowest common multiple*, and in appropriate situations can be synonymous with *least common denominator*, and *lowest common denominator*.

least squares fit
This term refers to a common method of fitting data with a theoretical curve (or model). The term "least squares" just refers to a quantity generated from the data and model that is examined and minimized as part of the process of obtaining the *best fit*.

least squares line
First look up *least squares fit* if you need to. The *least squares line* simply refers to the curve or model that is fitted to the data using the method of a *least squares fit*.

Leibniz
Gottfried Wilhelm *Leibniz* was a german mathematician and philosopher (1646–1716) who made many important contributions to mathematics. De-

tails are beyond the scope of this book so you should look him up if you are interested (see also *Leibniz's rule* below).

Leibniz's rule

A rule in *calculus* due to *Leibniz*, that provides two equivalent *expressions* for a particular double *operation*.

lemma

It is uncommon to come across this word in grade-school math, but it refers to a statement that is proved, in order to attempt to deduce the *proof* of a further statement. It is actually synonymous with *theorem*.

lemniscate curve

A graph of a particular class of *functions* that looks like the figure "8" on its side. The three-dimensional generalization has a toroidal shape (i.e., like a rubber tire, but with a cross-sectional shape that depends on the specific *equation*).

length

A measure of size, it is not always necessarily the longest *dimension* of an object. Sometimes the word *length* is used generically as a measure of size in any of the three spatial *dimensions*. Consult a textbook, your computer, or the internet for conversions between different units of measurement.

l'Hôpital's rule (after Guillaume de l'Hôpital)

Pronounced as "loppi-tahl's rule," it is a method in *calculus* to handle a particular "zero divided by zero" situation (when a *function* is a *ratio* of two *functions*). In order to understand further details, first look up *derivative* if you need to. *l'Hôpital's rule* states that the *functions* in the *numerator* and *denominator* should be replaced by their respective *derivatives* in this situation, after which the "zero divided by zero" problem may go way. Also known as Bernoulli's rule.

like terms

In the context of an *algebraic expression* or *equation* in general, one might be asked to "collect together *like terms*." This involves recognizing which *terms* can be added together without doing anything mathematically illegal and then merging two or more of such *like terms* together into one *term*.

limaçon

A curve formed by following a *point* inside, or on, a circle that rolls around on the *circumference* of another circle of equal radius. A *cardioid* curve is a special case of a limaçon, in which the point that generates the curve is on the *perimeter* of one of the circles.

limit

The general context for the usage of *limit* in grade-school math is varied. However, all of the meanings share the similar attribute that they convey the fact that the output (or result) of a *function* approaches a definite value as the input gets closer and closer to a particular value (the latter will be given in a specific problem). Often, that input value is *infinite* so it can never be reached. The *function* could also be the sum of an *infinite* number of *terms*. The concept of a *limit* is used frequently in *calculus* in a definitional context.

line graph

A simple graph showing the relation between two quantities, plotted using horizontal and vertical *axes*. Data points may be obtained from measurements, or they may be calculated from a *function*. The data points may or may not be marked with a symbol. They may or may not be joined up with line *segments*.

linear, linear equation, linear function

Usually, *linear* is an adjective that refers to a relationship between two quantities that is a *direct proportion* (i.e., changing the input by a given factor changes the output by the same factor). Graphically, such a relationship is a straight line. The corresponding *equations* for *linear* relationships are naturally called *linear equations*. The *functions* embodied in such *equations* are *linear functions*.

linear algebra

First look up *linear* and *matrices* if you need to. In grade-school math, *linear algebra* usually just refers to the topic of solving a system of *linear equations*, principally by the use of *matrices*. At college level and beyond, the term *linear algebra* refers to an enormous and formidable body of very scary mathematics.

linear equation

See *linear*.

linear factor

First look up *algebraic expression*, *variable*, and *power* if you need to. A *linear factor* is an *algebraic expression* that usually consists of not more than two *terms*, and in which no *variable* appears with a *power* higher than 1 (i.e., you will see no superscript written on the *variable*). As suggested by the name, if you graphed the *expression* versus any of the *variables*, it would be a straight line.

linear factorization theorem

First look up *polynomial* and *linear factor* if you need to. The *linear factorization theorem* pertains to the fact that, with certain provisions, a *polynomial* can be broken down into *linear factors*.

linear function

See *linear*.

linearly dependent

First look up *linear*, *power*, and *vector* if you need to. A set of mathematical entities known as *vectors* (which could represent multidimensional physical quantities or distances) is said to be *linearly dependent* if at least one member of the set can be expressed as a combination of the remaining members, without *raising any of them to a power*. The term may also refer to other entities such as *matrices*, with an analogous meaning. See also *linearly independent*.

linearly independent

First look up *linear*, *power*, and *vector* if you need to. A set of mathematical entities known as *vectors* (which could represent multidimensional physical quantities or distances) is said to be *linearly independent* if every member of the set cannot be expressed as a combination of any of the remaining members. The term may also refer to other entities such as *matrices*, with an analogous meaning. See also *linearly dependent*.

linear speed

The "straight-line" *speed*. The context is either to specify that something is in fact traveling in a straight line, or to describe what the state of motion would be if an object traveling in a curved path were to have all the *forces* on it turned off. In other words, in the absence of *force*, all objects travel in a straight line. For example, the *average linear speed* of the Earth's motion around the Sun can be estimated as the total curved distance traveled divided by the total time taken. See also *velocity*.

linear programming

This refers to a particular topic in mathematics that is concerned with solving certain types of optimization problems given various constraints, combining algebraic and graphical techniques. The *objective function* is the entity that is to be optimized. Note that "programming" in this context does not refer to computer programming, but rather, the "program" part is used here in the context of coming up with an optimal logistical program of action in a practical situation.

linear regression

First look up *regression* if you need to. A *linear regression* is the result of finding a best-fitting straight line to data. See also *regression coefficient*.

line of symmetry

Same as *axis of symmetry*.

litre

Abbreviation, L or *l*. One *litre* is a little over a quarter (0.264) of a US gallon, and a little under a quarter (0.220) of an imperial gallon. One litre of water has a mass of approximately 1 *kilogram (kg)*.

locus (plural: loci)

A path traced out by a *point*.

logarithm, logarithmic

The noun *logarithm* refers to a number generated from a given number according to a specific rule, designed to make very large and very small numbers easier to work with. The word *logarithm* is usually abbreviated to just *log*. The adjective *logarithmic* describes the behavior of a *function* if it involves a relationship between a set of numbers and the *logarithms* (or something closely related) of that set of numbers. See also *antilogarithm* (synonymous with *inverse logarithm*).

logic

An area of mathematics concerned with the study of reasoning from a starting point, to reach a conclusion in order to establish truth, assuming certain rules.

logistic function

A type of *function* in which the value of the *function* grows or decays, and then saturates, giving a stretched-out "S-shaped" curve. A common usage is in the study of population growth. The *basic logistic function* is a particular case of such a *function*, and it is one of the simplest of possible *logistic functions*. The *sigmoid function*, or *sigmoid curve*, is an even broader group of *functions* that have the same essential behavior as the *logistic function*.

longitude

Circles on a *sphere* that pass through the *poles*, used to mark an angular east-west distance *relative* to some agreed-upon reference line of longitude. On Earth, the reference line passes through the Greenwich Meridian in England, and is defined as zero degrees *longitude*. The lines of *longitude* are also known as meridians.

lowest common denominator (LCD)

Synonymous with *least common denominator*, which is the *least common multiple* of two or more *denominators*.

lowest common multiple (LCM)

Synonymous with *least common multiple*. The *least common denominator* is the *least common multiple* of two or more *denominators*.

– M –

Maclaurin series

See *Taylor series*.

magnitude

In grade-school math there are two common meanings. The first is that *magnitude* just means the size of a *variable*, or the size of a physical or geometrical quantity. In a more advanced context in applied math and science, *order of magnitude* means a factor of 10. An *order-of-magnitude* estimate means that the estimate is likely to be accurate to within a factor of 10 of the true value. The second meaning is somewhat related, but the process of calculating *magnitude* in that case is more complicated. For this second context first look up *complex number* and *vector* if you need to. Both *complex numbers* and *vectors* must be represented in a space with more than one *dimension*. The *absolute value* in this context is the actual length of either entity in that space. Another term that is synonymous with this meaning is *modulus*.

major axis

First look up *axis of symmetry*, *ellipse* and *hyperbola* if you need to. The *major axis* of an *ellipse* is the longer of the two *axes of symmetry*. See also *minor axis*. The *major axis* of a *hyperbola* is the distance between the two *vertices*, and is also known as the *transverse axis*.

mantissa

There are two different meanings that are relevant for grade-school math.
(1) First look up *scientific notation* and *floating point* if you need to. In this context, another word for *mantissa* is *significand*, and it refers to the part of a number expressed in *scientific notation* or *floating point representation* that contains the *significant digits*. In other words, it is that part of the number that does not involve an *exponent* or *power*; it is just the part that looks like a regular decimal number.

(2) First look up *common logarithm* if you need to. In another context, *mantissa* means the fractional part of a *common logarithm* (i.e., the part to the right of the decimal point).

many-to-one

The usual context refers to the fact that more than one input to a *function* (or equivalently, to a set of mathematical rules) results in the same output. Another way of saying this is that the *mapping* from the input(s) to the output is *many-to-one*. See also, *one-to-one*.

map, map onto, mapping

A *map*, or *mapping*, is a mathematical rule, or set of rules, that constitute a prescription of how to generate a particular output from a given input. The *mapping* is said to *map* the input onto the output.

mass

In applied math and physics, the *mass* of an object is a measure of the total amount of matter in the object. *Mass* is also a measure of its resistance to motion (in this context it is referred to as the *inertial mass*, but the two are numerically identical). *Mass* is not to be confused with *weight*: the latter depends on the local strength of gravity and on local *acceleration*, but the former does not.

matrix (plural: matrices)

Note: the entry for *matrix* has several subsections. A *matrix* consists of groups of mathematical objects in a specific arrangement. The mathematical objects may be numbers (of any kind), entire *algebraic expressions*, or even *functions*. Each of the mathematical objects in a *matrix* is called an *element*. A *matrix* has two or more *dimensions*, which can be thought of as the number of "identifying" attributes of each *element*. Only two-dimensional *matrices* can be written down easily on paper without splitting them up. In a two-dimensional *matrix*, the *elements* are arranged in a rectangular format of *rows* and *columns*. Grade-school math may involve up to three-dimensional *matrices*. One might ask what *matrices* are actually useful for. There are many answers to this, but a general answer is that many physical quantities cannot be expressed as a single number, and the laws of physics that operate on these physical quantities therefore demand multidimensional operators.

- **matrix addition**

    The process of adding *matrices* to form a new *matrix*. *Matrices can also be subtracted*. See also *matrix algebra*.

- **matrix algebra**

    The general process and set of rules governing the mathematical manipulation of *matrices*. General *matrices* must have the same *dimensions* in order to be able to perform mathematical operations between *matrices*. Sometimes the term *linear algebra* is used synonymously for *matrix algebra*.

- **matrix element**

    One of the mathematical entities in a *matrix*: see also *element(s) (of a matrix)*.

- **matrix inversion**

    The process of finding the *inverse* of a *matrix*, which is analogous to finding the *reciprocal* of an ordinary number. The *inverse matrix* multiplied by the original *matrix* is equal to a *matrix* that is the equivalent of the number one in regular algebra. The *matrix* that is equivalent to the number one is called the *identity matrix*, or the *unit matrix*. See crib sheet entry for *identity matrix*.

- **matrix multiplication**

    The process of multiplying two *matrices* together according to some special rules. See also *matrix algebra*.

maxima
The plural of *maximum*, in grade-school math the term *maxima* usually refers to the regions of the graph of a *function* that represent local *turning*

points, in which the *function* is changing from increasing to decreasing. See also *minima*.

maximum (of a function)

See *maxima*.

mean

Usually, the *mean* is equivalent to the *arithmetic mean*, or simple *average*. However, see also *geometric mean*, and *weighted mean*. If there is no qualifier on the word *mean* it usually just means the simple *average* (i.e., the total of all values of a quantity divided by the number of values).

measure (of an angle)

In *geometry* an angle can have attributes in addition to its actual size or numerical value, so the size or numerical value of an angle is referred to as its *measure*. An example of this in use might be, "The *measure* of angle A is 60 degrees."

median

There are two principal meanings in the context of grade-school math.

One is in *statistics*, where the *median* is the value that divides a *sample* of values of a quantity exactly in half. It is found by arranging the values in numerical order and picking the number in the middle (or the *average* of the middle two values, if there is an even number of values). Note that the *median* is equivalent to the 50th *percentile* and the second *quartile*.

The second context is in *geometry*, in which *median* refers to a line joining a point of a *triangle* (*vertex*), to a point on the opposite side that divides that side exactly into two equal *segments*. All *triangles* have three *medians*.

meter (m)

A unit of length equal to approximately 3.28 feet.

metric system

A decimalized system of measuring physical quantities. Lengths and distances are measured in *meters* (etc.), *mass* is measured in *kilograms*, and time is measured in seconds.

midpoint

Given a line *segment*, the *midpoint* divides the *segment* into two pieces of equal length.

midpoint theorem

First look up *coordinates* and *midpoint* if you need to. Given the *coordinates* of two *points*, the *midpoint theorem* gives a *formula* to calculate the *coordinates* of the *midpoint* of the straight-line *segment* joining the two given points.

minima

The plural of *minimum*, in grade-school math the term *minima* usually refers to the regions of the graph of a *function* that represent local *turning points*, in which the *function* is changing from decreasing to increasing. See also *maxima*.

minor (of a matrix element)

First look up *matrix* if you need to. The *minor of a matrix element* is a particular quantity formed from the *elements* of a *matrix*, according to special rules (which you can look up in a textbook).

minor axis

First look up *axis of symmetry* and *ellipse* if you need to. The *minor axis* of an *ellipse* is the shorter of the two *axes of symmetry*. See also *major axis*.

mnemonic

A "device" to aid your memory in recalling a *formula*, *equation*, or some set of rules or facts. The *mnemonic* may be some combination of letters making a word or "pseudo word," or it may be an entire phrase.

mode

In *statistics*, amongst a *sample* of values of a quantity, the *mode* is the value (or range of values), that occurs most often in the *sample*.

model

In applied math and science, *model* refers to a theoretical construction consisting of a *formula*, *formulas*, or tabulated numerical values, for direct comparison with data. The *model* usually has adjustable parameters in order to find the *best fit*. The parameters from the *best fit* are usually the desired end products of the process.

modulo (abbreviation "mod")

An *operation* on two numbers that returns the *remainder* when the first number is divided by the second number (for example, "12 mod 5" is equal to 2).

modulus

First look up *complex number* and *vector* if you need to. In grade-school math the usual meaning is synonymous with the *absolute value* of a *complex number* (see *absolute value*). This of course covers the case when the *complex number* is just an ordinary *real number*. The term *modulus* may also refer to the *absolute value* of the *length* of a *vector*.

modus ponens

In the field of *logic*, this is just a fancy term for a common method of *argument* involving an "if...then..." (conditional) statement that goes something like the following example. If your car runs out of gas then you will stop. Your car has run out of gas. Therefore you will stop. See also *modus tollens*.

modus tollens

A type of *argument* in the field of *logic* that involves an "if...then..." (conditional) statement, and goes something like the following example. If your car runs out of gas then it will stop. Your car has not stopped. Therefore you have not run out of gas. See also *modus ponens*.

moment

This has a special meaning in applied math and physics: in mechanics it measures the effectiveness of a *force* to turn something, or to make it deviate from straight-line motion. For example, it is easier to remove a screw using a screwdriver with a large handle than it is using a screwdriver with a smaller handle. There is a specific prescription for calculating the *moment* of a *force*. The term *moment*, in the sense described here, is synonymous with *torque*.

moment of inertia

A measure of the resistance of an object to being rotated. It depends on the object's *mass*, the distribution of *mass*, and the shape of the object.

momentum

In applied math and physics, *momentum* is an indicator of how much *force* needs to be applied over a given interval of time in order to reduce the straight-line motion of an object to zero (see *angular momentum* for curved motion). It is a law of physics that if the *momentum* of a system is to change, an external *force* (and therefore acceleration) has to be involved. Numerically, *momentum* is the product of *mass* and *velocity* and the rate of change of *momentum* with respect to time is equal to the *force* required to effect the change.

monomial

A particular type of *algebraic expression* that is characterized by only one *term* (which may, however, be composite), and is a *subset* of the class of *functions* known as *polynomials*.

monotonic

An adjective for a *function* that either always decreases or always increases. In other words, a given value of the *function* can never have an ambiguous input, except in regions in which the *function* is neither decreasing nor increasing.

multinomial

In *probability* theory, the *multinomial* is an extension of the case for which there are only two possible outcomes of a *random event* (*binomial*), to more than two possible outcomes. The *multinomial* is rarely formally encountered in grade-school math, although problems involving multiple outcomes are common. These are solved using *permutations* and *combinations*, but this amounts to the same thing as using *multinomials*.

multiplication property of equality

This is a theorem that states that if you multiply both sides of an *equation* by the same *real*, nonzero number, then the validity (or truth) of that *equation* is not affected. The *multiplication property of equality* holds if the multiplier is a *variable* or *algebraic expression* that represents a *real*, nonzero number. Recall that *real* numbers are just the regular numbers that you deal with (i.e., they can be represented on an arbitrary single number line).

multiplicative identity

A noun for a mathematical object that does not change another object of a given type under the *operation* of multiplication. For example, for ordinary numbers the *multiplicative identity* is 1. As another example, the *multiplicative identity* for *matrices*, under the *operation* of *matrix multiplication*, is the *unit matrix*.

multiplicative inverse

In regular grade-school arithmetic, the *multiplicative inverse* of a number is that which, when multiplied by the original number, yields the number 1. In practice, the *multiplicative inverse* is obtained by dividing 1 by the number in question. The *multiplicative inverse* of a number is therefore equivalent to the *reciprocal* of that number. More generally, *multiplicative inverse* may refer to objects that are not ordinary, *real* numbers. The principle is still the same, in the sense that an object multiplied by its *multiplicative inverse* should result in the appropriate *multiplicative identity*.

multivalued

An adjective describing a *function* that can have more than one output value for a single input value.

mutually exclusive

Usually encountered in *probability* theory, the term *mutually exclusive* refers to two or more events that cannot occur simultaneously. In other words if one of the events occurs, one can conclude that none of the other events occurred. For example, the outcomes of a particular team winning or losing a football game are *mutually exclusive* (the team cannot simultaneously win and lose). A counterexample is that of drawing a card at *random* from a full pack, amongst the possible outcomes of a card being a "Queen," and a card being red. These two possible events are not *mutually exclusive*.

mutually orthogonal

First look up *orthogonal* and *perpendicular* if you need to. Since *orthogonal* means *perpendicular*, *mutually orthogonal* refers to two or more mathematical or physical entities that are all *perpendicular* to each other.

mutually perpendicular

Same meaning as *mutually orthogonal*, except that *mutually perpendicular* usually refers to a two-dimensional situation. It is more common to use *mutually orthogonal* for three-dimensional situations.

– N –

nanometer (nm)
A unit of length equal to a billionth of a meter (10^{-9} m). Atoms are smaller than than a nanometer.

natural logarithm
First look up *base* and *logarithm* if you need to. The *natural logarithm* is a *logarithm* that has the special number *e* as its *base* (you can find information about *e* in the first entry under the letter "E").

natural numbers
This is just the name for the regular (whole and positive) counting numbers, 1, 2, 3.. etc. Zero may or may not be included (the definition varies). In other words, *natural numbers* are the nonnegative *integers*.

nautical mile
A measure of distance that is based on angular measure, so that it is more relevant for traveling on a curved surface such as that of the Earth. If we draw a line from the center of the Earth to a ship on the surface and then move that line through one-sixtieth of a degree, the ship will have traveled one nautical mile. It is about 15% longer than a regular mile (if it was straightened out).

negation
A term describing the process of changing the sign of a mathematical object from positive to negative or vice versa.

negative number
The subtraction of any positive number greater than zero from zero results in a *negative number*.

Newton's laws (of motion)
In applied math and physics, the three laws of motion due to Isaac Newton describe the mechanics of moving objects and the associated *forces* and accelerations. They are valid as long as the *speed* of any part of the system

relative to an observer is much less than that of light.

non-Euclidean (geometry)
Geometrical rules that are not *Euclidean* (see appropriate description of the latter).

noninvertible
Something that cannot be inverted, or something that does not have an *inverse*.

nonsingular matrix
See *inverse matrix*.

normal
In *geometry*, applied math and physics, the noun *normal* usually refers to a line that is *perpendicular* to something that is specified in the problem or statement.

normal curve
One of the formal names of the "*bell curve*," in the context of the *distribution* of the value of a quantity drawn randomly from a *sample*. See also *bell curve* and *Gaussian distribution* for more information.

normal distribution
Synonymous with *Gaussian distribution*, *bell curve*, and *normal curve*.

normalization, normalize
In general, the term *normalization* refers to a scaling factor of a *function*, graph of a *function*, or of data. Sometimes the term *renormalization* is used, which can mean the result of *normalizing* (the verb). However, the verb *renormalize* is usually used synonymously with *normalize*.

nth power
First look up *power* and *exponent* if you need to. The *nth power* refers to the result of multiplying a mathematical quantity or object (number, *variable*, or *expression* etc.), by itself n times. The number n need not be a whole number.

nth root

First look up *real numbers* and *complex numbers* if you need to. The *nth root* is an extension of *square root*, in which the *nth root* is the answer to the question, "What number, when multiplied by itself n times would give me the original number?" The "third root" is more commonly known as the *cube root*. The concept is not restricted to *real numbers* however, and can apply to various types of mathematical object, in which case there can be more than one solution. The *principal nth root* is the positive, *real number* solution.

number line

A line used to illustrate the *relative* positions of various types of numbers in numerical order.

numerator

The number (or *algebraic expression*) in a fraction that is on the top.

numerical integration

First look up *calculus*, *integral*, and *definite integral* if you need to. The term *numerical integration* refers to the process of estimating the numerical value of a *definite integral* (equivalent to the area under a curve between specified boundaries), using one of a variety of possible techniques. For example, see *trapezoidal rule*. The corresponding noun is *numerical integral*, which refers to the result of doing a *numerical integration*.

– O –

oblique triangle
Any *triangle* in which none of the three angles is 90 degrees. In other words, an *oblique triangle* is any *triangle* that is not a *right triangle*.

obtuse angle
An angle that is greater than 90 degrees and less than 180 degrees.

obtuse triangle
A *triangle* in which one of the angles is greater than 90 degrees (*obtuse*).

octant
First look up *coordinate system* if you need to. The most common meaning of *octant* in grade-school math is that it is a part of a three-dimensional space that is divided up by three *perpendicular axes* of a *rectangular coordinate system*. The space is thus divided into eight parts, or *octants*. The first *octant* is the one in which all coordinate values are positive, and it is usually the one on the top right-hand side, going into the page.

odd function
First look up *function* if you need to. An *odd function* is one that produces an output value that changes sign if the sign of input is changed (i.e., a positive output value becomes negative, or vice versa). Compare with *even function*.

one's complement
See *complement*.

one-to-one mapping
The usual context refers to the fact that a particular input to a *function* (or equivalently, a set of mathematical rules), gives one and only one unique output. Another way of saying this is that the *mapping* from the input to the output is *one-to-one*. See also, *many-to-one*.

open interval
An *open interval* is a numerical range of values that *does not* include the

boundary values of the interval.

operation

The process of applying a specific set of rules to one or more mathematical objects (inputs) in order to obtain a new mathematical object (output).

opposite side

Usually, this refers to one of the sides in a *triangle* in which one angle is 90 degrees. The *opposite side* is the one directly facing (opposite to) the 90 degree angle. However, the term is also used for *triangles* that don't have a 90 degree angle, in which case the *opposite side* just refers to the side opposite the angle that is specified.

ordered pair or ordered triple

In a two-dimensional graph, the term *ordered pair* refers to the pair of numbers that specify the position of a *point* on the graph (i.e., the *coordinates* of the *point*). In the most common type of graph encountered in grade-school math, the *ordered pair* refers to the x and y values of a *point*, where x is understood to be the first number in the pair. The term *ordered triple* is the corresponding generalization to a three-dimensional graph, for which three numbers are needed to specify a *point*. The order is x, y, and z.

order of a matrix

First look up *matrix* if you need to. A two-dimensional *matrix* has a certain number of *rows* and *columns*. The *order* of the matrix is equal to the number of *rows* times the number of *columns*. For a *matrix* with greater than two dimensions, the *order* is the product of the number of *elements* in each dimension.

order of magnitude

A factor of 10.

order of operations

If more than two numbers (or symbolic mathematical items), are combined with a mixture of arithmetic *operations* (addition, subtraction, multiplication, or division), the result is ambiguous without additional rules. This is because it matters which pairs of numbers (or items) are combined with which operation. Therefore, rules are required to establish how the items and *operations* are to be combined, and these rules are known as the *order of operations*. The rules state that, (1) items inside parentheses (or inside some other grouping device), are to be evaluated first, (2) multiplications and divisions are to be done next (from left to right), and (3) additions and subtractions are to be performed last (from left to right). Clearly, any *expressions* that are are superscripted (i.e., *powers* or *exponents*) should be evaluated and resolved first, using the same rules.

ordinal number

The numbers used to describe the order of events or things. For example, "first," "second," "third," etc.

ordinate

The usual context in grade-school math is that *ordinate* is a synonym for the *y-axis* of a graph (i.e., in a two-dimensional graph, the vertical *axis*).

origin

First look up *coordinate system* if you need to. In the context of grade-school math, the usual meaning of *origin* is the central reference *point* of a *coordinate system*, where all *coordinates* at that *point* have a value of zero (by definition).

orthocenter

First look up *altitude* (in a *triangle*) if you need to. The *orthocenter* of a *triangle* is the point at which the three *altitudes* of a *triangle* meet.

orthogonal

Usually synonymous with *perpendicular*, but the term *orthogonal* can be applied to situations in more than two *dimensions*. In general *orthogonal* refers to the fact that the projection of one mathematical object "onto" another has no overlap with the other, similar, mathematical object, when that projection is defined according to specific rules. The term *orthogonal* can apply to *functions*, *vectors*, *matrices*, and all sorts of other entities. However, in the simplest context, a set of three lines in three-dimensional space are *orthogonal* if each line is *perpendicular* to the other two.

orthogonal matrix

First look up *orthogonal*, *square matrix*, *transpose*, and *unit matrix* if you need to. An *orthogonal matrix* is a *square matrix* that is very special because when its *rows* are interchanged for its *columns* (the *transpose matrix*), and the resulting *matrix* is then premultiplied by the original *matrix*, the *unit matrix* is produced (i.e., the result has a "1" at every position on the *diagonal*, and is zero everywhere else). The reason why the original *matrix* is called *orthogonal* is that the *rows* can be thought of as *vectors* that are *orthogonal* to each other, and the same applies to the *columns*.

orthogonal vectors

See *vectors* and *orthogonal*.

orthographic drawing

A means of representing three-dimensional objects in two dimensions. The drawing is an *orthogonal* view of a slice cut through the object.

orthonormal basis vectors

First look up *vectors*, *basis vectors*, and *normalization* if you need to. A set of *orthonormal basis vectors* are *mutually perpendicular* to each other (*orthogonal*), and have the property that they are the only *vectors* needed to express any other *vector* in the domain of applicability and context (the "space") that is being considered. The "normal" in *orthonormal* means that all of the *basis vectors* are *normalized*, such that they have a length of exactly 1 (in whatever units are being considered).

oscillate, oscillation

The verb *to oscillate* means to vibrate repeatedly in some way (or go through a repetitive cycle of some sort). The noun *oscillation* is the motion that results from *oscillating*.

– P –

parabola
A curve that looks like a "U" (at a variable orientation). It is characteristic of a *function* that has a dependence on something *squared*. The "turnaround" point is called the *vertex*, and there is a point called a *focus* inside the "U." If *parallel* light rays entered a reflective *parabola*, parallel to the *symmetry axis*, all the rays would come together (*converge*) at the *focus*.

paraboloid
A three-dimensional version of a *parabola* (obtained by rotating a *parabola* around its *axis of symmetry*). An example of a *paraboloid* is the mirror behind a car headlamp, because the parabolic shape has the special property of focusing light into a beam of parallel rays, if the light source is placed at the special point called the *focus* of the *paraboloid*. In reverse, a reflective *paraboloid* focuses a parallel beam of light onto the *focal point*.

parallel lines
Straight lines that will never intersect each other, no matter how much they are extended.

parallelogram
A four-sided geometrical shape in which opposite sides are equal in length to each other and parallel to each other.

parallelogram rule
First look up *vector* and *resultant (of a vector)* if you need to. The *parallelogram rule* refers to a geometrical method for finding the sum (*resultant*) of two *vectors* in two *dimensions*. The two *vectors* form half of the *parallelogram*, and the diagonal of the *parallelogram* is the *resultant vector* (which indicates the net effect of the two individual component *vectors*).

parameter
In general, a *parameter* is a quantity that can be varied (a *variable*), and its

value affects the outcome of a mathematical *operation* or *function*.

parametric curve, parametric equation

These terms refer to situations in which a *function*, or set of mathematical rules, is given in terms of a *parameter* that does not correspond to one of the *axes* of a graph of the *function*, or set of rules. For example, instead of an *equation* giving y in terms of x, it may be possible to write an equivalent pair of *parametric equations* that relate y and x to a third *variable* (e.g., t). One advantage of doing this is that the resulting *parametric equations* may be easier to work with than the original (single) *equation*.

partial fraction

A complex *algebraic expression* that "looks like a fraction," consisting of a *numerator* and a *denominator*, might be amenable to be broken down into simpler *algebraic expressions* that still "look like fractions." These simpler *expressions* are known as *partial fractions*. They are usually encountered in certain types of *calculus* problems.

partial sums

There are two principal contexts in which this is used for grade-school math. The first refers to adding up (summing) only a specified *subset* of the *terms* in a *sequence* of numbers. The second meaning refers to a slightly different way of adding many-digit numbers together, compared with the standard method of "carrying over" digits to an adjacent column. The *partial sums* method explicitly adds the different columns separately (ones, tens, hundreds, etc.), after which these *partial sums* are all added together. While the method may have demonstration value to aid understanding, it really has no advantage. This is because you may have to end up using the carry-over method when adding the *partial sums* anyway, and then the method becomes much more long-winded and prone to error.

Pascal's triangle

A pattern of numbers arranged in a triangular format, in which each row is obtained from the previous row by adding the pair of numbers immediately to the left and to the right in the row above the current position. The numbers turn out to be useful, amongst other things, in *probability* theory, for events that have only two outcomes (as in a *binomial distribution*).

pentagon

A five-sided geometrical shape. In a regular *pentagon* all five sides have equal length.

percentile

A value that divides a *distribution* of a quantity into two parts, one part representing a percentage of the *distribution* that is the percentile. In other words, the *percentile* is a means of specifying where a particular value of a quantity falls in a *distribution* of that quantity. In the expression, "the nth *percentile* is X," it means that n percent of values in the *distribution* of the quantity of interest have a value less than (or equal to) X. The *distribution* itself must be specified in enough detail for the measure to have any meaning. For example, if you are told that your height is in the 47th percentile, it means that 47% of the people are as short, or shorter than you, but this doesn't mean anything if you are not told enough about the *population* on which the other measurements were made (for example, were those people living in the same country?). Note that the 50th percentile is equivalent to the *median* value of a sample, and is also equivalent to the second *quartile*.

perfect square

This usually refers to a number or *algebraic expression* that can be broken down into two identical quantities multiplied together.

perfect square trinomial

First look up *polynomial*, *binomial* and *trinomial* if you need to. A *perfect square trinomial* is a *polynomial* that contains three *terms* that can be expressed as the *square* of an *algebraic expression* that only has two *terms*. In other words, if a *binomial* (an *expression* with two terms) is multiplied by itself, the result is a *perfect square trinomial*.

perihelion

In applied math or physics, *perihelion* is the distance of closest approach of an object that is in orbit around the sun.

perimeter

The total length of the boundary of a two-dimensional geometric figure. It can be thought of as equivalent to the length of a piece of string that could be wrapped around the boundary. I will not give you all the different *formulas* for the *perimeters* of common shapes because you can find them in your child's textbook, usually collected together in the front or back of the book.

period, periodic

In grade-school math and physics, the term *periodic* is an adjective that describes a mathematical or physical quantity that is repetitive. The *period* (usually measured in units of time) is the interval between repetitions of a particular part of the cycle (which should be the same for any part of the cycle if the repetition is coherent). Examples that everyone is familiar with are phenomena related to the rotation of the Earth, which has a *period* of one day.

permutation

In grade-school math, *permutation* refers to one arrangement of the order of two or more items. For example, "CAT" is one possible *permutation* of the letters A, C, and T. The concept is used often in calculating *probabilities*.

perpendicular

An adjective describing a situation in which two mathematical or physical objects are at 90 degrees with respect to each other. Sometimes, *perpendicular* can be used as a noun, referring to an abstract line that is orientated at 90 degrees with respect to something else that is specified. See also *orthogonal*.

perpendicular lines

Lines that are *perpendicular* to each other. See *perpendicular* and *orthogonal*.

perspective

In *geometry*, the term refers to a drawing or representation of a three-dimensional object in two *dimensions*, in order to closely resemble how the object is seen by the eye. There is a more advanced meaning of *perspective* that is a property of pairs of *triangles*, but it is not encountered in grade-school math.

phase, phase shift
First look up *periodic* if you need to. The term *phase* has many different contexts, but the meanings are similar. It usually refers to some kind of repetitive or *periodic* variation of two different sources that have the same *period*, or *frequency*, but with a different reference point. In other words, at a given moment in time, the two variations will be in different parts of their cycle (or "out of phase"). The *phase shift* is a measure of the exact amount that any one of the variations would have to be shifted (in time) by, in order for the variations to be synchronous. The *phase shift* can be measured in various units, but an angle is a common one since a complete cycle can be thought of as stretching over 360 degrees.

pi (π)
I include an entry for π here, even though it should be familiar to everyone, because there is often some misunderstanding of its fundamental meaning. The fundamental definition is that it is equal to the *circumference* of a *circle* divided by its *diameter*. However, π happens to have the value that we are familiar with only in *Euclidean geometry* (for example, the geometry of the everyday world in which we live). In situations that the space cannot be described as *Euclidean* (for example, near a black hole), π would not have the *Euclidean* value.

pie chart
A method of graphically representing data that shows *relative* frequencies of occurrence of a quantity (in terms of fractions, or percentages). The *pie chart* is a *circle* consisting of *sectors* that represent labeled quantities. The *relative* frequencies of occurrence of the labeled items are *proportional to* the angles that the respective *sectors* make at the center of the *circle*.

piecewise
This is an adjective that usually refers to a graph or a *function* that is made up of disjoint *segments*, or pieces, for which each piece is specified by a unique set of rules.

planar
An adjective describing something that has the properties of a *plane*.

plane
In *geometry*, a *plane* is a two-dimensional (flat) surface that only requires two numbers to locate a *point* on it. Another way of defining a *plane* is that it is a surface on which all *perpendicular* lines to the surface are *parallel* to each other.

plane figure
In *geometry*, a two-dimensional (flat) shape.

point
A location in space that is uniquely specified by a set of values, the number of values (or *coordinates*), being equal to the number of *dimensions* of the space. In *geometry* a *point* has zero size, so it is actually an abstract concept (and in fact is one of the "undefined" entities in *geometry*).

point-slope form
For this, you may need to look up several terms, as necessary. The term *point-slope form* refers to the *equation* of a straight line. To unambiguously specify a straight line fixed in space, we need to specify either two *points* on it, or one *point* and the *slope* of the straight line (i.e., its orientation with respect to the horizontal *axis* of a graph). In the *point-slope form* of the *equation* of a straight line, the *coordinates* of any one *point*, and the *slope* of the line are explicitly specified in the *equation* (and can therefore be immediately read from the *equation*). Since there are an *infinite* number of *points* on a line, there are an *infinite* number of possible ways to write the *equation* but they all reduce to a single, unique *equation*. See also *slope-intercept form*.

Poisson distribution (after Siméon-Denis Poisson)
First look up *distribution* and *probability distribution* if you need to. For certain types of physical quantity that can take on only whole number values, many measurements, observations, or selections of that quantity result in a *distribution* that has a characteristic form, and it is called the *Poisson distribution*. If the *average* value over many trials or experiments is known, one can construct a *Poisson probability distribution*, and use the associated *formulas* to calculate the *probability* of obtaining a given whole number value of the quantity in question.

polar axis
Usually refers to a line passing through two *poles* on a *sphere*.

polar coordinates
First look up *coordinate system* and *coordinates* if you need to. The term *polar coordinates* refers to *coordinates* in a particular kind of *coordinate system* that is based on a *sphere* or a *circle*. The *coordinates* then specify distance along a *radius* and one or two angles, for two- and three-dimensional space respectively. The reference points are predefined by a suitable convention. Contrast *polar coordinates* with *Cartesian coordinates*, where the latter system is more suitable for rectangular entities.

polar equation
First look up *polar coordinates* if you need to. The *equation* of a *function* expressed in terms of *polar coordinates* is a *polar equation*.

pole
In grade-school math this usually refers to a *point* on a *sphere* that is in some way defined to be special (for example, an *axis* of rotation might pass through it).

polygon
A two-dimensional geometrical shape with more than three sides. In a regular *polygon* all the sides have equal length. Consult a textbook or other resource for listings and properties of various *polygons*.

polyhedron (plural: polyhedra)

For the purpose of grade-school math, a *polyhedron* is a three-dimensional geometric figure that has flat faces and straight edges. In a regular *polyhedron* the faces are regular *polygons* (i.e., all sides have equal length). Consult a textbook or other resource for listings and properties of various *polyhedra*.

polynomial

First look up *exponent* and *power* if you need to. A *polynomial* is an *algebraic expression* (consisting of *variables* and numbers) that (1) has no division *operation* in it (only addition, subtraction or multiplication), and (2) has no *powers* on the *variables* that are *fractions*. A *polynomial* cannot have an *infinite* number of *terms*, by definition. The degree of the *polynomial* is the highest sum of *powers* of the *variables* in any *term*.

population

In *statistics* the term *population* refers to a *sample* of any quantity that is being analyzed (i.e., it does not necessarily refer to a *population* of people). When a *subsample* is selected from the *population*, the original *population* (before selection) is often referred to as the *parent population*.

position vector

First look up *vector, coordinate system*, and *origin* if you need to. The term *position vector* specifically refers to a *vector* that gives the position of a *point, relative* to the *origin* of the *coordinate system*. This can be compared to *vectors* that are not *position vectors*, which may specify directions and distances between two *points* that do not include the *origin*.

postulate

See *hypothesis*. The noun *postulate* is synonymous with *hypothesis*. The verb *postulate* is synonymous with *hypothesize*.

potential energy

In applied math and physics, *potential energy* is stored *energy* that has the capacity, or potential, to change the *energy* content of other physical entities. Very often, mechanical *work* is done as part of the *energy* conversion process.

pound

A measure of *mass* equal to 0.453 *kilograms*.

power

The usual meaning in grade-school algebra refers to the superscript on a number, *algebraic expression*, or other mathematical object. In this context, *power* is synonymous with *exponent*. If the *power* is an *integer*, it has the simple meaning that an item with a superscript, or *power*, is multiplied by itself a number of times that is equal to the *power*. If the *power* is not an *integer*, the meaning is not so simple, and is beyond the scope of this crib sheet. The *power* itself could be an *algebraic expression*. The *operation* of applying a *power* is known as "raising to the *power* of" (whatever the *power* is).

Another meaning of *power*, encountered in applied math and physics, is the rate of consumption or emission of energy. It is usually measured in *Watts* (which is equivalent to *Joules* per second).

precision

A property of the representation of a number that reflects the degree of detail that the representation can record. It is very different to *accuracy* (see discussion for *accuracy*).

premise

In the field of *logic*, the term *premise* refers to an initial proposition. For example, consider the following argument. All giraffes are animals. There are giraffes in the zoo. Therefore there are animals in the zoo. The statement "All giraffes are animals," is the *premise*. It may or may not be true. The statement, "Therefore there are animals in the zoo," is the *consequent*, or conclusion.

prime factor

A *prime factor* is a number that is a *prime number* that divides exactly into another given number without a *remainder*. In other words, a *prime factor* of a number is a *factor* that itself has only 1 and itself as a *factor*.

prime number

A number that can only be divided exactly by 1 or itself, without a *remainder* (i.e., a *prime number* has only 1 and itself as *factors*).

prime polynomial

First look up *polynomial* if you need to. A *prime polynomial* is one that cannot be broken down into a product of two simpler *polynomials* that do not involve any numbers other than *integers*. In other words, if *factors* of a *polynomial* can be found that involve only *variables* and *integers*, then the *polynomial* is NOT *prime*.

prism

First look up *parallelogram, polygon* and *polyhedron* if you need to. A *prism* is a three-dimensional object (actually a *polyhedron*) that has two *parallel* faces that are *polygons*, and remaining sides that are *parallelograms*.

probability

A number or *fraction* between 0 and 1, or a *percentage*, enabling quantification of the expected (or *average*) number of times a particular event would occur if a measurement, observation, or realization could be repeated an arbitrarily large number of times. For example, if the *probability* that it will rain tomorrow is estimated to be 20%, and if there were 500,000 tomorrows, it might be expected to rain in 100,000 of them.

probability distribution

First look up *probability* if you need to. A *probability distribution* is a systematic quantification of the *probability* of obtaining various values of a mathematical or physical quantity (the *random variable*). In many ways, a *probability distribution* is simply a *histogram* showing the relative occurrence of all possible events, or values of the quantity in question.

probability density function

In some sense, *probability density function* is synonymous with *probability distribution*, except that sometimes the former refers to a mathematical *function* that is equivalent to the *probability distribution*. It is not always the case that such a mathematical *function* exists.

product

A noun describing the result of multiplying two mathematical objects together. The *operation* of multiplication may not be the regular one that applies to ordinary numbers, depending on the type of mathematical objects in question.

product rule

First look up *logarithm*, *derivative*, and *differentiation* if you need to. There are two principal situations in which a *product rule* is encountered in grade-school math. The first is in the context of the *logarithm* of a *product* of two mathematical objects, whereby the rule turns it into a sum of two *logarithms*. The second meaning is in the context of *calculus*, with respect to finding the *derivative* of, (or *differentiating*) a *product*. In that case, a different rule breaks down the process into two easier steps.

projectile

In applied math and physics, a *projectile* is an object that is given an initial *velocity*, after which the resulting motion under the influence of gravity is studied, the *projectile* having no power source of its own.

projection

In *geometry*, *projection* usually refers to either extensions of lines, or other geometrical constructions, or it might refer to the representation of an entire object mapped onto another surface or space. In physics, *projection* usually refers to the production of an optical image by means of the processing of light rays using optical devices (lenses, mirrors, etc.).

proof

A series of *arguments* that result in a conclusion about the truth of a proposition or statement.

proof by contradiction

A method of *proof* in which it is demonstrated that if the conclusion is not true, then there is a direct contradiction in two or more of the statements leading up to the false conclusion, implying that the conclusion cannot be false. For example, if one of the statements is "this is a straight line," and if assuming that the conclusion is not true implies that "this is a curved line," then there is an unresolvable contradiction because a line cannot be both straight and curved. Note that the term *proof by contradiction* is synonymous with *reductio ad absurdum*.

proof by induction

First look up *term* and *series* if you need to. A method of *reasoning* (establishing truth) for a *series* of *terms*. The method first establishes the truth of a statement for one *term*. Then truth is established for the next *term* in a manner that does not depend on what each *term* is. The truth for all *terms* is thereby established. Not to be confused with *inductive reasoning*.

proportion

The usual definition of *proportion* that you will find in many sources is that it refers to forcing equality between two *fractions* (or *algebraic expressions* that are *fractions*), or *ratios*. However, this does not tell you what it really means. WHY, for example, would you want to set two *fractions* equal to one another? A practical way of looking at *proportions* is that one of the *fractions* could represent a reference value of some kind, and the other could be variable. So, for example, we could say that the *proportion* of one variable quantity to another variable quantity is fixed at a value of 4:3, say. Therefore, when the second variable quantity is 12, the first variable quantity must be (4/3) times 12, or 16.

proportional to

First look up *proportion* if you need to. The term *"proportional to"* refers to a situation in which one mathematical or physical quantity varies as a function of some other quantity, in a such a way that the two quantities always maintain the same *proportion* (or *ratio*). Such a relationship is also called *linear*, because when the two quantities are plotted on a graph, the result is a straight line.

protractor

An instrument for measuring or constructing angles on a two-dimensional flat surface.

Pythagorean

An adjective describing something derived from *Pythagoras'* work.

Pythagoras' theorem

Pythagoras' theorem, also known as the *Pythagorean theorem*, is the famous *theorem* about *right-angled triangles* that states that adding the *squared* values of the two short sides of the *triangle* gives the *squared* value of the longest side of the *triangle* (*hypotenuse*). In grade-school math, the three-dimensional version of the *Pythagorean theorem* is also used. This version yields the straight-line distance between two *points* from the differences in *coordinates* in the three *mutually perpendicular* directions.

– Q –

quadrangle
Synonymous with *quadrilateral*.

quadrant
First look up *coordinate system* if you need to. The most common meaning of *quadrant* in grade-school math is that it is a part of a two-dimensional space that is divided up by the two *perpendicular axes* of a *rectangular coordinate system*. The space is thus divided into four parts, or *quadrants*. The first *quadrant* is the one on the top right (all coordinate values positive), and the rest are numbered numerically, going counterclockwise.

quadrantal angle
First look up *quadrant* if you need to. A *quadrantal angle* is one that is formed by "swinging" from the initial *standard position* (i.e., along the positive horizontal *axis*), to any one of the *axes* of the *coordinate system*. A *quadrantal angle* is therefore a multiple of ± 90 degrees.

quadratic, quadratic equation, quadratic function
First look up *power* and *polynomial* if you need to. The term *quadratic* is an adjective that describes a type of *algebraic expression* or *equation* in which the key *variable* appears *squared*, and with no higher *power*. However, it may appear with lower *powers* in addition to the *square*. The graph of a *quadratic function* looks like a "U" shape (but the orientation of the "U" is not restricted). Another way of describing a *quadratic function* is that it is a *polynomial* of degree two.

quadratic formula
First look up *real number* and *quadratic* if you need to. The *quadratic formula* gives the two solutions of a *quadratic equation* (which may not be *real numbers*). Graphically, the solutions correspond to the points of *intersection* of the "U"-shaped graph with the horizontal (x) *axis* (no *real number* solutions exist if the graph does not cross the line).

quadratic surfaces, quadric surfaces
First look up *conic section*, *plane*, and *quadratic function* if you need to. A *quadric surface* (equivalently, a *quadratic surface*), is the surface of a three-dimensional geometrical form that, when cut by a *plane* produces a cross section that is a *conic section*. It is characterized by an *equation* in which the *variables* for all three spatial *coordinates* appear as a *square* (and no higher *power*, but there may be lower *powers*).

quadrilateral
A four-sided geometrical shape. Note that *quadrilateral* is synonymous with *quadrangle* and *tetragon*.

quartic
First look up *polynomial* if you need to. A *quartic* is a *polynomial* in which the highest summed *power* of the *variables* in any *term* is four (i.e., it is a *polynomial* of degree four).

quartile
First look up *distribution* and *percentile* if you need to. In *statistics*, a *distribution* of data values from a *sample* can be sorted into numerical order, and then divided into four parts, each part containing 25% of the data. However, there are three *quartiles* because there are three values that are needed to split the data into four parts. The first *quartile* is the value of the data that separates out the lowest 25% of the values of the data. It is also known as the *lower quartile*, or 25th *percentile*. The second *quartile* splits the data at exactly the *midpoint*, and is therefore equal to the *median*. It is also known as the 50th *percentile*, because 50% of the data have values that lie on or below the second *quartile*, and the remainder of the data lie above the second *quartile*. The third *quartile* is the value of the data that separates out the highest 25% of the data. It is also known as the upper *quartile*, and the 75th *percentile* (because 75% of the data lie on or below the third *quartile*).

quintic
First look up *polynomial* if you need to. A *quintic* is a *polynomial* in which

the highest summed *power* of the key *variables* in any *term* is five (i.e., it is a *polynomial* of degree five).

quotient

A *quotient* is the result that is obtained by dividing one number or *algebraic expression* by another number or *algebraic expression*.

quotient identity

First look up *trigonometric functions* and *tangent* if you need to. The *quotient identity* refers to an *equation* relating the *tangent function* to the two principal *trigonometric functions*. Specifically, the *tangent function* is expressed as the *sine function* divided by the *cosine function*.

quotient rule

First look up *calculus* and *derivative* if you need to. The *quotient rule* in *calculus* is a procedure to find the *derivative* of a *compound function* that is made up of one *function* divided by another *function*.

– R –

radian

A measure of angle for which 360 degrees is equal to 2 times π *radians*. In other words, 360 degrees is equal to 6.28 *radians*, and 1 *radian* is equal to approximately 57.3 degrees.

radical

First look up *nth root* if you need to. In grade-school math, the "*square root*" symbol ($\sqrt{}$) is known as a *radical symbol*. There may be an additional number just over the "*square root*" symbol, extending the meaning to cover *nth roots*, not just the *square root*. For example, $\sqrt[3]{}$ means *cube root*. Underneath the *radical symbol* is the *radicand*, which may be a number or an *algebraic expression*.

radicand

The number or *expression* under a *radical* symbol. See entry for *radical*.

radius

The distance between the center of a *circle* and any point on the *circumference*. It is also the distance between the center of a *sphere* and any point on the surface of the *sphere*.

raise to the power of

See *power*.

random

This is a very difficult concept to define (despite what you may read elsewhere). The reason is that the question of predictability of the value of a variable quantity is central to the meaning of *random*, but the precise circumstances under which some types of quantity are predictable is debatable. Also, it is debatable whether we should consider the criterion that a quantity is predictable in principle or in practice. For the purpose of grade-school math it is sufficient to define *random* as a quantity (number) that is unpredictable in practice.

random fluctuations

Variations in the value of a quantity that are due to *random* processes, or otherwise essentially unpredictable processes. Synonymous with *statistical fluctuations*. See also *statistical error*.

random number

You may want to look up *random* because the meaning of *random* in math and science is nontrivial. The term *random number* usually refers to a *real number* that is selected at *random* from a prespecified range and *distribution*. If the *distribution* happens to be *uniform*, then the *random number* is also *unbiased*.

random sample

A *sample* of values selected from a larger collection of values of a mathematical or physical quantity, in which the selection is not prescribed by any rule that would destroy the unpredictability of values in the new *sample*.

random variable

An algebraic or numerical quantity whose value is *random*. You may want to look up *random*, because the meaning of *random* in math and science is nontrivial.

range

In grade-school math, *range* usually refers to the set of valid values of a *function*, or graph of a *function*, that results from a valid input (the *domain*). The *range* can include *infinity*. In a graph of y versus x, the *range* is a set of valid values of y.

rate

This is a commonly misused term. It refers to how much a mathematical or physical quantity changes in a given amount of time. In other words, it is the mathematical or physical quantity divided by time. For example, *speed* is the *rate* of change of distance. A common mistake is to say "rate of *speed*." What is wrong here is that *speed* is already a *rate*. One should either say, "*rate* of change of distance," or just "*speed*," not "*rate of speed*."

ratio

The *ratio* of two numbers, *algebraic expressions*, or other pair of mathematical or physical quantities, is a measure of how many times one quantity is larger than the other. It is simply equal to one quantity divided by the other. A *ratio* can also be expressed as a *fraction* or a *proportion*. For example, something that is split into two parts according to a proportion of 3 : 5 has a *ratio* for the smaller part to the larger part of 3/5, or 0.60. In terms of *fractions* of the whole, the smaller and larger parts are equivalent to 3/8 and 5/8 respectively.

rational expression

First look up *polynomial* if you need to. A *rational expression* looks like a *fraction*, except that the *numerator* and *denominator* are *algebraic expressions* that are *polynomial functions*. The *numerator* could be just a number because that is a special case of a *polynomial*, one having a *degree* of zero. The *denominator* could of course also be just a number, but then the entire *expression* would simply be a regular *polynomial*.

rationalizing the denominator

In situations where a *function* has the form of one *algebraic expression* divided by another, the *denominator* may, for one of several reasons, be awkward to work with. For example, a *square root* or a *complex number* in the *denominator* is difficult to work with. It is possible to transform the *function* so that the *denominator* is greatly simplified (in the example above, there would be no *square root* or *complex number* in the *denominator*). The transformation is made at the expense of making the *numerator* more complicated, but the whole *expression* may still be easier to manipulate and work with than the original. The process is known as *rationalizing the denominator*, and it is also used when the *denominator* is simply the *square root* of a *real number*.

rational number

First look up *integer* and *ratio* if you need to. A *rational number* is any number that can be expressed as the *ratio* of two *integers* (except that the *divisor* or *denominator* cannot be zero). Thus, all regular *integers* (including zero), are *rational numbers* because they are a special case of the general definition.

rational root theorem

First look up the following if you need to: *rational number*, *polynomial*, and *root*. The *rational root theorem* is a method for determining possible solutions (i.e., *roots*) of a *polynomial equation* that are *rational numbers*. The method does not solve the *equation*, but just narrows down the possible solutions.

real number

At the level of grade-school math, an adequate definition of *real numbers* is that they can be represented by single *points* somewhere along a single, *infinitely* long number line. They include *rational numbers* (which themselves include *integers*), and *irrational numbers*. In contrast, *complex numbers* cannot be represented by a *point* on a line, but instead need a two-dimensional space.

real roots

First look up *roots* if you need to. The term *"real roots"* simply refers to those solutions of equations that are *real numbers*, as opposed to *complex numbers*. Graphically, the former correspond to the points at which the graph of the *function* crosses the horizontal *axis*, but in the latter case the graph does not actually cross the horizontal *axis* anywhere.

rearrange

The term usually refers to the rearrangement of algebraic quantities in an *equation*, according to the rules of *algebra*, for the purpose of *simplifying* the *equation* and/or *solving* it.

reciprocal

The *reciprocal* of a number, or *algebraic expression*, is equal to "1 divided by that number or *algebraic expression*."

rectangle

A four-sided geometrical shape in which all the *interior angles* are 90 degrees (*right angles*), and in which pairs of sides are *parallel* to each other, and equal in length.

rectangular coordinates, rectangular coordinate system

The term *rectangular coordinates* is synonymous with *Cartesian coordinates*. A *rectangular coordinate system* is a *coordinate system* based on a grid of rectangular "building blocks." See appropriate crib sheet entries.

recurrence relation

See *recursive*.

recurring decimal

In decimal notation, some numbers have the properties that they have an *infinite* number of digits after the decimal point, and that they have a group of digits that repeat indefinitely. For example, when 1/6 is written as a decimal number, it has a "1" after the decimal point, which is then followed by an *infinite* number of occurrences of the digit "6." Symbolically, one convention for indicating the digits that repeat over and over in a *recurring decimal* is to place a dot over each digit that is to be repeated. Thus, 1/6 would be written as $0.1\dot{6}$, and 9/11 would be written as $0.\dot{8}\dot{1}$. A *recurring decimal* is also known as a *repeating decimal*, and contrasts with a *terminating decimal*, which only has a *finite* number of digits.

recursive

A rule or phenomenon that either repeats the "rule within the rule" ("nesting"), or a rule that only yields a result in terms of another result. The latter is the most common situation encountered in grade-school math, in the context of *recursive formulas*, or *recursive rules*. These are usually *algebraic expressions* for the *terms* of a *series* that generate the next *term*, given the current *term*. In order to obtain a *formula* or rule for an arbitrary *term*, some algebraic work is required. The terms *recursive formula*, *recurrence relation*, and *recursive rule* are all synonymous.

recursive formula, recursive rule

See *recursive*.

reduced fraction

A *fraction* for which there is no equivalent *fraction* that has smaller numbers in the *numerator* and *denominator*.

reduced row echelon form

First look up *matrix* if you need to. A *matrix* that is in *reduced row echelon form* is one that has been manipulated according to specific rules. Usually, this is done so that the *matrix* is in a form that makes it easier to solve an *equation* involving the original *matrix*.

reductio ad absurdum

Synonymous with *proof by contradiction*.

reflection

Usually used in the context of *symmetry* in *geometry*. One side of a two-dimensional figure with an *axis of symmetry* can be generated by a *reflection* of the other side by an imaginary mirror along the *axis of symmetry*.

reflexive property

This is really one of those things in *mathematics* that seems like it is unnecessary. The *reflexive property* simply states that something, anything, is equal to itself. This is in essence a definition of equality, since one could ask the question, "When is something not equal to itself?" The *reflexive property* is just a formal answer to that question (never). See also *symmetric property* and *transitive property*.

regression

The term *regression* refers to the result of fitting a theoretical *model* (a mathematical *function* that may or may not describe a physical process), to data. The purpose of finding the *best fit* is to test a *hypothesis* (of a theory against data), and/or to be able to estimate values that the data would have, where there is no actual data (*interpolation*). A *linear regression* is one in which the *model* is a straight line. The best-fitting line is called the *regression line*. The *regression coefficient* is a measure of how well the theoretical *model* fits the data. A *significance* value (or *confidence level*) can also be calculated by standard methods, in order to estimate the probability that such a good fit was obtained purely by chance (due to *random fluctuations* in the data and measurements conspiring to cause a spuriously good fit).

regression coefficient

See *regression*. The term *regression coefficient* is also used synonymously with *correlation coefficient*.

regression line

See *regression*.

regular

Obviously there are many different contexts, but a common one is in *geometry*, in which the adjective *regular* describes a geometric figure in which all the sides have equal length, and all the angles at each *vertex* are equal to each other.

relative, relative velocity

The adjective *relative* describes a large variety of mathematical and physical quantities that are not *absolute*, but instead are referenced to the value of the same quantity in a different situation or object. In applied math and physics, *relative velocity* is a common example because ALL *velocities* can only be defined in relation to something else, since there is no such thing as an *absolute* state of rest.

remainder

Division can be performed not only on two ordinary numbers, but also on two *algebraic expressions* (that satisfy certain conditions). In general, a *remainder* is the mathematical object that is left over after the division, if the *divisor* is not a *factor* of the *dividend*. The *remainder* may be a number or an *algebraic expression*.

remainder theorem

The *remainder theorem* is a *theorem* concerning the division (actually referred to as *synthetic division*), of two *algebraic expressions*. The *theorem* is a rule prescribing a method to find the *remainder* without actually going through the process of performing the division. If the *remainder* is zero, it means that the *divisor* is a *factor* of the *algebraic expression* that is the *dividend*.

renormalization, renormalize

See *normalize*.

repeated root

Some types of *equation* have more than one solution (*root*), and sometimes two or more of the solutions (*roots*) turn out to be identical. These identical solutions are called *repeated roots*.

residuals

For grade-school math, the term *residuals* usually refers to remainders that are left over after fitting a theoretical *model* (or mathematical *function*) to a set of data points. In other words, each data point has a *residual* that is a measure of how good or bad the fit is at that point. The *residuals* can be expressed in various ways, the most common being a simple difference between the data and the model. *Residuals* can also be expressed as percentage deviations (relative to either the *model* or the data). A *residual* of zero indicates a perfect fit (by any measure).

resultant

First look up *vector* if you need to. When one or more *vectors* are added together, the single *vector* that is equivalent to all the *vectors* added together is called the *resultant*. For example, the combined effect of the *force* of wind and engine thrust on a plane is a net (*vector*) motion that has a *magnitude* and a direction that is not equal to either of the two individual *vectors*.

rhombus

A four-sided geometrical figure (*quadrilateral*) in which all sides are equal in length. Pairs of directly opposing angles are also equal to each other.

Riemann sum (after Bernhard Riemann)

First look up *calculus*, *integral*, and *definite integral* if you need to. *Riemann sum* is a generic term that refers to the formulation of approximations for calculating the area under a curve, or equivalently, the value of a *definite integral* of a *function* between specified boundaries.

right angle
An angle equal to 90 degrees.

right circular cone
A *cone* in which the *axis of symmetry* passing through the *vertex* is *perpendicular* to the base of the *cone*.

right triangle, right-angled triangle
A *triangle* in which one of the angles is 90 degrees.

rigid body
A term used in applied math and physics that refers to a three-dimensional object that retains its shape, despite the application of *forces* on the object. Something that is not rigid might be described as elastic, or liquid, for example.

Romberg integration (after W. Romberg)
First look up *calculus, integration,* and *definite integral* if you need to. *Romberg integration* is a method of estimating the area under a curve (for example, the graph of a *function*), that can used to numerically estimate the value of a *definite integral* in *calculus*. *Romberg's method* is more accurate than the *trapezoidal rule* and *Simpson's rule*.

root, roots
The term *root* usually means a solution to an *equation*. It is not to be confused with the word "root," as in "*square root*", "*cube root*," etc.

root mean square (r.m.s.)
In *statistics*, the *root mean square* (r.m.s.) value of a set of data is the *square root* of the *average* of the sum of the *squared* values of the data. The reason why it is useful is that the simple *average* is not appropriate in some situations in which the data can be both negative and positive because it could lead to a situation in which the simple *average* is zero. That would not give any idea about the range of the data, so the *r.m.s.* value can be used instead, because it turns the negative values of the data into positive ones (because of the "squaring").

rose curve

A description of the graphs of a class of *functions* that look like leaves or petals arranged *symmetrically* about a center (the number of leaves depends on the *equation*).

rotational symmetry

A three-dimensional object that has *rotational symmetry* around a particular *(rotational) axis of symmetry* is unaltered in appearance as it is rotated, possibly only at discrete positions around the *axis*.

rounding

The process of approximating a numerical value by terminating the number at a given place after the decimal point, OR by keeping a specified number of *significant figures*. The last digit of the truncated number is adjusted if necessary, in order to best represent the original number to the specified level of *precision*. See detailed discussion under *significant figures* for examples.

rows

Usually refers to the *rows* in a rectangular grid (array) of *elements* that form a *matrix*. See crib sheet entries for *matrix* for more details.

– S –

saddle point

A point on a curve at which the curvature instantaneously ceases to change. See also *inflection*.

sample

In statistics, *sample* is a noun or verb related to the selection of a set of mathematical or physical quantities from a larger collection of such quantities. An *unbiased sample* is one in which the data values were selected without any condition imposed on the values of the data (so in some sense, the selection is *random*). In practice, it may only be possible to investigate the extent to which the *sample* is *unbiased* after the selection has been done, because the method of selection may not be able to avoid bias.

scalar

There are many types of mathematical objects, and a *scalar* is one of the simplest, being just a single number. Temperature is an example of a *scalar*. On the other hand, objects such as *vectors* need more than one number to describe them completely. *Velocity* is an example of something that is not a *scalar*. However, *speed* is a *scalar*.

scalar product

First look up *scalar* and *vector* if you need to. The *scalar product* is an *operation* on two *vectors* using specific rules that result in an answer that is a *scalar* (i.e., just a single number). The result is related to the angle between the *vectors*, and to the size of the *vectors*. The term *scalar product* is synonymous with *inner product* and *dot product*.

scalene triangle

A *triangle* in which all three sides have different lengths.

scatter plot

A graph plotting two quantities against each other, with each pair of values of data represented by a single marker (or "point"). If the two quantities are related to each other, then the scatter of points will form a definite pattern.

scientific notation

A method of representing numbers that accommodates situations in which a number is extremely small, or extremely large. The standard notation consists of two parts:

(1) A *mantissa* or *significand* (synonymous terms), that is a decimal number between 1 and 10, multiplied by

(2) a *power* of 10 (the *exponent*).

secant

First look up *cosine* (or *cos*) if you need to. The *secant* (pronounced seek-ant), is a derived *trigonometric function* (of an angle), that is equal to "1 divided by the *cosine* (or *cos*) *function*."

second quartile

See *quartile*.

sector

A portion of a *circle* that is enclosed by two straight lines that extend from the center to points on the *circumference*, and the part of the *circumference* that is included by the two lines.

segment

The usual context refers to a portion of a straight line that has a definite length (as opposed to being *infinite*).

semicircle

One of the halves of a *circle* that is formed by dividing the *circle* into two parts at a *diameter*.

semimajor axis

First look up *ellipse*, *hyperbola*, and *major axis* if you need to. The *semimajor axis* is half of the *major axis* of an *ellipse*.

semiminor axis

First look up *ellipse* and *minor axis* if you need to. The *semiminor axis* is half of the *minor axis* of an *ellipse*.

sequence

A collection of ordered numbers, or *algebraic expressions*, in which each *term* is usually generated by a definite rule. See also *arithmetic series*, and *geometric progression*.

series

Usually synonymous with *sequence*.

set(s), set theory

A *set* is a collection of mathematical objects in which each member of the *set* satisfies particular rules to qualify for membership to the *set*. Naturally, the field of *set theory* concerns the study of *sets*, and their mathematical properties.

sigmoid function

See *logistic function*.

significance, significant

In *statistics* the term *significance* is used to describe the *probability* that a particular result might have been obtained by chance, and not as a result of the truth of the *hypothesis* being tested. *Random fluctuations* can conspire to give the same result. The *significance* is usually given as a percentage *probability*. If the *significance* is LOW, the result is said to be highly statistically *significant*. The terminology is confusing and unfortunate, because the first use of the word *significance* in the previous sentence refers to the *probability* that the *hypothesis* is false, but the use of the word *significant* later in the same sentence refers to the the *probability* that *hypothesis* is true.

significand

Synonymous with *mantissa*.

significant figures

This term describes the approximate representation of a number to a specified *precision* according to the number of *significant digits* that are retained. The number of *significant digits* includes zeros at the extreme right-hand side of the final number, but not to the extreme left-hand side. The *preci-*

sion in terms of *significant digits* is not to be confused with the *precision* specified in terms of the number of decimal places retained. For example, the number 4.92301 specified to 4 decimal places is 4.9230, but to 4 *significant figures* it is 4.923. These are NOT the same thing, even though they are the same number! This is because, if we were just given the rounded numbers, in the former case the original number could be anywhere in the range 4.92295 to 4.92304, but in the latter case, the original number could be anywhere in the range 4.9225 to 4.9234. Thus, the different meanings give extremely different ranges for the original numbers.

similar (triangles, figures)

In *geometry*, two geometrical shapes or figures are said to be *similar* if they are related to each other by a simple scaling factor. In other words, one figure could be transformed into the other by photocopying and zooming. Thus the *proportion*, or *ratio*, of pairs of corresponding sides of *similar figures* is the same for all pairs of sides. Moreover, all angles are preserved. In other words, pairs of corresponding angles in *similar figures* are equal to each other.

simple harmonic motion

See the explanation for *harmonic motion*.

simple interest

Simple interest that accrues on a debt or on a savings account refers to decrements or increments (respectively) per accrual period that are calculated using a predetermined percentage of the initial balance of funds at the very beginning of the term of accrual. Contrast *simple interest* with *compound interest*, which has a decrement or increment that is a predetermined percentage of the balance in the previous accrual period, not the initial term balance.

simplify, simplification

Usually, the verb refers to the process of using the rules of *algebra* to convert an *algebraic expression*, or *equation*, into another one that has fewer *terms*, and that has redundant complexity eliminated.

Simpson's rule (after Thomas Simpson)

First look up *calculus*, *integration*, and *definite integral* if you need to. *Simpson's rule* is a method for estimating the area under a curve (for example, the graph of a *function*), that can used to numerically estimate the value of a *definite integral* in *calculus*. *Simpson's rule* is more accurate than the *trapezoidal rule*, but less accurate than *Romberg's method*.

simultaneous equations

First look up *linear* and *matrix* if you need to. A mathematical or physical problem may need more than one *equation* to describe it completely. In general, for a problem that has a certain number of *unknown variables* that we are attempting to solve for, we need to have the same number of *equations* as there are *unknown variables*, in order to solve the problem completely. The *equations* are then *simultaneous equations*, because they describe constraints that must be satisfied simultaneously for the *unknown variables*. In grade-school math, the *simultaneous equations* that are encountered are often not more complex than *linear*, and are usually solved by the method of *elimination* and *substitution*, or by the use of *matrices* and *matrix algebra*.

sine, sin

One of the two principal *trigonometric functions* of angle (the other is *cosine*, or *cos*). You can visualize this *function* by imagining swinging your arm in a circle, pivoted at your shoulder. If you start with your arm horizontal, the vertical distance between the end of one of your fingers and the reference level where your arm is horizontal, traces the *function*. The *function* repeats every 360 degrees. The *sine function* can also be expressed as a *ratio* of the side of a *right-angled triangle* opposite to the angle in question, to the longest side (the *hypotenuse*).

sine rule

First look up *sine* if you need to. The *sine rule* gives a *formula* for the length of a side of a *triangle* if you know two angles and one side, or it can give you an angle, if you know the length of two sides and one angle. The *formula* involves only the *sine functions* of the angles, so the angles have to be converted for input to the *formula*, and the output *sine* value has to be converted back to an angle.

singular matrix

See discussion for *inverse matrix*.

sinusoid

First look up *sine* and *cosine* if you need to. The term *sinusoid* is a noun that describes something (usually a wave), that looks like the *sine* or *cosine functions* (i.e., a repetitive, *periodic* wavelike pattern).

slope

The *slope* of the graph of a *function* is a measure of how fast the *function* is changing at any given position on the graph. If the graph is a *function* of time, then the *slope* is the instantaneous *rate* of change of the *function*. The *slope* can be found by graphical construction, or by the use of *calculus*. If the *function* is a straight line then the *slope* is just the change in the vertical direction on the graph of the *function* divided by the corresponding change in the horizontal direction.

slope-intercept form

For this, you may need to look up several terms, as necessary. The term *slope-intercept form* refers to the *equation* of a straight line. To unambiguously specify a straight line fixed in space, we need to specify either two *points* on it, or one *point* and the *slope* of the straight line (i.e., its orientation with respect to the horizontal *axis* of a graph). In the *slope-intercept form* of the *equation* of a straight line, the crossing *point* on the vertical *axis* (i.e., the *y-intercept*), and the *slope* of the line are explicitly specified in the *equation* (and are therefore immediately apparent from the *equation*). See also *point-slope form*.

speed

Speed is the *rate* of change of distance (or *displacement*) with respect to time. *Speed* is distinguished from *velocity* because it is just a single number, but *velocity* includes information about the direction of travel (it is a *vector*), and requires more than one number to describe it.

sphere

A three-dimensional object for which any point on the surface is located at a *constant* distance from a fixed reference point that is the center of the *sphere*.

spheroid

First look up *ellipse*, *minor axis*, and *major axis*. A *spheroid* can be formed by an *ellipse* that is revolved around the *major axis* or *minor axis* to create a three-dimensional solid. A *prolate spheroid* is one that is formed by a revolution around the *major axis*, and an *oblate spheroid* is one that is formed by a revolution around the *minor axis*. The former looks like a an american football, and the latter looks like a pumpkin.

spline

First look up *model*, *curve fitting*, and *piecewise* if you need to. The term *spline fit* refers to a set of *functions* that are used to approximate a given set of data, in a *piecewise* manner. In other words, a single *function* may be inadequate to represent all of the data with sufficient accuracy, so a number of *functions* are used to fit different portions of the data.

spurious correlation

First look up *correlation* and *significance* if you need to. A *spurious correlation* is a *correlation* between two quantities that is obtained by chance, and that may not represent a real relationship between the two quantities. Measurement errors and *statistical fluctuations* (i.e., *random fluctuations*) in the data may cause a *spurious correlation*.

square, squared

The noun *square* has two meanings in grade-school math. The first meaning is that it is the name for the geometrical shape that has four sides of equal length, and *vertex* angles all equal to 90 degrees. The second meaning refers to a mathematical object that is a *perfect square* in the sense that it can be broken down into a product of two identical numbers or *algebraic expressions*. The verb *square* refers to the process of multiplying two items together. A number or *algebraic expression* "*squared*" refers to the result of *squaring* the number or *algebraic expression* respectively.

square matrix

First look up *matrix* if you need to. A *square matrix* is one that has an equal number of *rows* and *columns*. In other words, a *square matrix* is a square grid of items (which could be numbers, or other kinds of mathematical object).

square root

Given a number or *algebraic expression*, the *square root* is that which when multiplied by itself, results in the given number or *algebraic expression*.

SSA (or equivalently, ASS)

In *geometrical proofs*, "SSA" is an acronym for "side-side-angle," referring to two *triangles* that have the same values for two corresponding sides, and one angle that is NOT included by the two sides. Additional information is required to prove whether the two *triangles* are equivalent (*congruent*), because SSA does not give a unique *triangle*. SSA can be written equivalently as ASS (angle-side-side).

SSS

In *geometrical proofs*, "SSS" is an acronym for "side-side-side," referring to the fact that if you can prove that the length of three sides of a *triangle* are equal to the corresponding sides for another *triangle*, then the two *triangles* are equivalent (*congruent*).

standard deviation

In *statistics*, the *standard deviation* gives a particular measure of the spread in data pertaining to a particular quantity. See also *dispersion*. If the data are drawn from a quantity that has a *distribution* that is a *bell curve*, the *standard deviation* is a measure of the width of that curve. More specifically, it indicates that approximately 68% of the values in the *distribution* of the quantity in question lie in the range covered by the *average* value, plus or minus one *standard deviation*.

standard position
First look up *coordinate system* of you need to. The term *standard position* refers to an angle that is located so that its *vertex* is at the center of a *rectangular coordinate system* (the *origin*), and one of the rays lies along the positive horizontal *axis*. In this case the *ray* that lies on the horizontal *axis* is called the *initial side*, and the other *ray* defining the angle is called the *terminal side*.

static
In applied math and physics, *static* refers to situations in mechanics problems in which there is no motion, and all *forces* (and *torques*) balance to zero.

static friction
In applied math and physics, *static friction* refers to the friction between surfaces that are stationary with respect to each other (but *forces* exist that are trying to cause *relative* motion). Contrast with *kinetic friction*.

stationary point
Aside from the usual meaning of lack of motion, in mathematics a *stationary* point on a curve or graph of a *function* is a point at which the curvature either changes direction, or ceases to change instantaneously. In other words, the *function* changes from increasing to decreasing or vice versa, or momentarily stops increasing or decreasing. See also *inflection* and *saddle point*. Another synonymous term for *stationary point*, is *turning point*.

statistic
When used as a noun, *statistic* usually refers to a quantity that is constructed from data and a *model* (that is being fitted to the data). The *statistic*, as constructed, helps to gauge the goodness of fit, and to help iterate to find the *best fit*. A common *statistic* used for this purpose is *chi-squared* (χ^2), but there are others.

statistical error
Certain physical quantities, when they are measured, by nature will not give identical values if the measurements are repeated many times. Usu-

ally, this is because a *random* process may be responsible for producing the physical quantity. An example is the number of light rays emitted by a shining object in a given amount of time. However, the *average* of the measurement of a large number of the physical events being measured does produce consistent results. The *random* nature of the responsible process, or processes, then leads to an inherent uncertainty on the *average* value, and that uncertainty is called the *statistical error*. The larger the number of events that are sampled, the smaller the *statistical error* will be.

statistical fluctuations

Usually synonymous with *random fluctuations*. See also *statistical error*.

statistical significance

See *significance (statistical)*.

statistics

The study of the collective, or aggregate, behavior and properties of a system composed of many components. Sometimes the term *statistics* is used as a noun, as in "The data had good statistics," meaning that the *statistical errors* on the data were favorably small.

statute mile

This is the full name for the regular mile, internationally agreed to be equal to 1609.344 meters. See also *nautical mile*.

stem-and-leaf plot

A method of organizing and displaying data in a table format that brings out certain attributes of the data "at a glance," such as the number of items per equal intervals of the numerical value. The "stem" is a column showing the left-most digit of an interval (for example, tens), and the "leaf" is a row of data following each stem, such that values of the stem combined with each item in the "leaf" give back the original data values in that stem group.

step function

A *function* that is made up of multiple disjoint pieces of horizontal *line segments*. A specific special case is called the *Heaviside step function* (after Oliver Heaviside), which consists of only two pieces, forming a "sudden" jump. Its graph looks like a step on a staircase.

subset

A collection of items drawn from a larger collection of items.

substitution

Replacement of a *variable* in an *algebraic expression* or *equation*, with a number or another *algebraic expression*. The purpose may be to either numerically *evaluate* a *function*, or to *simplify* an *algebraic expression*, or to solve an *equation*, or to *eliminate* a *variable*.

substitution property

This is a formalization of the simple concept that if one mathematical *variable* or *expression* is equal to another, then one can be substituted for the other (and vice versa) in any *equation* or *algebraic expression* involving the original item (*variable* or *expression*).

sum of a series

First look up *sequence* if you need to (*series* is synonymous with *sequence* in this context). The *sum of a series* is the result of adding up all the *terms* of a *sequence*, starting and ending at places in the *series* that are specified in the problem. The result may be a number, or it may be an *algebraic expression*. The phrase "sum to N terms" means start from the first *term* and add up all the *terms*, up to and including the Nth *term*.

sum to infinity

First look up *sum of a series* if you need to. The *sum to infinity* of an *infinite series* usually refers to the result of adding up all *terms*. Obviously it is not possible to do this by examining each *term*, but there are techniques for finding the *sum to infinity*. Only certain classes of *infinite series* have *sums to infinity* (i.e., those that do not have sums become infinitely large as the number of *terms* increases).

supplementary angle

Given an angle, the *supplementary angle* is equal to 180 degrees minus the given angle. The two angles therefore add up to 180 degrees.

surface area

The total area on the surface of a three-dimensional object. A summary of the *formulas* for the *surface area* of some common geometrical forms can often be found at the back of a textbook.

syllogism

In the field of *logic*, the term *syllogism* refers to a type of *argument* in which there are two propositions (*premises*), followed by a conclusion that is true if the *premises* are true (but the *syllogism* does not prove that the *premises* are true). One of the propositions is a major *premise*, and the other (second) proposition is a minor *premise*. For example, the following is a *syllogism*: All giraffes are animals. There are giraffes in the zoo. Therefore there are animals in the zoo.

symmetric property

This is one of those "stating-the-obvious" properties in math, which simply formalizes the statement that if an item is equal to a second item, then the second item is equal to the first item.

symmetry

In grade-school math, the study of *symmetry* is essentially restricted to

(1) *axes of symmetry* dividing two-dimensional geometric shapes into two mirror images, and

(2) *rotational symmetry*, pertaining to an object that, when rotated around a particular *(rotational) axis of symmetry*, is unaltered in appearance as it is rotated (possibly only for special positions around the *axis*).

synthetic division

First look up *polynomial*, *degree*, and *linear factor* if you need to. *Synthetic division* is a shorthand method of dividing a *polynomial* by a *polynomial* having a smaller *degree* (for example, a *linear factor*). The method avoids having to write out all the *variables*, because only numbers have to be written down and manipulated.

– T –

tangent

For grade-school math there are two principal meanings of the word *tangent*.

(1) The first meaning is in the context of *geometry* and *trigonometry*. First look up *sine* (or *sin*) and *cosine* (or *cos*) if you need to. The *tangent* (of an angle) is a derived *trigonometric function* that is equal to the *sine* (or *sin*) *function* divided by the *cosine* (or *cos*) *function*. The *tangent* of an angle is usually abbreviated as *tan*. In terms of the sides of a *right-angled triangle*, the *tangent function* can be expressed as the *ratio* of the shortest side to the second-shortest side of the triangle.

(2) The second meaning of *tangent* is connected with the relation between a straight line and a curve, and the *functions* that describe them. This meaning has a geometrical interpretation as well. Specifically, the *tangent* line at a given *point* on a curve is a line that just touches the curve, but does not cross it. In other words the *tangent* line has only ONE *point* of intersection with the curve, and no more.

tautology

A statement in which the proposition trivially implies the conclusion. In other words, the proposition is equivalent to the conclusion. For example, $1 = 1$ is a tautology. This is a very simple example, but in more complicated situations, one could make a *truth table* and show that it is entirely equivalent to the *truth table* of some different *logical expression*, in which case the two *expressions* would be *tautologies*.

Taylor series (after Brook Taylor)

First look up *function*, *power*, *derivative*, and *sum to infinity* if you need to. A *Taylor series* is a *sequence* of *terms* that is constructed to represent a *function* in the neighborhood of a particular input value, if the *derivatives* of that *function* can be calculated. A *Taylor series* has an *infinite* number of *terms* (involving *powers* of the key *variable*), whose sum is equivalent to the *function* in question. A *Maclaurin series* (after Colin Maclaurin) is the special case of a *Taylor series* that is centered on an input value of zero.

term

First look up *algebraic expression*, *complex numbers*, and *function* if you need to. A *term* is part of an *algebraic expression*, or *equation*, that is a mathematical object in its own right, or a *term* can be a combination of such objects that are combined only with multiplication or division. The objects making up a *term* may be ordinary numbers, *complex numbers*, or entire *functions*. Usually the only thing that separates *terms* is a "+" or "−" sign, so the constitution of a "*term*" is rather arbitrary, but the label, *term*, is convenient for talking about different parts of an *algebraic expression*.

terminating decimal

A number that has a *finite* number of digits following a decimal point, when the number is represented in decimal notation.

tessellation

A system of tiles made up of one or more two-dimensional geometrical shapes that completely fills an arbitrary two-dimensional surface, without any gaps.

tetragon

Synonymous with *quadrilateral*.

tetrahedron (plural: tetrahedra)

A three-dimensional geometrical figure (*polyhedron*) that is made of four triangular faces. In a regular *tetrahedron*, all the faces are *equilateral triangles* (and are therefore identical to each other).

theorem

A set of statements leading to a conclusion that does not trivially follow from each of the isolated statements. A *theorem* is generally something that has been established to be true based on mathematical rules and logic, but a *theory* (in science) has not necessarily been proven to be generally true.

third-degree polynomial

First look up *power, term, variable,* and *polynomial* if you need to. A *third-degree polynomial* is a *polynomial* in which the highest summed *powers* of the *variables* in any *term* is 3. Such a *polynomial* is also known as a *cubic*.

third quartile

See *quartile*.

three-body problem

This is not commonly encountered in grade-school math. The term *three-body problem* refers to the problem of solving the mechanics of three objects that are subject to mutual *forces* (and possibly external *forces* as well).

topology, topologically equivalent

A field of mathematics that concerns the deformation and distortion of geometrical objects, whilst preserving the essential connections (i.e., no cutting and sticking together is allowed). An object after such a deformation is said to be *topologically equivalent* to the object before the deformation. A common example is a map of an underground rail system. Such a map shows the correct relationship between the railway lines and the stations, but the distances between the stations, and the shapes of the railway lines are usually distorted for convenience. The map of the underground railway is a *topological* representation of the physical map.

torque

The term *torque* refers to the turning effect of a *force* (it has units of a *force* times distance). In applied math and physics at grade-school level, the term *torque* is often used synonymously with the term *moment*.

trace

First look up *matrix* and *diagonal of a matrix*, if you need to. The *trace* of a *square matrix* is the sum of its *diagonal elements*.

transcendental number

First look up *e, rational number, irrational number, complex number,* and *polynomial* if you need to. The term *transcendental number* is a very difficult concept to define, and the *proof* of whether a given number is *tran-*

scendental has challenged the greatest mathematicians. Fortunately, for grade-school math, you only need to know the following.

(1) *Transcendental numbers* are those that cannot be expressed as functions of *rational numbers* using a number of terms that is not *infinite* (formally, *transcendental numbers* are not the solutions to *polynomial* equations with *rational coefficients*).

(2) There are an uncountable number of *transcendental numbers* and each of them requires an *infinite* number of decimal places to be represented.

(3) All *transcendental numbers* are *irrational*, BUT all *irrational numbers* are NOT *transcendental numbers*.

(4) *Transcendental numbers* need not be *real numbers*, but may be *complex numbers*.

Two common examples of *transcendental* numbers are π and e. An example of a number that is *irrational* but NOT *transcendental* is $\sqrt{2}$.

transformation

There are several terms that you may need to look up, as needed. In *geometry*, a *transformation* usually refers to changing a geometrical object in one of four ways: (1) moving it (*translation*), (2) reflecting it in an imaginary mirror, (3) rotating it, or (4) shrinking or enlarging it, whilst preserving *relative proportions*. In *algebra*, *transformation* usually means applying an *operation* on sets of *coordinates* to obtain new *coordinates*. Although related to the geometrical meaning, in *algebra*, a *transformation* is not restricted to the four *operations* described for geometry, and the *transformation* may not necessarily have a physical correspondence. A *geometric* or *algebraic transformation* may involve the use of *matrices*, or the *transformation* itself may refer to generating a new *matrix*. The term *transformation* may also refer to the manipulation of an *equation* to change it into a different form.

transitive property

This concerns two statements of equality or *inequality*, with reference to three items (which could be numbers or *algebraic expressions*). In the case of *equality*, if the first item is equal to the second item, and if the second item is equal to the third item, then the first item is equal to the third item. The logic proceeds analogously for *inequalities*. For example, if the first item is greater than the second item, and the second item is greater than the third item, then the first item is greater than the third item.

translation

First look up *coordinate system* if you need to. The term *translation* usually means moving a geometrical object, or a graph of data, or a graph of a *function*, to a different position in a *coordinate system*. There are specific ways to change a *function*, or to manipulate data points, in order to move the graph to a different position in space *relative* to the fixed *coordinate axes*.

transpose

You may need to look up *matrix* first. There are two common meanings of *transpose* for the purpose of grade-school math. The first relates to the fact that the phrase "*transpose* an *equation*," is usually synonymous with *rearranging* an *equation*, either to solve it, or to *simplify* it. The second meaning refers to the *transpose* of a *matrix*, which is another *matrix* that is constructed by interchanging the *rows* and *columns* of the original *matrix*.

transversal

In *geometry*, a *transversal* is a line that cuts across (traverses) some other lines. A particular case of interest in *geometry* is a *transversal* that cuts *parallel lines* (e.g., see *corresponding angles*).

transverse axis (of a hyperbola)

See *major axis*.

trapezoid, trapezium

A four-sided geometrical shape (*quadrilateral*), that has one pair of sides that are *parallel* to each other. Note that somewhat different meanings of the two terms, *trapezoid* and *trapezium*, may be in use in different countries, but one thing for sure is that they are both *quadrilaterals*. See also *isosceles trapezoid*.

trapezoidal rule, trapezoid rule, trapezium rule

First look up *calculus*, *integration*, and *definite integral* if you need to. The *trapezoidal rule* is a method for estimating the area under a curve (for example, the graph of a *function*), that can used to numerically estimate the value of a *definite integral* in *calculus*. The *trapezoidal rule* is less accurate than *Simpson's rule* and *Romberg's method*.

tree diagram

In *probability* theory, a *tree diagram* is useful for laying out all of the various possible outcomes of chains of events, in order to compute the *probability* of occurrence of a given final outcome.

trend

Usually refers to a pattern in graphed data, showing that one of the quantities represented by the data might be related to another quantity drawn from the same sample or experiment. The relationship need not be a straight line, but if there is an apparent *trend*, there are various methods to quantify the *probability* that the *trend* is not due to *random* "coincidences." See also *correlation* and *regression*.

trial

Although the word *trial* is used in grade-school math with a standard meaning, as in "trying out" an estimated solution to a problem, it also has another meaning, in the context of *probability* theory. Suppose that there is some process that is being studied, and suppose that the process produces some set of possible outcomes every time that it is invoked. Further suppose that at each invocation, or "realization" of the process, the outcomes are not necessarily the same each time. Examples of such a process are the toss of a coin, the roll of a die, and so on. Formally, each invocation, or "realization" of the process, is called a *trial*, and you may come across phrases such as, "After N trials..." (where N is the number of *trials*).

triangle

A two-dimensional geometric shape with three sides. In ordinary space (i.e., in *Euclidean geometry*) the three angles of a *triangle* add up to 180 degrees.

triangular number

If a number of dots can be arranged in the shape of a *triangle*, then that number is a *triangular number*. In other words, each row of dots in the arrangement has one more dot than the previous row. An equivalent definition of a *triangular number* is therefore that it is the cumulative sum of the *integers* starting from 1. The first ten *triangular numbers* are thus 1, 3, 6, 10, 15, 21, 28, 26, 45, 55.

triangularize, triangularization (of matrices)

Watch out! Do not confuse *triangularize* with *triangulate*! First look up *matrix* if you need to. The term *triangularize* refers to the process of manipulating a *matrix* (using the rules of *matrix algebra*) to produce a new *matrix*, in which the visual pattern of numbers (not counting zeros) forms a *triangular* shape. The reason for doing this is that the resulting triangular *matrix* allows an easier solution of *matrix equations* that involve the original *matrix*.

triangulate

The verb to *triangulate* refers to a process involving *geometry* to locate the position of a remote object or event. It is based on the principle that you can know everything about a *triangle* (the lengths of all three sides and the *measure* of all three angles), if you know (1) only the length of all three sides, or (2) the length of one side and the two angles at each end of that side. The remote object or event that you are trying to locate will be at one point (*vertex*) of a *triangle*.

Method (1) can be used for situations such as locating the center of an Earthquake. At a location far from the Earthquake, the time delay between two kinds of signal will tell you how far the Earthquake is from that point, but it will not tell you the direction. That's one side of a *triangle*. In a different city you can do the same thing. That's a second side of the *triangle*. You can measure the distance between the two cities. That's the third side of the *triangle*. This solves the triangle but it does not solve for the location of the Earthquake because there are two solutions due to the fact that the same *triangle* can be flipped over and still be a solution. In other words, the two solutions are located at an equal *perpendicular* distance either side of the baseline that connects the two cities. Without any other information you then have to take a measurement at one more city and then only one *triangle* will fit the data, and the Earthquake will be located at the *vertex* that does not coincide with one of the cities.

Method (2) can be used for situations such as locating the position of a radio beacon. The signal strength picked up from the beacon by a receiver has a directional dependence, and this fact is used to figure out two angles of a *triangle*. The signal is measured from two different locations and the orientation of the receiver is rotated for maximum signal strength at each location. The distance between the two locations is measured, and the optimum angle of the receiver *relative* to the line joining the two locations is noted for each location. Thus we have the length of one side of a *triangle* and two angles, so the *triangle* is solved completely. The radio beacon will then be located at the *vertex* of the *triangle* that does not coincide with either of the locations that measurements were made.

trichotomy property

This is just a fancy way of saying that when two numbers are compared, there are only three possible outcomes concerning the *relative* size of the two numbers (i.e., they are either equal, or one is smaller or larger than the other).

trigonometry

Trigonometry is the study of *triangles* and the relationships concerning the sides and angles of *triangles*.

trigonometric addition formulas

First look up *trigonometry* and *trigonometric function* if you need to. The *trigonometric addition formulas* are a set of relations that allow you to calculate values of the principal *trigonometric functions* for the sum OR difference of two angles, if you know the values of the principal *trigono-*

metric functions for the individual angles.

trigonometric function

This term usually refers to the principal *functions* that arise in *trigonometry*. Although the *trigonometric functions* are generated by the consideration of *triangles*, they have natural circular properties (see definitions of the individual *functions*: *sine, cosine, tangent, cosecant, secant,* and *cotangent*). Sometimes these *functions* are called "trig" *functions* for short.

trigonometric identity

An equality involving some combination of *trigonometric functions* (there are several common identities).

trinomial

First look up *polynomial* if you need to. A *trinomial* is a *polynomial* consisting of three *terms*.

truncated decimal

A decimal number that has been truncated by removing all digits to the right of a prespecified position after the decimal point. Note that this is NOT the same as *rounding*.

truth table

In the field of *logic*, a *truth table* shows all the possible outcomes (true or false), of applying a logical *operation*, or set of *operations*, on a number of "input" logical *variables*. Logical *variables* can only take on one of two values, namely true or false. The *truth table* may help to replace a complex logical *operation* with a simpler one that is exactly equivalent.

turning points

Synonymous with *inflection* and *stationary point* (look up *inflection*).

two-body problem

In applied math and physics, the term *two-body problem* refers to the problem of solving the mechanics of two objects subject to mutual *forces* (as well as possible external *forces*).

two's complement

See *complement*.

– U –

unbiased

An adjective for a quantity that is not affected by particular factors that are specified. For example, the tossing of a coin may be *unbiased* with respect to the local temperature, but it may or may not be *unbiased* with respect to the initial spin and height of the drop. This would have to be assessed experimentally. See also discussions for *sample* and *uniform*.

unbiased sample

Synonymous with *uniform distribution*. See discussions under *unbiased*, *uniform* and *sample*.

unbounded

This usually refers to a *function* that increases or decreases without limit (presumably to "plus or minus" *infinity*), as the input to the *function* approaches one or more "special" values or regimes.

uniform

An adjective that usually describes a quantity that does not depend on other physical parameters (which must usually be specified). For example, *uniform speed* means that the *speed* (of an object) does not change with respect to distance or time (i.e., the speed is *constant* with respect to those parameters). Another common usage is in the term *uniform distribution*. This means that a mathematical or physical quantity is distributed in such a way that the amount of the quantity in arbitrary, equal intervals is the same. In other words, a *uniform distribution* is *unbiased* towards any particular range of values of the key *variable*. For example, the outcome of the roll of a fair dice has a *uniform distribution* of integers in the range 1 to 6, inclusive. Each of the six outcomes are equally likely.

union

First look up *set* and *set theory* if you need to. In *set theory*, the *union* of two *sets* is a larger set that is formed by including members of both *sets*.

unit, units

There are many possible contexts but the most common one is the one that is most familiar, referring to the physical standards of reference that real measurements pertain to. See discussion on *dimensions*. Another meaning occurs as in the phrase, "...per *unit* length," or "...per *unit* (something)." In this context, *unit* literally means the number 1 (in whatever system of measurement that is relevant in the context). For example, saying, "My *speed* is greater than yours," is equivalent to saying, "I cover more distance in unit time than you do."

unit matrix

First look up *matrix*, *element*, and *diagonal* if you need to. A *unit matrix* is a *square matrix* whose *diagonal elements* are all equal to 1, and whose *nondiagonal elements* are all equal to zero. The term *unit matrix* is synonymous with *identity matrix*.

universal set

First look up *set theory* if you need to. The *universal set* is the *set* that includes everything, including itself.

unknown

Usually, *unknown* refers to the *unknown* values of *variables* in an *equation*, or set of *equations*. However, you will often see, or read about, *unknown* as if it were a noun. For example, in the sentence, "In order to solve a system of *equations* completely, the number of independent *equations* must be at least equal to the number of *unknowns*," the term *unknowns* is used as a (plural) noun.

unlike terms

See *like terms*. *Unlike terms* in an *algebraic expression* are those that are not *like terms*.

– V –

variable

When used as a noun, *variable* refers to something that stands in place of a variety of mathematical objects including numbers (of various kinds), entire *algebraic expressions*, or *functions*. Even objects in the field of *logic* are referred to as *variables* (logical *variables*), and as such may represent statements, or "truth" values. In a given application, the context should define precisely what all of the *variables* represent. If they represent numbers, their numerical value may not be known. In mathematics (as opposed to computer science), a *variable* is an item that is usually "named" by a letter of an alphabet (not necessarily English). More than one letter is rarely used because it would be confused for multiplication of two *variables*. Instead, subscripts can be used (but the rules are more complicated in more advanced mathematics applications). The term *variable* may also be used as an adjective, describing a quantity that varies, as opposed to having a fixed value.

variance

First look up *standard deviation* if you need to. In *statistics*, the *variance* is equal to the *square* of the *standard deviation*. It is therefore, like the *standard deviation*, a measure of how good or bad a proposed *model* is, for the purpose of representing a collection of data.

varies directly

See *direct variation*.

varies inversely

See *inversely proportional*.

vector

A *vector* is a mathematical object that needs more than one number to describe it (those numbers are generally known as the *components* of the vector). In grade-school math, *vectors* describe several types of physical quantities that cannot be defined by a single number (for example, a *velocity* or a *force*). In contrast, physical quantities that can be described by a single number are called *scalars* (for example, temperature).

vector analysis

First look up *vector* if you need to. The term *vector analysis* refers to the process of manipulating mathematical *expressions* and *equations* involving *vectors*, using the established rules for *vector operations*.

vector cross product

See *vector product*.

vector product

First look up *vector* if you need to. Due to the fact that a *vector* is made up of more than one number (i.e., it has several *components*), multiplication in the ordinary sense does not have any meaning because there are many possible ways that multiplication could be defined for *vectors*. The *vector product* is a predefined prescription for combining two *vectors* in order to form a new *vector*. The definition is deliberately designed to mirror certain physical process in order for *vectors* to be useful for real problems. For example, the so-called *coriolis force* that is associated with hurricanes on Earth, at a basic level involves *vector products* of physical quantities. Although the *vector product* is written with a "×" symbol, it is not simple multiplication: it involves multiplication, addition, and subtraction. See also *inner product* (or synonymously, *scalar product*), which is a different definition of a procedure for combining two *vectors*, and it also useful for solving real-world problems. Note that the terms *cross product* and *vector cross product* are synonymous with the term *vector product*.

velocity

The *rate* of change of distance with respect to time, with a specification of the direction of motion. Not to be confused with *speed*, which only gives the *rate* of change of distance with respect to time, and no information on the direction of motion. See also *vector* and *scalar*.

Venn diagram (after John Venn)

First look up *sets* and *set theory* if you need to. A Venn diagram is a visual display of all the *sets* in a given problem, depicting information about the overlap properties of all the *sets* with respect to each other. The *sets* are usually drawn as *circles* inside a *rectangle*.

vertex (plural: vertices)

For the purpose of grade-school math, *vertex* has two meanings. One is in *geometry*, in which a *vertex* is a *point* where the lines or edges that define a geometric shape meet. In three dimensions the *vertices* are the points where the edges of a geometric figure meet. The second meaning is synonymous with a point of *inflection* on the graph of a *function* (look up *inflection* if you need to).

volume

A measure of the three-dimensional space that is occupied by an object or physical entity. A summary of the *formulas* for the *volume* of some common shapes can usually be found at the back or front of a school textbook.

– W –

Watt (after James Watt)
A measure of *power* that is equivalent to *Joules* per second.

weight
The *weight* of an object is a measure of the reaction *force* at the point of contact on a surface, under the influence of gravity, and any other local accelerations. The *weight* of an object should not be confused with its *mass*, because the former depends on the local gravity and acceleration, but the latter does not (as perceived by an observer moving with the object itself). In applied math and physics, *weight* is actually measured in the same *units* as *force*, but in everyday usage it is measured in the same *units* as *mass*.

weighted mean (weighted average)
The *weighted mean* of a collection of data values is an *average* that takes account of the measurement uncertainties and any other uncertainties in the data values (i.e., it takes account of the error bars on the data points). Data points with small uncertainties influence the value of the *weighted mean* more than data points with large uncertainties. The motivation is that the *average* value of the data should reflect the higher quality, and more reliable data.

work
In applied math and physics, *work* has the same *units* as *energy*, and is entirely equivalent to *energy*. *Work* is the mechanical manifestation of *energy*, produced in the process of converting *energy* from one form to another.

wrapping function
This refers to a specific *function* that takes a straight line of *real numbers* and wraps it around a *circle* that has a *radius* of one unit. The input to the *wrapping function* is a single number that corresponds to the length around the *circumference* from some reference point. The output of the *wrapping*

function is a pair of numbers that correspond to the *coordinates* of the end of the line that is wrapped around the *circle*, the latter being centered at the intersection of the horizontal and vertical *coordinate axes*.

– X –

x-axis

In a regular two-dimensional graph (technically, a *Cartesian coordinate system*), the x-axis is the horizontal line that is used to place the position of a *point* in the horizontal direction from the center of the graph (its *origin*). For the generalization to three dimensions, see z-axis.

x-intercept

See *intercept*.

– Y –

y-axis

In a regular two-dimensional graph (technically, a *Cartesian coordinate system*), the y-axis is the vertical line that is used to place the position of a *point* in the vertical direction from the center of the graph (its *origin*). For the generalization to three dimensions, see z-axis.

y-intercept

See *intercept*.

– Z –

z-axis

First look up *coordinate system*, *Cartesian coordinates*, *x-axis*, and *y-axis* if you need to. In a three-dimensional graph (in several different *coordinate systems*, but most commonly in *Cartesian coordinates*), the z-axis is *perpendicular* to the *plane* defined by the other two *coordinate axes*, and passes through the the center of the system (its *origin*). By convention, in a three-dimensional *Cartesian coordinate system*, the x-axis goes from left to right (negative to positive, respectively), the y-axis goes from into, and out of the page (positive into the page), and the z-axis therefore goes from bottom to top (positive up).

zero factor theorem

If the product of a number of *algebraic expressions* is equal to zero, then the *zero factor theorem* simply states that at least one of those *algebraic expressions* must itself be equal to zero. There is otherwise no way that the product of all the *algebraic expressions* could be equal to zero.

zero matrix

First look up *matrix* if you need to. A *zero matrix* is one in which all of the *elements* of the *matrix* have a value of zero.

zeros (of a function)

A *function* operates on inputs (independent *variables*) to give an output (the value of the *function*). The *zeros* of a *function* are the values that the input *variable* must have for the *function* value (output) to be zero. The *variable* that is being solved for should of course be specified in the problem (but often there may only be one such *variable*).

z-intercept

See *intercept*.

Appendix A

Oral Drills

I have talked about the importance of practicing oral drills in several places in this book (§2.7, §3.6, and §5.5.6), and you are advised to read the entire book before working with your child on the oral drills. The drills are organized into three categories, according to elementary-school level, middle- to high-school level, and a special set for precalculus and calculus students.

There are several sets of oral drills in each category, with various levels of difficulty. A list of drill topics is given at the beginning of each of the three groups of drills. Each drill has an approximate response-time goal, which is meant only as an approximate guide on what to aim for. Within each of the groups of drills there is obviously a range in academic level and readiness. You should exercise judgement as to when your child is ready for each drill and each drill should be mastered at the earliest time that your child is ready. This can be facilitated by following what your child is doing at school.

In some of the drills in the middle-school and high-school category, it is not indicated whether a drill is appropriate at the middle-school level or the high-school level. Again, exercise judgement and introduce each drill at the earliest time that your child is ready for it. You may find it helpful to encourage your child to use the "money rule" (discussed in §2.4) in order to facilitate speed and accuracy with the mental arithmetic, where appropriate.

The drills are to be performed *only* orally. *No writing is allowed.* Obviously, no calculators are allowed either. However, the student *can* (if requested) be shown the questions and hints (if there are any) briefly, before an oral drill is administered. In that case, in order to avoid recall from memory, mix up the order of the questions. The purpose of these oral drills is principally to develop *speed* in response time, whilst maintaining *accuracy*. The number of questions in each drill is small. The topics covered are not exhaustive, and the idea is to give you something to *start* with for each different drill. You can supplement what is given with your own extensions of the drills, or completely new drills with different topics, if or when that becomes necessary. You can find some useful pointers to resources to help you do this at the website `http://www.helpyourchildwithmath.com`. The drills that are given here in this appendix are intended mainly to illustrate the sort of exercises that are required, although they do cover some very essential and fundamental skills.

The oral drills also encourage personal interaction and encourage parent and child working together. Whilst the questions in each drill may seem simple, the power of the drills should not to be underestimated because they build *speed and accuracy*. These oral drills are brain training exercises, and *not* "rote learning." It is important to remember that the less time a student spends on the easier material in a real test or exam situation, the more time that there will be available for the more difficult material. The drills will also reduce the chances of making mistakes with a wide range of material in a real test or exam situation. This is particularly vital when you consider that making a simple mistake at the beginning of a more advanced problem (such as in calculus), can affect the outcome of the entire problem. A mistake at the beginning of a complex problem, if it is not caught, can lead to a journey that becomes long and time-consuming, only to end up producing something that is wrong.

Remember that, especially for the precalculus and calculus drills, *you do not have to know the material yourself* in order to be able to administer the drills. Just read out the drills and listen for the correct answer (which is given for every part of every drill).

A.1 Elementary-School Level

Drills in this section:

Addition of Two Numbers	328
Addition of Three Numbers	329
Missing Number in Addition of Two Numbers	330
Subtraction of Two Numbers	331
Multiplication of Two Numbers	332
Multiplication of Three Numbers	333
Division of Two Numbers	334
Addition and Subtraction of Fractions	335
Multiplication and Division of Fractions	336
Percentages (Forward)	337
Percentages (Reverse)	338
Estimation Skills	339

Addition of Two Numbers

Response-time goal: 1–2 seconds or better (dependent upon grade level).

(1) 1 + 3 = **4**
(2) 2 + 7 = **9**
(3) 6 + 2 = **8**
(4) 7 + 5 = **12**
(5) 4 + 5 = **9**
(6) 1 + 5 = **6**
(7) 7 + 3 = **10**
(8) 11 + 2 = **13**
(9) 9 + 6 = **15**
(10) 6 + 4 = **10**

Add additional drills here:

Addition of Three Numbers

Response-time goal: 2–3 seconds or better (dependent upon grade level).

(1) $1 + 2 + 1 = $ **4**
(2) $1 + 1 + 1 = $ **3**
(3) $2 + 0 + 3 = $ **5**
(4) $0 + 0 + 7 = $ **7**
(5) $1 + 2 + 3 = $ **6**
(6) $5 + 1 + 2 = $ **8**
(7) $9 + 1 + 2 = $ **12**
(8) $5 + 5 + 1 = $ **11**
(9) $6 + 2 + 1 = $ **9**
(10) $4 + 2 + 2 = $ **8**

Add additional drills here:

Missing Number in Addition of Two Numbers

Response-time goal: 2–3 seconds or better (dependent upon grade level).

(1) 1+ what = 5? (**4**)
(2) 0+ what = 12? (**12**)
(3) 2+ what = 6? (**4**)
(4) 1+ what = 11? (**10**)
(5) 3+ what = 7? (**4**)
(6) 2+ what = 5? (**3**)
(7) 9+ what = 10? (**1**)
(8) 8+ what = 11? (**3**)
(9) 4+ what = 7? (**3**)
(10) 6+ what = 6? (**0**)

Additional drills here:

Subtraction of Two Numbers

Response-time goal: 1–2 seconds or better (dependent upon grade level).

(1) $5 - 4 = \mathbf{1}$
(2) $4 - 0 = \mathbf{4}$
(3) $1 - 1 = \mathbf{0}$
(4) $7 - 2 = \mathbf{5}$
(5) $4 - 1 = \mathbf{3}$
(6) $5 - 2 = \mathbf{3}$
(7) $6 - 1 = \mathbf{5}$
(8) $9 - 1 = \mathbf{8}$
(9) $14 - 2 = \mathbf{12}$
(10) $11 - 2 = \mathbf{9}$

Add additional drills here:

Multiplication of Two Numbers

Response-time goal: 2–5 seconds or better (dependent upon grade level). Note that students should build speed and accuracy with *all* of the multiplication tables from 1 through 12, in addition to these drills. The oral drill here is just a "spot check" for the purpose of revealing any potential problems.

(1) $4 \times 3 = \mathbf{12}$
(2) $5 \times 7 = \mathbf{35}$
(3) $1 \times 3 = \mathbf{3}$
(4) $5 \times 2 = \mathbf{10}$
(5) $2 \times 6 = \mathbf{12}$
(6) $2 \times 3 = \mathbf{6}$
(7) $3 \times 3 = \mathbf{9}$
(8) $4 \times 4 = \mathbf{16}$
(9) $4 \times 1 = \mathbf{4}$
(10) $4 \times 2 = \mathbf{8}$

Add additional drills here:

Multiplication of Three Numbers

Response-time goal: 2–6 seconds or better (dependent upon grade level).

(1) $2 \times 3 \times 2 = $ **12**
(2) $1 \times 4 \times 2 = $ **8**
(3) $0 \times 1 \times 3 = $ **0**
(4) $1 \times 1 \times 1 = $ **1**
(5) $4 \times 2 \times 2 = $ **16**
(6) $3 \times 2 \times 2 = $ **12**
(7) $2 \times 2 \times 2 = $ **8**
(8) $1 \times 2 \times 2 = $ **4**
(9) $3 \times 3 \times 1 = $ **9**
(10) $5 \times 2 \times 2 = $ **20**

Add additional drills here:

Division of Two Numbers

Response-time goal: 1–2 seconds or better (dependent upon grade level).

(1) $6 \div 3 = \mathbf{2}$
(2) $4 \div 2 = \mathbf{2}$
(3) $9 \div 3 = \mathbf{3}$
(4) $8 \div 2 = \mathbf{4}$
(5) $10 \div 5 = \mathbf{2}$
(6) $12 \div 3 = \mathbf{4}$
(7) $6 \div 2 = \mathbf{3}$
(8) $8 \div 4 = \mathbf{2}$
(9) $12 \div 4 = \mathbf{3}$
(10) $1 \div 1 = \mathbf{1}$
(11) $0 \div 1 = \mathbf{0}$
(12) $0 \div 12 = \mathbf{0}$

Add additional drills here:

Addition and Subtraction of Fractions

Response-time goal: 2–4 seconds or better (dependent upon grade level). For earlier elementary-grade levels, make up some easier drills if this one is too difficult. If the student has not yet formally studied the addition and subtraction of fractions, use the drill for estimating decimal equivalents or simple fractions, making use of the money rule (see §2.4) as an intermediate mental "lever" if necessary.

(1) $\frac{1}{2} + \frac{3}{2} = 2$

(2) $\frac{3}{2} - \frac{1}{2} = 1$

(3) $\frac{2}{3} + \frac{1}{6} = \frac{5}{6}$

(4) $\frac{2}{3} - \frac{1}{2} = \frac{1}{6}$

(5) $\frac{3}{4} + \frac{1}{2} = 1\frac{1}{4}$

(6) $\frac{1}{7} + \frac{1}{3} = \frac{10}{21}$

(7) $\frac{7}{8} - \frac{3}{16} = \frac{11}{16}$

(8) $\frac{7}{4} + \frac{5}{2} = 4\frac{1}{4}$

(9) $\frac{4}{3} - \frac{2}{5} = \frac{14}{15}$

(10) $\frac{12}{8} + \frac{10}{4} = 4$

Add additional drills here:

Multiplication and Division of Fractions

Response-time goal: 2 seconds or better.
The answers should be in the simplest form.

(1) $\frac{1}{2} \times \frac{1}{3} = \frac{1}{6}$

(2) $\frac{2}{3} \times \frac{6}{1} = 4$

(3) $\frac{5}{7} \times \frac{1}{2} = \frac{5}{14}$

(4) $\frac{4}{3} \times \frac{6}{7} = 1\frac{1}{7}$

(5) $\frac{2}{5} \times \frac{1}{3} = \frac{2}{15}$

(6) $\frac{3}{2} \div \frac{1}{2} = 3$

(7) $\frac{2}{3} \div \frac{1}{3} = 2$

(8) $\frac{5}{6} \div \frac{1}{2} = 1\frac{2}{3}$

(9) $\frac{5}{6} \div \frac{2}{3} = 1\frac{1}{4}$

(10) $\frac{7}{12} \div \frac{1}{4} = 2\frac{1}{3}$

Add additional drills here:

Percentages (Forward)

Response-time goal: 2–4 seconds or better (dependent upon grade level).

(1) What is 200 increased by 5%? Answer: **210**
(2) What is 3% of 200? Answer: **6**
(3) What is 120 decreased by 10%? Answer: **108**
(4) What is 50 increased by 100%? Answer: **100**
(5) What is 30 increased by 200%? Answer: **90**
(6) What is 40% of 12? Answer: **4.8**
(7) What is 12 increased by 50%? Answer: **18**
(8) What is 18 decreased by 50%? Answer: **9**
(9) What is 99 decreased by 100%? Answer: **0**
(10) What is 70 increased by 20%? Answer: **84**

Add additional drills here:

Percentages (Reverse)

Response-time goal: 2–4 seconds or better (dependent upon grade level).

(1) What reduced by 20% gives 80? Answer: **100**
(Hint: $80 \div (1.00 - 0.20) = 100$.)

(2) What increased by 50% gives 9? Answer: **6**
(Hint: $9 \div (1.00 + 0.50) = 6$.)

(3) What increased by 10% gives 11? Answer: **10**
(Hint: $11 \div (1.00 + 0.10) = 10$.)

(4) What reduced by 50% gives 90? Answer: **180**
(Hint: $90 \div (1.00 - 0.50) = 180$.)

(5) What reduced by 25% gives 3? Answer: **4**
(Hint: $3 \div (1.00 - 0.25) = 4$.)

(6) What increased by 25% gives 50? Answer: **40**
(Hint: $50 \div (1.00 + 0.25) = 40$.)

(7) What reduced by 10% gives 90? Answer: **100**
(Hint: $90 \div (1.00 - 0.10) = 100$.)

(8) What reduced by 30% gives 7? Answer: **10**
(Hint: $7 \div (1.00 - 0.30) = 10$.)

(9) What increased by 200% gives 600? Answer: **200**
(Hint: $600 \div (1.00 + 2.00) = 200$.)

(10) What increased by 40% gives 14? Answer: **10**
(Hint: $14 \div (1.00 + 0.40) = 10$.)

Add additional drills here:

Estimation Skills (Elementary Level)

Response-time goal: 2 seconds or better.

(1) Approximately what do you need to multiply 3 by to get 80?
Answer: **27** (Hint: $3 \times 3 \times 9 = 81$.)

(2) Approximately what do you need to multiply 4 by to get 50?
Answer: **12** (Hint: $4 \times 12 = 48$.)

(3) Approximately what do you need to multiply 5 by to get 49?
Answer: **10** (Hint: $5 \times 10 = 50$.)

(4) Approximately what do you need to multiply 6 by to get 31?
Answer: **5** (Hint: $6 \times 5 = 30$.)

(5) Approximately what do you need to multiply 7 by to get 50?
Answer: **7** (Hint: $7 \times 7 = 49$.)

(6) Approximately what do you need to divide 50 by to get 8?
Answer: **6** (Hint: $8 \times 6 = 48$.)

(7) Approximately what do you need to divide 22 by to get 3?
Answer: **7** (Hint: $7 \times 3 = 21$.)

(8) Approximately what do you need to divide 25 by to get 4?
Answer: **6** (Hint: $6 \times 4 = 24$.)

(9) Approximately what do you need to divide 80 by to get 9?
Answer: **9** (Hint: $9 \times 9 = 81$.)

(10) Approximately what do you need to divide 98 by to get 10?
Answer: **10** (Hint: $10 \times 10 = 100$.)

Add additional drills here:

A.2 Middle- to High-School Level

Drills in this section:

Multiplication of Two (Small) Numbers	342
Division of Two Numbers	343
Multiplication of Two (Larger) Numbers	344
Harder Division of Two Numbers	345
Multiplication of Three Numbers (Middle School)	346
Multiplication of Three Numbers (High School) ..	347
Squares of Integers	348
Square Roots	349
Sum and Difference of Factors	350
Harder Addition and Subtraction of Fractions	351
Fraction to Decimal Conversion (Estimation)	352
Percentages (Forward)	354
Percentages (Reverse)	355
Percentages for No Net Change (High School) ...	356
Estimation Skills (Middle School)	358
Estimation Skills (High School)	360

Multiplication of Two (Small) Numbers

Response-time goal: 2 seconds or better.

Note that students should build speed and accuracy with *all* of the multiplication tables from 1 through 12, in addition to these drills. The oral drill here is just a "spot check" for the purpose of revealing any potential problems.

(1) $7 \times 8 = $ **56**
(2) $9 \times 8 = $ **72**
(3) $7 \times 12 = $ **84**
(4) $8 \times 12 = $ **96**
(5) $6 \times 8 = $ **48**
(6) $12 \times 9 = $ **108**
(7) $6 \times 9 = $ **54**
(8) $11 \times 9 = $ **99**
(9) $7 \times 6 = $ **42**
(10) $7 \times 9 = $ **63**

Add additional drills here:

Division of Two Numbers

Response-time goal: 2 seconds or better.

(1) $64 \div 4 = \mathbf{16}$
(2) $45 \div 9 = \mathbf{5}$
(3) $120 \div 6 = \mathbf{20}$
(4) $24 \div 3 = \mathbf{8}$
(5) $48 \div 6 = \mathbf{8}$
(6) $81 \div 3 = \mathbf{27}$
(7) $72 \div 6 = \mathbf{12}$
(8) $56 \div 8 = \mathbf{7}$
(9) $108 \div 3 = \mathbf{36}$
(10) $84 \div 7 = \mathbf{12}$

Add additional drills here:

Multiplication of Two (Larger) Numbers

Response-time goal: 3 seconds or better.

(1) $15 \times 9 = $ **135** (Hint: $150 - 15$.)
(2) $25 \times 8 = $ **200**
(3) $16 \times 12 = $ **192** (Hint: $160 + 32$.)
(4) $13 \times 13 = $ **169**
(5) $18 \times 6 = $ **108** (Hint: 9×12.)
(6) $14 \times 15 = $ **210** (Hint: $140 + 70$.)
(7) $17 \times 12 = $ **204** (Hint: $170 + 34$.)
(8) $13 \times 19 = $ **247** (Hint: $(13 \times 20) - 13$.)
(9) $11 \times 17 = $ **187** (Hint: $170 + 17$.)
(10) $31 \times 12 = $ **372** (Hint: $(3 \times 120) + 12$.)

Add additional drills here:

Harder Division of Two Numbers

Response-time goal: 3 seconds or better.

(1) $625 \div 5 = \mathbf{125}$
(2) $128 \div 4 = \mathbf{32}$
(3) $65 \div 5 = \mathbf{13}$
(4) $1024 \div 4 = \mathbf{256}$
(5) $84 \div 6 = \mathbf{14}$ (Hint: $84 = 2 \times 42$.)
(6) $108 \div 3 = \mathbf{36}$ (Hint: $108 = 12 \times 9$.)
(7) $980 \div 7 = \mathbf{140}$ (Hint: $98 = 2 \times 49$.)
(8) $288 \div 12 = \mathbf{24}$
(9) $112 \div 4 = \mathbf{28}$
(10) $4096 \div 8 = \mathbf{512}$ (Hint: $96 = 12 \times 8$, and $4000 = 500 \times 8$.)

Add additional drills here:

Multiplication of Three Numbers (Middle School)

Response-time goal: 3–5 seconds or better.

(1) $5 \times 4 \times 6 = $ **120**
(2) $4 \times 3 \times 7 = $ **84**
(3) $6 \times 2 \times 4 = $ **48**
(4) $3 \times 2 \times 3 = $ **18**
(5) $4 \times 1 \times 9 = $ **36**
(6) $4 \times 3 \times 2 = $ **24**
(7) $5 \times 9 \times 1 = $ **45**
(8) $6 \times 0 \times 3 = $ **0**
(9) $8 \times 4 \times 5 = $ **160**
(10) $6 \times 3 \times 3 = $ **54**

Add additional drills here:

Multiplication of Three Numbers (High School)

Response-time goal: 3 seconds or better.
The student should be able to break some of the numbers into factors in order to make the mental calculation easier and quicker.

(1) $7 \times 8 \times 3 = $ **168**
(2) $12 \times 4 \times 5 = $ **240**
(3) $9 \times 3 \times 4 = $ **108**
(4) $11 \times 2 \times 6 = $ **132**
(5) $12 \times 12 \times 4 = $ **576** (Hint: double 144 twice.)
(6) $5 \times 8 \times 8 = $ **320**
(7) $7 \times 6 \times 4 = $ **168**
(8) $7 \times 7 \times 8 = $ **392**
(9) $6 \times 3 \times 7 = $ **126**
(10) $9 \times 7 \times 6 = $ **378** (Hint: $(60 \times 6) + (3 \times 6)$.)

Add additional drills here:

Squares of Integers

Response-time goal: 1 second or better.
These should be committed to memory as they will need to be recalled quickly, extremely often.

(1) 7^2: What is 7 squared? Answer: **49**
(2) 11^2: What is 11 squared? Answer: **121**
(3) 2^2: What is 2 squared? Answer: **4**
(4) 5^2: What is 5 squared? Answer: **25**
(5) 8^2: What is 8 squared? Answer: **64**
(6) 3^2: What is 3 squared? Answer: **9**
(7) 6^2: What is 6 squared? Answer: **36**
(8) 4^2: What is 4 squared? Answer: **16**
(9) 9^2: What is 9 squared? Answer: **81**
(10) 12^2: What is 12 squared? Answer: **144**
(11) 10^2: What is 10 squared? Answer: **100**
(12) 1^2: What is 1 squared? Answer: **1**
(13) 13^2: What is 13 squared? Answer: **169**
(14) 25^2: What is 25 squared? Answer: **625**
(15) 15^2: What is 15 squared? Answer: **225**

Square Roots

Response-time goal: 1 second or better.
These should be committed to memory as they will need to be recalled quickly, extremely often.

(1) $\sqrt{64}$: What is the positive square root of 64? Answer: **8**
(2) $\sqrt{4}$: What is the positive square root of 4? Answer: **2**
(3) $\sqrt{25}$: What is the positive square root of 25? Answer: **5**
(4) $\sqrt{49}$: What is the positive square root of 49? Answer: **7**
(5) $\sqrt{9}$: What is the positive square root of 9? Answer: **3**
(6) $\sqrt{16}$: What is the positive square root of 16? Answer: **4**
(7) $\sqrt{81}$: What is the positive square root of 81? Answer: **9**
(8) $\sqrt{121}$: What is the positive square root of 121? Answer: **11**
(9) $\sqrt{100}$: What is the positive square root of 100? Answer: **10**
(10) $\sqrt{144}$: What is the positive square root of 144? Answer: **12**
(11) $\sqrt{1}$: What is the positive square root of 1? Answer: **1**
(12) $\sqrt{36}$: What is the positive square root of 36? Answer: **6**
(13) $\sqrt{225}$: What is the positive square root of 225? Answer: **15**
(14) $\sqrt{169}$: What is the positive square root of 169? Answer: **13**
(15) $\sqrt{625}$: What is the positive square root of 625? Answer: **25**

Sum and Difference of Factors

Response-time goal: 2 seconds or better.
This drill is useful to students for factorizing *quadratic equations*.

(1) What factors of 12 have a sum of 7 and a difference of −1?
Answer: **(3, 4)**

(2) What factors of 8 have a sum of 6 and a difference of 2?
Answer: **(4, 2)**

(3) What factors of 6 have a sum of −5 and a difference of −1?
Answer: **(−3, −2)**

(4) What factors of 21 have a sum of 10 and a difference of −4?
Answer: **(3, 7)**

(5) What factors of 16 have a sum of 10 and a difference of 6?
Answer: **(8, 2)**

(6) What factors of 42 have a sum of −17 and a difference of −11?
Answer: **(−14, −3)**

(7) What factors of 15 have a sum of 16 and a difference of 14?
Answer: **(15, 1)**

(8) What factors of 56 have a sum of 30 and a difference of 26?
Answer: **(28, 2)**

(9) What factors of 12 have a sum of −8 and a difference of −4?
Answer: **(−6, −2)**

(10) What factors of 16 have a sum of 8 and a difference of 0?
Answer: **(4, 4)**

Additional drills here:

Harder Addition and Subtraction of Fractions

Response-time goal: 2–4 seconds or better (dependent upon grade level). This drill can be used for both exact answers and for estimating (either decimal equivalents or simple fractions). For exact answers the student should use whatever method appears to be easiest, so several trials with the drill may be required before the response time is satisfactory. For estimating, the student could use the money rule (see §2.4) as an intermediate mental "lever" if necessary. On a related note, if the drill is used for exact answers, and the student responds with an answer that is "way off," ask the student to use the money rule to do a quick "sanity check."

(1) $\frac{7}{12} + \frac{2}{3} = 1\frac{1}{4}$

(2) $\frac{5}{9} - \frac{1}{2} = \frac{1}{18}$

(3) $\frac{2}{3} + \frac{5}{8} = 1\frac{7}{24}$

(4) $\frac{6}{7} - \frac{1}{3} = \frac{11}{21}$

(5) $\frac{1}{18} + \frac{2}{3} = \frac{13}{18}$

(6) $\frac{3}{4} + \frac{1}{5} = \frac{19}{20}$

(7) $\frac{5}{3} - \frac{1}{6} = \frac{3}{2} = 1\frac{1}{2}$

(8) $\frac{1}{2} + \frac{9}{5} = 2\frac{3}{10}$

(9) $\frac{1}{8} + \frac{1}{5} = \frac{13}{40}$

(10) $\frac{2}{9} + \frac{2}{11} = \frac{40}{99}$

Add additional drills here:

Fraction to Decimal Conversion (Estimation)

Response-time goal: 2–4 seconds or better (dependent upon grade level).

(1) Estimate the decimal equivalent of $\frac{3}{7}$. Answer: **0.42**
(Hint: $14 \times 7 = 98$, or approximately 100; "exact" answer is 0.429.)

(2) Estimate the decimal equivalent of $\frac{2}{9}$. Answer: **0.22**
(Hint: $11 \times 9 = 99$, or approximately 100, and $11 \times 2 = 22$; "exact" answer is 0.222 recurring.)

(3) Estimate the decimal equivalent of $\frac{4}{15}$. Answer: **0.28**
(Hint: $15 \times 7 = 105$, or approximately 100, and $4 \times 7 = 28$; "exact" answer is 0.266 recurring.)

(4) Estimate the decimal equivalent of $\frac{2}{17}$. Answer: **0.12**
(Hint: $2 \times 8 \times 12 = 192$, or approximately 200; "exact" answer is 0.118.)

(5) Estimate the decimal equivalent of $\frac{5}{7}$. Answer: **0.70**
(Hint: $14 \times 7 = 98$, or approximately 100, $14 \times 5 = 70$; "exact" answer is 0.714.)

(6) Estimate the decimal equivalent of $\frac{1}{6}$. Answer: **0.17**
(Hint: $17 \times 6 = 102$, or approximately 100; "exact" answer is 0.166 recurring.)

(7) Estimate the decimal equivalent of $\frac{3}{11}$. Answer: **0.27**
(Hint: $9 \times 11 = 99$, and $9 \times 3 = 27$; "exact" answer is 0.273.)

(8) Estimate the decimal equivalent of $\frac{12}{7}$. Answer: **1.68**
(Hint: $14 \times 7 = 98$, or approximately 100, and $14 \times 12 = 144 + 24$; "exact" answer is 1.714.)

Continued on next page.

(9) Estimate the decimal equivalent of $\frac{5}{12}$. Answer: **0.40**
(Hint: $12 \times 8 = 96$, or approximately 100, and $8 \times 5 = 40$; "exact" answer is 0.416 recurring.)

(10) Estimate the decimal equivalent of $\frac{7}{60}$. Answer: **0.117**
(Hint: $\frac{6}{60} + \frac{1}{60} = 0.1 + [0.1 \times \frac{1}{6}]$; "exact" answer is 0.1166 recurring.)

Add additional drills here:

Percentages (Forward)

Response-time goal: 2 seconds or better (dependent upon grade level).

(1) What is 30 increased by 15%? Answer: **34.5**
(Hint: $(0.1 \times 30) \times 1.5 = 4.5$.)

(2) What is 40 decreased by 15%? Answer: **34**

(3) What is 200 decreased by 80%? Answer: **40**

(4) What is 300 increased by 70%? Answer: **510**
(Hint: $70 \times 3 = 210$.)

(5) What is 12 increased by 20%? Answer: **14.4**
(Hint: $2 \times 1.2 = 2.4$.)

(6) What is 15 decreased by 30%? Answer: **10.5**
(Hint: $3 \times 1.5 = 4.5$.)

(7) What is 400 increased by 55%? Answer: **620**
(Hint: $400 + 200 + 20$.)

(8) What is 88 increased by 25%? Answer: **110**
(Hint: $88 \div 4 = 22$.)

(9) What is 75% of 80? Answer: **60**
(Hint: $3 \times (80 \div 4)$.)

(10) What is 60 decreased by 75%? Answer: **15**
(Hint: $60 \div 4 = 15$.)

Add additional drills here:

Percentages (Reverse)

Response-time goal: 2 seconds or better (dependent upon grade level).

(1) What reduced by 15% gives 170? Answer: **200**
(Hint: $(2 \times 85)/(1.00 - 0.15) = 2 \times (85/0.85)$.)

(2) What reduced by 30% gives 210? Answer: **300**
(Hint: $(3 \times 70)/(1.00 - 0.30) = 3 \times (70/0.70)$.)

(3) What increased by 12% gives 56? Answer: **50**
(Hint: $112 = 2 \times 56$; calculate $(0.5 \times 112)/(1.00 + 0.12)$.)

(4) What increased by 3% gives 27.81? Answer: **27**
(Hint: $27.81 = 3^3 + (3^4/100) = 3^3 \times (1.00 + 0.03)$.)

(5) What reduced by 65% gives 7? Answer: **20**
(Hint: $7/(1.00 - 0.65) = (2 \times 3.5)/0.35$.)

(6) What reduced by 35% gives 1.3? Answer: **2**
(Hint: $1.3 = 2 \times 0.65$; calculate $(2 \times 0.65)/(1.00 - 0.35)$.)

(7) What increased by 15% gives 3.45? Answer: **3**
(Hint: $3.45/(1.00 + 0.15) = (3 \times 1.15)/1.15$.)

(8) What increased by 45% gives 29? Answer: **20**
(Hint: $29 = 2 \times 14.5$; calculate $(2 \times 14.5)/(1.00 + 0.45)$.)

(9) What increased by 28% gives 0.256? Answer: **0.2**
(Hint: $0.256 = 2 \times 0.128$; calculate $(2 \times 0.128)/(1.00 + 0.28)$.)

(10) What reduced by 17% gives 830? Answer: **1000**
(Hint: divide by $(1.00 - 0.17)$.)

Add additional drills here:

Percentages for No Net Change (High School)

Response-time goal: 2–5 seconds or better (dependent upon grade level). A very common mistake that students make is to suppose that a percentage change of a given quantity can be reversed by applying the same percentage change in the opposite sense, in order to recover the original value of the given quantity. However, this procedure does *not* recover the original value. For example, 100 increased by 25% is 125, but 125 decreased by 25% is *not* 100 (it is 93.75). In the following drills the student has to find the percentage value that must follow the given increase or decrease in order to recover the original quantity. The worked solutions show the required mental processes in some detail, since students generally find this topic quite tricky. The student is allowed to study the solutions before doing the oral drill because the drill is designed with the assumption that the student has learned how to solve these problems. However, mix up the order of the questions when administering the drill, and make up new, similar questions.

(1) A reduction of 25% followed by what percentage increase gives the original value? Answer: $\mathbf{33\frac{1}{3}\%}$
(Solution: $(1.00 - 0.25) = (3/4)$, and $(3/4)$ must be multiplied by $(4/3)$ in order to give exactly 1.00; i.e. $(3/4)(4/3) = 1$, and $(1.00 - 0.25)(1.00 + 0.33\dot{3}) = 1$, from which $33.3\dot{3}\%$ can be picked out.)

(2) An increase of 25% followed by what percentage decrease gives the original value? Answer: **20%**
(Solution: the reciprocal of $(1.00 + 0.25) = (5/4)$ is $(4/5) = 0.80$, and $0.80 = (1.00 - 0.20)$, hence 0.20, or 20%.)

(3) A reduction of 10% followed by what percentage increase gives the original value? Answer: $\mathbf{11\frac{1}{9}\%}$
(Solution: the reciprocal of $(1.00 - 0.10) = (9/10)$ is $(10/9) = 1 + (1/9)$, so $(1/9)$ is the fractional increase, which is $(100/9) = 11\frac{1}{9}\%$.)

(4) An increase of 10% followed by what percentage decrease gives the original value? Answer: $\mathbf{9\frac{1}{11}\%}$
(Solution: the reciprocal of $(1.00 + 0.10) = (11/10)$ is $(10/11) = 1 - (1/11)$, so $(1/11)$ is the fractional decrease, which is $(100/11) = 9\frac{1}{11}\%$.)

(5) A reduction of 50% followed by what percentage increase gives the original value? Answer: **100%**
(Solution: the reciprocal of $(1.00 - 0.50) = (1/2)$ is $2 = 1.00 + 1.00$, so the fractional increase is 1.00, or 100%.)

(6) An increase of 50% followed by what percentage decrease gives the original value? Answer: **$33\frac{1}{3}\%$**
(Solution: the reciprocal of $1.00 + 0.50 = (3/2)$ is $(2/3) = 1.00 - (1/3)$, so the fractional decrease is $(1/3)$, or $33\frac{1}{3}\%$.)

(7) A reduction of 80% followed by what percentage increase gives the original value? Answer: **400%**
(Solution: the reciprocal of $1.00 - 0.80 = (1/5)$ is $5.00 = 1.00 + 4.00$, so 4 times the original number must be added, so it is 400%.)

(8) An increase of 80% followed by what percentage decrease gives the original value? Answer: **44%**
(Solution: the reciprocal of $1.00 + 0.80 = (9/5)$ is $(5/9) = 1.00 - (4/9)$, so the fractional decrease is $(4/9)$, or $(44/99)$, or approximately 44%.)

(9) A reduction of 40% followed by what percentage increase gives the original value? Answer: **$66\frac{2}{3}$**
(Solution: the reciprocal of $1.00 - 0.40 = (6/10)$ is $(10/6) = 1.00 + (4/6)$, and $(4/6) = (2/3) = 66\frac{2}{3}\%$.)

(10) An increase of 60% followed by what percentage decrease gives the original value? Answer: **37.5%**
(Solution: the reciprocal of $1.00 + 0.60 = (16/10) = (8/5)$ is $(5/8) = 1.00 - (3/8)$, and $(3/8) = (12.5 \times 3)/(12.5 \times 8) = (37.5/100)$.)

Add additional drills here:

Estimation Skills (Middle School)

Response-time goal: 4 seconds or better.
Note that "≈" means "approximately equal to," and "d.p." means "decimal place." Make decisions for rounding up or rounding down that are most appropriate, according to the particular approximations that are made.

(1) As a *simple* fraction, approximately what is $\frac{7}{9} - \frac{1}{5}$? Answer: $\frac{3}{5}$
(Hint: $11 \times 9 \approx 100$, $0.77 - 0.20 = 0.57 \approx 0.6$).

(2) To 1 d.p., approximately what is 1.2×0.79? Answer: **1.0**
(Hint: $12 \times 8 = 96$; "exact" answer is 0.948.)

(3) To 1 d.p., approximately what is 1.41×0.42? Answer: **0.6**
(Hint: $14 \times 4 = 2 \times 7 \times 4 = 56$; "exact" answer is 0.592.)

(4) To 1 d.p., approximately what is the circumference of a circle that has a diameter of 4.2 meters? Answer: **13.0**
(Hint: $\pi \approx 3$, round up 12.6; "exact" answer is 13.2.)

(5) To the nearest 1%, approximately what percentage of the circumference of a circle is its radius? Answer: **16%**
(Hint: $\pi \approx 3$, $(100/3)/2 \approx (33/2)$; "exact" answer is 15.9%.)

(6) To 1 d.p., approximately what is 7.3 divided by 2.3? Answer: **3.0**
(Hint: $12 \times 6 = 72$ and $(7.3/2.3) \approx (72/24) = (6/2)$; "exact" answer is 3.17.)

(7) To 1 d.p., approximately what is 92.3 divided by 8.2? Answer: **11.5**
(Hint: $12 \times 8 = 96$, $(92.3/8.2) \approx (96/8) = 12$, $(96 - 92)/8 \approx 0.5$; "exact" answer is 11.26.)

(8) To 1 d.p., approximately what is the square root of 0.80? Answer: **0.9**
(Hint: $\sqrt{(81/100)} = (9/10)$; "exact" answer is 0.894.)

Continued on next page.

(9) To 1 d.p., approximately what is the square root of 10? Answer: **3.1** (Hint: $\sqrt{9} < \sqrt{10}$; "exact" answer is 3.16.)

(10) To 1 d.p., approximately what is the square root of 8.0? Answer: **2.9** (Hint: $\sqrt{10} > 3$ and $\sqrt{(81/10)} > \sqrt{8}$; "exact" answer is 2.83.)

Additional drills here:

Estimation Skills (High School)

Response-time goal: 4 seconds or better.
Note that "≈" means "approximately equal to," and "d.p." means "decimal place." Make decisions for rounding up or rounding down that are most appropriate, according to the particular approximations that are made.

(1) To 1 d.p., approximately what is 1.2 squared divided by π?
Answer: **0.5** (Hint: $(150/3) = 50$; "exact" answer is 0.46.)

(2) To 1 d.p., approximately what is the square root of 1000 divided by the square root of 11? Answer: **10.0**
(Hint: $\sqrt{1000} = \sqrt{10}\sqrt{100}$, and $\sqrt{11} \approx \sqrt{10}$; "exact" answer is 9.53.)

(3) To 1 d.p., approximately what is the square root of 5? Answer: **2.3**
(Hint: $\sqrt{5} \approx \sqrt{(49/10)}$, and $(7/3) = 2 + (1/3)$; "exact" answer is 2.24.)

(4) To the nearest 100, approximately what is π times 27 squared?
Answer: **2,200** (Hint: $3 \times 3 \times 9 \times 3 \times 9 = 81 \times 3 \times 9 \approx 2,430 - 240$; "exact" answer is 2,290.22.)

(5) To 1 d.p., approximately what is 2.6 squared? Answer: **6.8**
(Hint: $(2 \times 13)^2/100$, and $170 \times 4 = 680$; "exact" answer is 6.76.)

(6) To 1 d.p., approximately what is the ratio of the long side to the short side of a piece of paper that has dimensions of 11.0 inches and 8.5 inches?
Answer: **1.3** (Hint: $(110/85) = 1 + (25/85) \approx 1 + (1/3)$; "exact" answer is 1.29.)

(7) To 1 d.p., approximately what is the square root of 2? Answer: **1.4**
(Hint: $\sqrt{2} = \sqrt{(200/100)} \approx \sqrt{(4 \times 49)/100} = (2 \times 7)/10$; "exact" answer is 1.414.)

(8) To 1 d.p., approximately what is the length of the diagonal of a piece of paper that has dimensions of 11.0 inches and 8.5 inches? Answer: **13.9**
(Hint: $\sqrt{[(11^2) + (8.5^2)]} < \sqrt{(121 + 80)} \approx \sqrt{200} \approx \sqrt{4 \times 49}$; "exact" answer is 13.90.)

Continued on next page.

(9) If a circle is drawn inside a square so that the circle touches all four sides of the square, to the nearest 5%, what is the approximate area of the circle as a percentage of the area of the square? Answer: **75%**
(Hint: $(\pi r^2)/(2r)^2$; "exact" answer is 78.5%.)

(10) A sphere is placed inside a cubic box and the sphere just touches all six sides of the box. To the nearest 5%, approximately what percentage of the volume in the box is not occupied by the sphere? Answer: **50%**
(Hint: $[(4/3)\pi r^3]/(2r)^3$; "exact" answer is 47.6%.)

Additional drills here:

A.3 Precalculus and Calculus

Note that the oral drills in this section do not contain any actual calculus material. What the drills *do* contain are some very basic precalculus topics that I have found are very often not given enough attention by students. Failure to develop speed and accuracy in the topics in the drills significantly impairs a student's performance in precalculus and calculus. The material practiced in these drills comes up extremely frequently, over and over again, in precalculus and calculus problems. However, even the topics covered here are only a bare minimum. By the time a student is studying precalculus and calculus, he/she should be independent enough to construct additional appropriate drills himself/herself, as or when needed.

Drills in this section:

Degrees to Radians Conversion ...	364
Radians to Degrees Conversion ...	365
Trigonometric Function Values	366
Logarithms and Inverse Logarithms	367
Exponents	368

Degrees to Radians Conversion

Response-time goal: 2 seconds or better.
Students may need to review relevant material before doing these drills for the first time.

Convert the following from degrees to radians.
(1) 0°; Answer: **0**
(2) 270°; Answer: Three pi over two (**3π/2**)
(3) 90°; Answer: pi over two (**π/2**)
(4) 360°; Answer: Two pi (**2π**)
(5) 45°; Answer: pi over four (**π/4**)
(6) 60°; Answer: pi over three (**π/3**)
(7) 30°; Answer: pi over six (**π/6**)
(8) 180°; Answer: pi (**π**)
(9) 135°; Answer: Three pi over four (**3π/4**)
(10) 120°; Answer: Two pi over three (**2π/3**)

Additional drills here:

Radians to Degrees Conversion

Response-time goal: 2 seconds or better.
Students may need to review relevant material before doing these drills for the first time.

Convert the following from radians to degrees.
(1) Pi over two ($\pi/2$); Answer: **90°**
(2) Zero; Answer: **0**
(3) Three pi over two ($3\pi/2$); Answer: **270°**
(4) Two pi (2π); Answer: **360°**
(5) Pi (π); Answer: **180°**
(6) Pi over four ($\pi/4$); Answer: **45°**
(7) Pi over six ($\pi/6$); Answer: **30°**
(8) Pi over three ($\pi/3$); Answer: **60°**
(9) Five pi over three ($5\pi/3$); Answer: **300°**
(Hint: $\frac{6\pi}{3} - \frac{\pi}{3} = \frac{5\pi}{3}$.)
(10) Five pi over four ($5\pi/4$): Answer: **225°**
(Hint: $\frac{4\pi}{4} + \frac{\pi}{4} = \frac{5\pi}{4}$.)

Additional drills here:

Trigonometric Function Values

Response-time goal: 2 seconds or better.
Students may need to review relevant material before doing these drills for the first time.

(1) Sine of zero degrees ($\sin 0°$); Answer: **0**
(2) Cosine of 90 degrees ($\cos 90°$); Answer: **0**
(3) Cosine of 60 degrees ($\cos 60°$); Answer: $\frac{1}{2}$
(4) Sine of 180 degrees ($\sin 180°$); Answer: **0**
(5) Sine of 45 degrees ($\sin 45°$); Answer: $1 \div \sqrt{2}$, or $1/\sqrt{2}$
(6) Cosine of 45 degrees ($\cos 45°$); Answer: as for (5), or $1/\sqrt{2}$
(7) Sine of 30 degrees ($\sin 30°$); Answer: $\frac{1}{2}$
(8) Cosine of zero degrees ($\cos 0°$); Answer: **1**
(9) Sine of 90 degrees ($\sin 90°$); Answer: **1**
(10) Sine of 360 degrees ($\sin 360°$); Answer: **0**
(11) Cosine of 30 degrees ($\cos 30°$); Answer: $(\sqrt{3})/2$
(12) Sine of 60 degrees ($\sin 60°$); Answer: $(\sqrt{3})/2$
(14) Tangent of 45 degrees ($\tan 45°$); Answer: **1**
(15) Tangent of 30 degrees ($\tan 30°$); Answer: $1/\sqrt{3}$
(16) Tangent of 60 degrees ($\tan 60°$); Answer: $\sqrt{3}$

Additional drills here:

Logarithms & Inverse Logarithms

Response-time goal: 2 seconds or better.

(1) Log in base 10 of 10? Answer: **1**
(2) Log in base 10 of 1? Answer: **0**
(3) Log in base 10 of 100? Answer: **2**
(4) Log in base 10 of one million? Answer: **6**
(5) Log in base 10 of 0.1? Answer: **−1**
(6) Inverse log in base 10 of 3? Answer: **1000**
(7) Inverse log in base 10 of 0? Answer: **1**
(8) Inverse log in base 10 of 1? Answer: **10**
(9) Inverse log in base 10 of 2? Answer: **100**
(10) Inverse log in base 10 of −2? Answer: **0.01**

Additional drills here:

Exponents

Response-time goal: 2 seconds or better.

(1) What is 10 to the power of 0? Answer: **1**
(2) What is e to the power of 1? Answer: **e**
(3) What is 2 to the power of 3? Answer: **8**
(4) What is e to the power of 0? Answer: **1**
(5) What is 2 to the power of -1? Answer: **0.5**
(6) What is 10 to the power of -1? Answer: **0.1**
(7) What is 2 to the power of 0? Answer: **1**
(8) What is 10 to the power of -3? Answer: **0.001**
(9) What is 2 to the power of -2, *as a fraction*? Answer: $\frac{1}{4}$
(10) What is 3 to the power of -2, *as a fraction*? Answer: $\frac{1}{9}$

Additional drills here:

Index

χ^2 and χ^2 distribution, *see* chi-squared
Å, *see* Angstrom

AAA, 169
AAS, 169
abelian, 169
abilities (for math), 6, **13**, **14**, **23**, **25**, 27, **28**, **32**, **33**, 37, 73, 114, **121**, 151
abscissa, plural abscissae, 169
absolute value, **170**, **251**, **256**, 289
acceleration, **170–171**, 223, 252, 257, 260, 319
accuracy
 meaning of, **171**, 275
 numerical, 147, **171**
 of work, 37, 39, **138**, 151, **157**, **324**
ACT (exams), 112, 141, 144, 150
active memory, *see* memory, active
active studying, *see* studying, active
acute
 angle, **171**, 172
 triangle, 171
addend, 171
addition formulas, *see* trigonometric addition formulas
additive
 identity, 172
 inverse, **172**, 193
adjacent
 angle, 172
 side, **172**, 219
AEA, *see* alternate exterior angles

agility, mental, *see* mental agility
AIA, *see* alternate interior angles
algebra, 27, 59, 113, 116, 123, **162**, **172**, 193, 201, 224, 227, **247–248**, 253, 275, **286**, **296**, 297, 308
 Boolean, *see* Boolean logic
 linear, **247–248**, 253
algebraic
 expression, 26, **71**, 72, 73, 146, **146**, **150**, **162**, 170, **173**, 190, 191, **213**, **215**, 219, 221–223, 233, 242, **246**, 248, **252**, 257, 261, 268, 269, 274, 275, 278, 280, 282, 285–287, 289, 290, 295, 296, 299, 300, **303**, **306**, 308, 316, 317
 number, 173
alternate
 exterior angles, 173
 interior angles, 173
altitude, **173**, 213, 265
analytic, 173
 geometry, *see* coordinate geometry
 skills, 13, 162
angle
 -angle-angle, *see* AAA
 -angle-side, *see* AAS
 -side-angle, *see* ASA
 -side-side, *see* SSA
 acute, *see* acute angle
 adjacent, 172

bisector, **174**, 234
central, *see* central angle
complementary, *see* complementary angle
coterminal, *see* coterminal angle
Euler, *see* Euler angle
measure of, *see* measure of an angle
obtuse, *see* obtuse angle, 263
right, *see* right angle
supplementary, *see* supplementary angle
Angstrom, 174
angular momentum, **174**, 257
angular speed, 174
antecedent, 174
antilog, *see* antilogarithm
antilogarithm, 174, 250
aphelion, 175
apothem, **175**, 237
aptitude (for math), *see* intuition
arc, 175
arccos, arccosine, 175
arccosec, arccosecant, 175
arccot, arccotangent, 175
Archimedes, 175
arcminute, 176
arcsec
    (arcsecant), 176
    (arcsecond), 176
arcsin, arcsine, 176
arctan, arctangent, 176
area, 33, **176**, 205, 230, **234**, 238, 262, 290, 291, 297, **304**, 310
Arg, 176, 177
Argand diagram, **176**, 177
argument, **177**, 179, 211, 212, 256, 277, 304
arithmetic
    mean, 177
    mental, *see* mental arithmetic
    progression, *see* arithmetic series

    sequence, *see* arithmetic series
    series, 178, 192
ASA, 178
aspect ratio, 178
ASS, *see* SSA
associative property, 178
astronomy, 47–48
asymptote, 63, 66, 69, 70, **178**
attitude
    (as in spatial orientation), 179
    positive, 25, 122
    to math, 17, **18–20**, 23, 25
    to studying, 17
augmented matrix, 179
average, 29, 92, 148, 149, 171, 177, **179**, **218**, **244**, 254, 273, **276**, **291**, 300, **302**, 319
axes, *see* axis
axiom, 179, 227
axis, 60–64, 66, 67, 69, 158, 159, 169, **179**, **198**, **199**, 204, 234, 239, 263, 265, 268, 280, 294, 309, **321–322**
    of rotation, 215, 273, **292**
    of symmetry, **179**, 195, 251, 255, 267, **288**, 291, **304**
    polar, 273

bar graph, 60, 62, **181**, 230
base, **181**, 182, 189, 192, 260, 367
basic logistic function, *see* logistic function
basis vectors, *see* vectors, basis
bearing, 182
bell curve, **182**, **187**, 226, 261, 300
best fit, **182**, 245, 256, 288, 301
best use of tutoring, *see* tutoring, optimal use of
biconditional, 182
binary, 181–182
binomial, **183**, 257
    coefficients, 183

probability distribution, **183**, 269
series, 183
bisect, 183
bisector, 184, 190
   of an angle, **174**, 234
blackouts (in exams), 122, 161
Boolean algebra, *see* Boolean logic
Boolean logic, 184
boundary conditions, 184
bounded, 184, 185
   above, 184, 185
   below, 185
boundedness, 185
box and whisker plot, 185
Boyle's law, 185
branches
   of a graph, 64–66, **75–82**, **185**, 231
   of a hyperbola, **185**, 231
breaks (in studying), *see* concentration

calculator, 17, 26, **27**, 31, **146**, 147, 171, 173, 324
   graphing, *see* graphing calculator
   limitations of, 27, 32–33, 72–84, 324
   problems with, 27, 32–33
calculus, 12, 14, 25, 26, 38, 40, 50, 56, **72**, 100, 105, 135, **186**, 188, 189, **205**, **207**, 222, **238**, **239**, 246, 247, **262**, 268, 277, 282, 290, 291, 297, 298, 310, 323–325, **363–368**
calorie, **186**, 215, 243
capacity, 133
   potential energy, 274
   volume, 187
cardinal number, 186
cardioid curve, 186, 247
Cartesian, 186
   coordinates, **187**, **198**, **199**, 227, 273, 287, 321
case studies, 25–27, 116–119

center of coordinates, 187
centimeter, 170, **187**
central
   angle, 187
   limit theorem, 187
centroid, **187**, 217
Ceva's theorem, 188
Cevian, 188
   circle, 188
   triangle, 188
chain rule, 188
change
   of base, 189
   of variable, 189
characteristic polynomial, 189
Charles's law, 189
checklist for
   graphing, 158–159
   homework, 55–56
   tutoring criteria, 90–93, 103
chi-squared (χ^2), **189**, 232, 301
   distribution, **189**, 232
chord, 190
circle, 62, 159, 175, 187, **190**, 196, 200, 202, 206, 213–215, 218, 223, 230, 237, 244, 271, 273, 283, 294, 297, 318
circular function, 190
circumcenter, **190**, 217
circumference, 187, **190**, 202, 215, 244, 271, 283, 294
circumscribed (circle), 190
closed
   interval, 190
   solution, 190
closure property, 190
cm, *see* centimeter
coaching, *see* tutoring
coefficient, 191
   binomial, 183
   correlation, 191, **199**, **288–289**
   leading, 244

polynomial, 191
regression, 191, **199**, **288–289**
cofactor, 191
cofunction, 191
cognitive
    abilities, *see* mental abilities
    skills, *see* mental skills
college, 98, 100, **134**, 248
collinear, 191
columns (of a matrix), **191**, 206, **252**, 264, 266, 300, 309
combinations, combinatrics, 191
common
    denominator, **192**, 227, 245
    difference, 178, 192
    logarithm, **192**, 252
    mistakes, *see* mistakes
    ratio, **192**, 226
communication with your child (about math), *see* personal interaction
commutative property, 169, **192**
complement, 193
complementary angle, 193
completing the square, 193
complex
    conjugate, **193**, 196
    fraction, *see* compound fraction
    harmonic motion, *see* harmonic motion
    number(s), 72, 170, **176–177**, **193–194**, 196, 204, 217, **233**, 251, 256, 286
    roots, 194
component (of a vector), *see* vector components
composite
    function, *see* compound function
compound
    fraction, 194
    function, 189, **194**, 225, 239, 282
    interest, **195**, 228

computers, **17**, 20, **31**, 44, 72, 79, 83, 84, 173, 193, 209, **222**, 246, 316
    applications for math, *see* software tools
concave, 195
concentration (for studying), 54, 123
concurrent, 195
conditional
    equation, 195
    probability, 195
    statement, 147, 174, **182**, **195**, 256
cone, **195**, 196, 291
confidence building, 25, 52, 139, 140
confidence level (statistics), **195**, 288
congruence, *see* congruent
congruent, 196
conic sections, **196**, 204, 208, 222, 231, 244, 281
conjecture, 196
conjugate, 196
    axis of a hyperbola, 196
    of a complex number, 193, 196
    of a matrix, 196
consequent, 197, 275
constant, 197
    in quadratics, 193
continuity
    in problem solving, 56, 160
    in tutoring, 89, 92
    of a function, **197**, 209, 240
continuous, 185, **197**, 209
contrapositive, 197
converge, **197**, 210
convergence, *see* converge
converse, 198
convex, 195, **198**
coordinate
    axes, 179, **198**, 309, 321
    geometry, 174, **198**
    plane, 199
    system, 187, 198, **199**, 227, 263,

265, **273**, 274, 280, 287, 309, 321
coordinates, **72**, 76, 187, **199**, 255, 264, 265, 272, **273**, 281, 308
    Cartesian, **187**, **198, 199,** 227, 273, 321
    center of, 187
    polar, 273
    rectangular, **187**, 263, 280, **287**
coplanar, 199
corollary, 199
correlation, **199**, 310
    coefficient, 191, **199, 288–289**
    spurious, 289, 299
corresponding angles, 173, **200**
cos, *see* cosine
cosec, *see* cosecant
cosecant, 175, **200**, 313
cosh, *see* hyperbolic functions
cosine, 175, 190, **200, 201,** 208, 294, 297, 298, 305, 313, **366**
    rule, 200
cot, *see* cotangent
cotangent, 175, **201**, 313
coterminal angle, 201
Cramer's rule, 201
crib sheet, 163–322
    how to use, **7–10**, 52–53, 165–167
    when to use, 52–53
cross product, *see* vector product
cube root, **201**, 262, 283
cube, cubed, cubing, 201
cubic, 201, 307
curve fitting, 182, 191, **202**, 204, 245, 249, **288**
cycloid, 202
cylinder, 202

damped harmonic motion, 203, 229
damped oscillation, 203, 229
damping, 203, 229
dates (on notes and worksheets), 50–51

dB, *see* decibel
De Moivre's theorem, 204
De Morgan's law, 205
decibel (dB), 203
deductive reasoning, 177, **203**, 235
definite integral, **203**, 234, 262, 290, 291, 297, 310
degenerate, 204
degree (of a polynomial), **204**, 223, 274, 280–282, 307
degrees of freedom, 204
denominator, **192**, 194, **205**, 227, 230, 234, 245, **268**, 286, 288
density, 170, 187, **205**
dependent
    event, 205
    variable, **205**, 233, 235
derivative, 189, **205, 207**, 233, 277, 282
Descartes' rule of signs, 205
determinant, 206
diagnostic testing, 99, 105, **108–110**, 116, 138
diagonal (of a matrix), 206, 315
diagrams, 49, 55, **115**, 125, **135**, 160, 163
    tree, 310
    Venn, 317–318
diameter (of a circle or sphere), **206**, 271, 294
difference of two squares, 206
difference quotient, 207
differentiable, 207
differential, 207
differential equation, 207
differentiation, **186, 205**, 207, 233, 277
dihedral angle, 207
dimensional analysis, 146, 207
dimensions
    as in units, 163, **207**, 246, 315
    matrices, 72, 252, 253, 264
    spatial, 169, 170, 179, 187, **199**, 217, 218, 227, 230, 233, 237,

239, 242, 246, 251, 263–267, 270–274, 276, 278, 280, 281, 286, 288, 291, 292, 299, 304, 306, 318, 321
direct variation, 209
directed distance, 208
direction angle, direction cosine, 208
directly proportional, *see* direct variation
directrix, **208**, 244
discipline, 133–134, 138
discontinuity, 209
discrete, discrete mathematics, 209
discriminant, 209
dispersion, **210**, 240, 300
displacement, **210**, 298
distance formula, 210
distractions (from studying), *see* concentration
distribution, **210**, 218, 269, 281, 300
    binomial, 183
    chi-squared (χ^2), 189
    frequency, 224, 230
    Gaussian, **226**, 261
    normal, 182, 226, **261**
    Poisson, 273
    probability, 182–183, 187, 189, 210, 226, 261, 269, 273, **276**
distributive law, *see* distributive property
distributive property, 210
diverge, divergent, 210
divergent series, 210, 211
dividend, **211**, 289, 290
divisor, 211
DMS, 211
dodecahedron, dodecahedra, 211
domain, 211, 284
dot product, *see* scalar product
double valued, 212
double-angle formulas, 211
drills, oral, *see* oral drills

e, **213**, 217, 219
eccentricity, **213**, 214
eigenvalues, 213
element(s) (of a matrix), 193, 196, 206, 209, **213**, 233, **252**, **253**, 255, 264, 292, 315, 322
elevation, 213
elimination
    of a variable, **214**, 297, 303
    of causes of difficulty, 54
    of multiple-choice answers, 143, 145–154
    of tutoring candidates, 102
ellipse, **196**, **213**, **214**, 223, 251, 255, 294
ellipsoid, 214
empathy (for attitude to math), 18–19, 21
empirical, **214**, 235
empty set, 214
end behavior, 214
energy, 186, **215**, 243, 274, 275, 319
    kinetic, 243
    potential, 274
equation(s)
    conditional, 195
    differential, 207
    general, 5, 19, 125, 126, 135, 160, 162, 190, **195**, 197, 204, 214, **215**, 218, **223**, 224, 233, 236, 237, 246, **286**, 292, **296–297**, **303**, 306, **315**
    implicit, 233, 234
    integral, 238
    linear, 201, **247**, 288, 297
    matrix, **72**, 179, 206, 209, 213, 248, 288, **297**, 311
    mnemonics for, 255
    of a conic section, 204, 231, 267, **281**
    parametric, 268
    polar, 273

polynomial, 205, 286, 308
quadratic, 16–18, 129, **280**, 281, 350
simultaneous, 179, 201, 206, 214, 288, **297**
solution of, **72**, 163, 172, 179, 190, 193, 194, 201, **204**, 205, 206, 209, 213, **214–215**, 219, 238, 247, **286**, 288, 290, **291**, 297, 303, 308, 309, 311, 315
transposing, 309
trigonometric, 211
vector, 317
with complex numbers, 204
equator, **215**, 244
equiangular, 215
equiangular triangle, *see* equilateral triangle
equidistant, 190, 215
equilateral, 215
  polygon, 216
  triangle, 215, **216**, 233, 306
equilibrium, 216
equivalent fractions, 216
escape velocity, 216
estimation, 276
  by extrapolation, 220, 288
  of tutoring costs, 90–96
  oral drills, 40–41, 339, 352–353, 358–361
  order of magnitude, 163, **251**
  skills, 34–37, 40–41, 43, 146–147, 163, 339, 352–353, 358–361
Euclidean (geometry), **216**, 261, 271
Euler
  angles, 216
  constant, 217
  formula, 217
  line, 217
  number, 213, 217, 219
evaluation (of a function), **71**, 72, 74, 150, 203, **217**, 303

even function, 218
exams
  blackouts in, 122, **161**
  critical keywords for, 156
  graphing checklist, 61–64, 158–159
  graphing in, 158–159
  maximizing performance in, 7, **121–127**, 137, **140**, 141
  mental preparation for, 140
  mistakes in, 39, **40**, **42–43**, 56, 59, 139–140, **144–145**, **150–151**, **156**, 157, 160, 162–163
  night before, 140
  order of attacking questions in, 155–156
  preparation courses, 111–113, 141
  preparation for, *see* exams, studying for
  reviewing for, 51, 104, **125**, **129–135**, **137–141**
  simulated, 123, 133, **137–141**, 156, 157
  standardized, 110, **111–112**, **141**, 144–145, **150–154**
  strategy during, 137, 154–163
  studying for, **54–55**, **59–66**, **110–113**, **121–135**, 137–141
  timekeeping during, 39, 40, 43, 50, 99, 104, 138, **156–158**
excircle, 218
expectation value, 218
expected value, *see* expectation value
explicit
  equation, *see* explicit function
  formula, *see* explicit function
  function, 218, 233
  rule, *see* explicit function
exponent, 105, **218**, 219, **224**, 235, 251, 261, 274, 275, **294**, 368
exponential, **219**, 228
  decay, 219, **228**

function, 213, 217, **219**, 231
   growth, 219, **228**
   number (the), 213
expression, *see* algebraic expression
exterior angles, 173, 200, **219**
extraneous solution, 219
extrapolate, extrapolation, 220

factor, **38**, **221**, 227, 230, 247, 276, **289**, 290, 347
   linear, 26, **248**, 304
   prime, 275
   scale, **61**, **261**, 296
factorial, 221
factoring, 221
factorization, **221**, 248, 276, **350**
factors
   holding students back, 25–27, 31–33, 40, 61, 73–84, 112
   of polynomials, 221
Fibonacci number, Fibonacci sequence, 221
finite, 190, **221**
   difference, 222
   number of pixels, 74
   numerical resolution, 74
   sequence, 222
first
   octant, *see* octant
   quadrant, *see* quadrant
   quartile, *see* quartile
fitting, *see* curve fitting
floating point (representation), **222**, 251
focal length, 222
foci, *see* focus
focus, 222, 267
FOIL (method), 221, 223
force, 174, **223**, 224, 234, **236**, 249, 256, 257, **260**, 291, 301, **307**, 313, 316, **317**, **319**
formula, **126**, **135**, **146**, 160, 176, 192, 202, 204, 214, 215, **217**, **223**, **224**, 231, 234, 255, **255**, 270, 304
   crib sheet entry, 223
   distance, 210
   midpoint, 255
   quadratic, 193, **280**
   recursive, 287
   trigonometric, 200, 211, 229, 297, 312
fourth-degree polynomial, 223
fractal, 223
fraction
   as a probability, 276
   as in proportions, **278**, 285
   complex, *see* compound fraction
   compound, 194
   equivalent, 216
   general, 5, 16, 17, **28**, **35**, 192, 205, 224, 245, 262
   improper, 234
   in an exponent, **224**, **252**, 274
   in oral drills, 335–336, 351–353
   partial, 268
   reduced, 288
free fall, 224
frequency, **224**, 230, 271
   distribution, 182, **224**, **230**
friction, 224
   kinetic, **243**, 301
   static, 243, **301**
function, **224**, **306**, 314, 316
   argument to a, 177
   calculator, **32**, **71**, 72, 74, 79
   composite, *see* compound function
   compound, 189, **194**, 225, 239, 282
   continuity of, **197**, 209, 240
   evaluation of, 71, 72, **74**, **150**, 203, **217**, 303
   even, 218
   explicit, 218

exponential, 213, 217, **219**, 231
graph of, **62–65**, 71, 72, 74, **75**, **76**, 78, **79**, **185**, 204, 237, 239, 253–255, 268, 272, 291, 297, **298**, 301, 303, 309, 310, 318
hyperbolic, 231
implicit, 233
inverse, 241
linear, 247
logarithmic, 250
odd, 263
of a function, 225
polynomial, 183, 201, 204, 205, 257, **274**
quadratic, 280
slope of a, **298**, 301
step, 302
trigonometric, 73, 175, 176, 190, 200, 201, 211, 217, 229, 294, 297, 305, 312, **313**
wrapping, 319
zeros of a, 322
fundamental theorem of algebra, 225

gallon, *see* litre
Gaussian, 226
 distribution, 182, **226**, 261
generating function, 226
geometric
 mean, 226
 progression, 192, 226
 proof, 6, 16, 17, **100**, **135**, 169, 178, **226**, 300
 ratio, *see* common, ratio
 series, *see* geometric progression
geometry, 99, 105, 123, **135**, 173, 188, 190, 196, 200, 207, 215, **226**, **227**, 254, **271**, 272, 277, 288, 289, 296, 308, 309, **311**, 318
 analytic, *see* coordinate geometry
 coordinate, 174, **198**

Euclidean, **216**, 261, 271
non-Euclidean, **261**, 271
glossary, *see* crib sheet
goals
 achievement of, 4, **19**, 21, 101, **119**
 for review sessions, 129–130
 for tutorials, 85, 93, 95, 96, **99**, **104, 105**
golden ratio, 227
grade level, 1, **2, 3, 7**, 8, 9, 25–27, 30, **32**, **38**, 40, **50**, **53**, **56**, **90**, 99, **99, 100**, 101, 114, **121**, 140, 146, 162, **165**, **323–368**
grades
 dropped, 33, 116–119
 good, 13, 19, 24, **32**, **37**, **40**, 85, 106, **122**, 139
 poor, **116–119**, 121, 122, **156**
gradient (of a function), *see* slope
graphing
 by hand, 59–66, 114, 158–160
 checklist, 61–64, 158–159
 general, 57–84, 158–159
 mistakes in, *see* mistakes in graphing
 problems with, 60–61, 64
 skill in, *see* skills, graphing
graphing calculator
 developing intuition for, 72–84, 99, 113–114
 general, 59, 71–84
 major pitfalls of, 72–84
 matrix calculations, 72
 memory jogger for, 71, 84
 problems with, 64, 65, 72–84
 unique capabilities of, 59, 71–72
graphs
 checklist for, 61–64
 scale, axes, and resolution, 60–61
 types of, 59–60, 64
greatest common

denominator, 227
divisor, 227
factor, 227
grid, 227
grid-ins, 144–145
group (theory), 169, 228
growth rate, 219, **228**

half-angle formulas, 212, **229**
half-life, 229
half-plane, 229
hand-drawn graphs, *see* graphing by hand
harmonic motion, 203, **229**, 296
    complex, 229
    damped, 229
    simple, 229
Heaviside step function, *see* step function
helical, 229
helices, 230
helix, 230
hemisphere, **230**, 244
Heron's (or Hero's) formula, 230
Hertz, 230
highest common denominator (HCD), *see* greatest common denominator (GCD)
highest common divisor (HCD), *see* greatest common divisor (GCD)
highest common factor (HCF), *see* greatest common factor (GCF)
histogram, 60, 181, **224**, **230**
homework, 16, **33**, **51**, **73**, 106, 116, 131, **165**
    checking for mistakes, 33
    checklist, 55–56
    helping with, 33, 53–56, 120
    organization of, 50–51
    problems with, 53–55
    taking too long, 54
Hooke's law, 230
horizontal-line test, 231
hyperbola, 185, 196, 223, **231**, 294
hyperbolic, 231
hyperbolic functions, 231
hypotenuse, 172, **232**
hypothesis, 177, 189, **195**, **196**, 204, **232**, 274, 288, 295
    null, 232
    testing, 232
hypothesize, 232, 274
Hz, *see* Hertz

icosahedra, 233
icosahedron, 233
identity
    additive, 172
    general, 233
    matrix, **233**, 253, 258, 266, 315
    multiplicative, 258
    trigonometric, 313
imaginary number, 193–194, **233**
implicit
    differentiation, 233
    equation(s), 233
    function, 233
improper fraction, 234
incenter, **234**, 237
inch, 187, **234**
inclined plane, 234
indefinite integral, 203, **234**
independent
    event, 205, **235**
    tutor, **86–89**, 90, 94, 95, **98–103**
    variable, 205, 219, 233, **235**, 322
index, 218, 235
induction, *see* proof by induction
inductive reasoning, 177, 203, **235**, 278
inequality, **236**, 308
inertia, inertial mass, **236**, 252

inexpensive tutoring, *see* tutoring, ideas for reducing cost of
infinite, 177, 190, 221, 222, **236**, 247, 274, 286, 294, **303**, **308**
  sequence, *see* infinite series
  series, 183, 210, **236**, 303
infinitesimal, 237
infinity, 178, **236**, 284, **303**, 314
inflection (or inflexion), **237**, 293, 301, 313, 318
initial side, 301
initial value(s), 237
inner product, *see* scalar product
inradius, 175, **237**
inscribed
  circle, 175, **237**
  triangle, 237
inspiration, 21, 90, 150
integer, 26, 183, **186**, 192, **209**, 218, 221, 227, **237**, 241, 260, 275, 276, 285, 286
integrable, 238
integral, **203–204**, **234**, **238**, **262**, 290, 291, 297, 310
  definite, **203**, 234, **262**, 290, 291, 297, 310
  equation, 238
  indefinite, 203, **234**, 239
integrand, 238
integrate, 238
integration, 186, **238**, **239**, 262, 291, 297, 310
  by parts, 239
  constant, 239
  numerical, 262
intercept, 239
interest
  compound, **195**, 228
  simple, 296
interior angles, 173, 200, **239**, 286
intermediate value theorem, 240
internet, **3**, **9–10**, 16, 41, 53, 96, 98, **166**, 246
math aids and resources, 9–10, 41–48
websites, 3, 8, 53
interpolate, interpolation, 240
interpretation (of exam questions), 60, 114–115, 155–156
interquartile range, 240
intersection, 188, 190, **240**, 280
intuition
  for math, learning and developing, 21–48, 73
  graphing calculator, *see* graphing calculator, developing intuition for
  hinderances to developing, 41–48, 65, 73, 126, 151
invariant, 240
inverse
  additive, **172**, 193
  cosine, *see* arccos
  function, 241
  general, 241, **241**, 261
  logarithm, *see* antilogarithm
  matrix, **241**, 253
  multiplicative, 258
  of a function, 241
  sine, *see* arcsin
  tangent, *see* arctan
inversely proportional, 241
invertible, 241
irrational number, **241**, 286
irreducible, 242
isobar, 242
isometric projection, 242
isometry, 242
isosceles
  trapezoid, 242
  triangle, 242
isothermal, 242
isotropic, 242

Joule, 186, 215, **243**, 319

kg, *see* kilogram
kilogram (kg), 243
kilometer (km), 243
kinetic
    energy, 243
    friction, **243**, 301
km, *see* kilometer

l'Hôpital's rule, 246
L, *l*, *see* litre
large numbers
    law of, 218, **244**, 276, 302
    multiplication of, 244, **344**
latitude, 244
lattice multiplication, 244
latus rectum, 244
law of cosines, *see* cosine rule
law of large numbers, 218, **244**, 276, 302
law of sines, *see* sine rule
layout of work (in problem solving), 55–56, 160
leading coefficient, leading term, 244
leaf-of-stem plot, *see* stem-and-leaf plot
learning
    intuition for math, 21–48, 73
    receptiveness to, 17, 21, 30
    speed in mental arithmetic, *see* mental, arithmetic, speed in
least common
    denominator (LCD), 245
    multiple (LCM), 245
least squares
    fit, 245
    line, 245
Leibniz, 245
Leibniz's rule, 246
lemma, 246
lemniscate curve, 246

length, 170, 173, 184, **187**, 200, **208**, 215, 216, **227**, 242, **246**, 251, **254**, 255, 267, 269, 270, 273, 274, 287, 289, 290, 293, 294, 297, 299, 311, 312, 315
like terms, **246**, 315
limaçon, 186, 247
limit (of a function), 247
line graph, 247
line of symmetry, *see* axis of symmetry
linear, **247**, 278
    algebra, **247–248**, 253
    equation, 201, **247**, 288, 297
    factor, *see* factor, linear
    factorization theorem, 221, **248**
    function, 247
    growth rate, 228
    interpolation, 240
    programming, 249
    regression, 249, **288**
    speed, 249
linearly
    dependent, 248
    independent, 248
litre, 249
loci, 249
locus, 190, 249
log, *see* logarithm
logarithm, 105, **175**, **192**, 241, **249**, 260, 277, **367**
    common, 192
    natural, 260
logarithmic, 249
logic, 177, **184**, 193, 205, **250**
logistic function, 250
longitude, 250
lower quartile, *see* quartile
lowest common denominator, *see* least common denominator
lowest common multiple, *see* least common multiple

m, *see* meter
Maclaurin series, *see* Taylor series
magnitude, 163, 170, **251**
major axis, **251**, 294
mantissa, **251**, 294, 295
many-to-one, 252
map, map onto, **252**, **263**, 277
mapping, **252**, 263
    many-to-one, 252
    one-to-one, 263
mass, 205, **208**, 223, **236**, **252**, 254, 319
materials and supplies checking, 52
math terms, *see* crib sheet
matrices, *see* matrix
matrix, 252–253
    addition, 253
    additive identity, 172
    additive inverse, 172
    algebra, 253, 311
    augmented, 179
    cofactor, 191
    columns, *see* columns (of a matrix)
    complex conjugate of a, **193**, 196
    conjugate of a, 196
    determinant of a, 206
    diagonal of a, **206**, 315
    discriminant of a, 209
    element(s) of a, 193, 196, 206, 209, **213**, 233, **252, 253**, 255, 264, 292, 315, 322
    equation, **72**, 213, **297**, 311
    inverse, 241, 253
    inversion, 253
    multiplication, 253, 258
    nonsingular, 241
    order of a, 264
    orthogonal, 266
    reduced row echelon form, 288
    rows, *see* rows (of a matrix)
    singular, 241
    square, 206, 233, 241, 266, **300**

trace of a, 307
transpose of a, 266, **309**
triangular, 311
triangularization of a, 311
unit, 233, 253, 258, 266, **315**
zero, 322
maxima, maximum, 237, **253**
mean, 254
    arithmetic, 177
    geometric, 226
    weighted, *see* weighted mean
measure of an angle, 244, 254, 278, 283, 311
median
    in statistics, 185, 240, **254**
    in triangles, 188, **254**
memory
    active, 55, 123–125, 130–133, 135, 137, 138
    aids, 125–127, 133, 255
    jogger, 8, 71, 84, 106, 125, 132, **165**
    long-term, 55, 125, 133
    passive, 130
mental
    abilities, 13–14, 17, 29, 30
    agility, 29, 37, 323–368
    arithmetic, 27–32, 34, 35, 323–368
    speed in, 26, 37–39, 44, 50, 324
    preparation (for exams), 140
    skills, 13–14, 17, 29, 32, 34, 38, 39, 55, 60, 123, 132, 324
mentoring, *see* tutoring
meter, 187, 254
metric system, 254
midpoint, 188, 255
    theorem, 255
mile
    nautical, 260
    statute, 302
minima, minimum,

minor
    axis, **255**, 294
    of a matrix element, 255
mistakes in
    graphing, 52, 55, 59–61, 63–66, 73, 160
    study techniques, 130, 132
    your own work, learning to find, 31–33, 41–44, 49, 73, 114, 147, 163
mnemonics, 126, 223, **255**
mod, *see* modulo
mode (statistics), 255
model, 182, **255**, **288**, 301, 316
modulo, 256
modulus, 256
modus ponens, 256
modus tollens, 256
moment, 256, 307
moment of inertia, 257
momentum, 174, **257**
money rule (for mental arithmetic), 28–31
monomial, 257
monotonic, 257
motivation for studying, 11–18, 20, 133–134
multinomial, 257
multiple choice, *see* multiple-choice questions
multiple-choice questions
    elimination techniques, 143, 145–154
    general, 130, 139–154
    guessing, 147–150
    mistakes in, 144–145, 151
    pick-a-number strategy, 150–154
    timekeeping for, 143–144
    with penalties, 148–150
multiplication
    drills, **38**, 40, **332–333**, 342, **344–347**

lattice method, 244
of matrices, 253
tables, **26**, 27, **34**, 40, 50, 105
multiplication property of equality, 258
multiplicative
    identity, 258
    inverse, 258
multivalued, 212, 258
music (while studying), 123
mutually
    exclusive, 258
    orthogonal, 208, **259**
    perpendicular, 182, 208, **259**, 266

nanonmeter (nm), 260
natural
    logarithm, 260
    number, 186, 191, 237, **260**
nautical mile, 260
neatness, importance of, 55, 61–62, 159–160
negation, 260
negative number, 170, **172**, 191, **193**, 194, 237, **260**
Newton's laws (of motion), 12, 260
nm, *see* nanometer (nm)
non-Euclidean (geometry), **261**, 271
noninvertible, 261
nonsingular matrix, 241
normal
    curve, 261
    direction in geometry, 261
    distribution, 182, 226, **261**
normalization, normalize, **261**, 266
notes
    dating, 50–51
    organization of, 50–51
    use of, 124, 130, 131
nth power, 261
nth root, 226, **262**, 283
null hypothesis, 232
number

algebraic, 173
cardinal, 186
complex, 72, 170, **176–177**, **193–194**, 196, 204, 217, **233**, 251, 256, 286
imaginary, **193–194**, 233
integer, 237
irrational, 241, 286
line, 262
natural, *see* natural number
negative, 170, **172**, 191, **193**, 194, 237, **260**
ordinal, 265
prime, 275, 276
random, 284
rational, 285, 286
real, 194, 241, 280, **286**
transcendental, 307
triangular, 311
numerator, 194, 234, **262**, 268, **288**
numerical integration, 262

objective function, *see* linear programming
oblique triangle, 263
obtuse
    angle, 263
    triangle, 263
octant, 263
odd function, 263
one's complement, 193
one-to-one mapping, 263
open interval, 263
operation, 264
opposite side, 264
oral drills, 10, 28, **34–41**, 44, 50, **56–57**, 115–116, **323–368**
    addition, 328–330
    degrees to radians, 364
    division, 334, 343, 345
    estimation, 339, 352–353, 358–361
    exponents, 368
    factors, 350
    fractions, 335–336, 351–353
    help from tutor, 115–116
    how to use, 323–325
    logarithms, 367
    multiplication, 332–333, 342, 344, 346–347
    percentages, 336–338, 351–357
    radians to degrees, 365
    square roots, 349
    squares, 348
    subtraction, 331
    trigonometric functions, 366
order
    of a matrix, 264
    of a polynomial, *see* degree (of a polynomial)
    of magnitude, 163, 251, **264**
    of operations, 210, **264**
ordered pair, or ordered triple, 264
ordinal number, 265
ordinate, 265
organization of work, 50–51
origin (of coordinate system), 187, **265**, 274
orthocenter, 217, **265**
orthogonal, 199, 259, **265**
    matrix, 266
    vectors, 182, **265–266**
orthographic drawing, 266
orthonormal basis vectors, 266
oscillate, oscillation, 266

panic (over tests and exams), 122, 161
parabola, 196, 208, 223, **267**
paraboloid, 267
parallel, 272
parallel lines, 267
parallelogram, 267
    rule, 267
parameter, 256, 267

parametric
    curve, *see* parametric equation
    equation, 268
parent population, *see* population
parental
    concerns, 5, 71, 112–113, 141
    role (in helping with math), 6–11, 29–31, 37–41, 47–50, 54–57, 114, 134, 138
partial
    fraction, 268
    sums, 268
Pascal's triangle, 268
pentagon, 211, **269**
percentile, 254, **269**
perfect square, 269
    trinomial, 269
performance
    poor, 23, 49, 54, 56, 61, 108, 114–119, 125, 129, 131, 137, 138
    ways to improve, 2, 28, 29, 40–41, 49, 51, 56, 61, 85, 99, 109, 112, 114–115, 118–119, 125
perihelion, 269
perimeter, 175, **270**
period, periodic, **229**, **270**, 271, 298
permutation, 192, **270**
perpendicular, 259, 265, **270**, 272
    lines, 270
    normal, 261
    vectors, 182
personal interaction, 3, 7–11, 44, 50, 52–53, 324
perspective (geometry), 270
phase, phase shift, 271
pi (π), 271
pie chart, 62, **271**
piecewise, 272
planar, 272
plane, 199, 207, 229, **272**
    figure, 272
    inclined, 234

point, **264**, 265, **272**, 273, 274, 299
point-slope form, 272
Poisson distribution, 273
polar
    axis, 273
    coordinates, 273
    equation, 273
pole (spherical geometry), 250, **273**
polygon, 175, 215, 216, **273**, 276
polyhedron (plural polyhedra), 211, **274**, 276, 306
polynomial, 183, 201, 204, 205, 257, **274**, 281, 286, 307, 313
    coefficients, 191
    degree of a, **204**, 223, 280–282, 307
    factorization of a, **221**, 248
    interpolation, 240
    prime, 276
    quadratic, 280
    synthetic division of a, 304
population (statistics), 182, 226, 269, **274**
position vector, 274
positive
    affirmations, 25
    attitude, 25, 122
postulate, 274
potential energy, 274
pound, 275
power
    as in energy, 203, **275**, 319
    as in exponents, 181, 183, 191, 201, 204, **219**, 224, 235, 248, 251, 261, 274, **275**, 280–282, **294**, 307
practical uses of math skills, 30–31, 41–44, 47–48
precalculus, 38, **56**, 100, 105, **186**, **323**, 325, **363–368**
precision, **171**, 202, **275**, 295, 296
premise, 177, 197, 203, **275**, 304

prime
    factor, 275
    number, 275, 276
    polynomial, 276
principal nth root, 262
prism, 276
probability, 205, 235, 244, 257, 258, **276**, 288, 295
    conditional, 195
    confidence level, 195, 196
    density function, 276
    distribution, 187, 210, **276**
        binomial, **183**, 269
        chi-squared (χ^2), 189
        Gaussian, **226**, 261
        normal, 182, **261**
        Poisson, 273
    significance level, 200, 295
problems with
    calculators, 27, 32–33
    graphing, 60–61, 64
    graphing calculator, 64, 65, 72–84
    homework, 53–55
product, 277
product rule, 277
proficiency
    lack of, and improving, 31, 40, 105, 113
    with a graphing calculator, *see* graphing calculator, developing intuition for
    with mental arithmetic, *see* skills, mental arithmetic
projectile, 277
projection, 242, **277**
proof, 162, 179, 246, **277**
    by contradiction, **277**, 288
    by induction, 235, **278**
    geometric, 6, 16, 17, **100**, **135**, 169, 178, **226**, 300
    strategies for, 135, 162
proportion, 227, **278**, 296

proportional to, 247, 271, **278**
protractor, 278
PSAT/NMSQT, 112, 141, 144, 150
Pythagoras' theorem (or Pythagorean theorem), 279
Pythagorean, 279

quadrangle, *see* quadrilateral
quadrant, 78, **280**
quadrantal angle, 280
quadratic, 280
    equation, 193, **280**, 281, 350
    formula, 193, **280**
    function, 280
    surfaces, 281
quadric surfaces, *see* quadratic surfaces
quadrilateral, **281**, 290, 309
quartic, 223, 281
quartile, 185, 240, **281**
quintic, 281
quotient, 282
    identity, 282
    rule, 282

radians, 283, 364
radical, 283
radicand, 283
radius, 175, 237, 273, **283**
raise to the power of, *see* power, as in exponents
random, 195, 257, 259, **283**, 284, 302, 310
    fluctuations, 196, **284**, 289, 295, 299, **301–302**
    number, 284
    sample, 182, 261, **284**
    variable, 276, **284**
range
    in data, 60, 291
    of a function, 284
rate, 275, **284**, 298, 317
ratio, 192, 203, 226, 241, 246, **278**, **285**, 296

common, 226
    geometric, *see* common ratio
    golden, 227
rational
    expression, 285
    number, 3, 9, **285**, 286
    root theorem, 286
rationalizing the denominator, 285
ray, 301
real
    number, 194, 241, 280, **286**
    roots, 194, 280, **286**
rearrange (an equation), 286
reasoning
    deductive, 177, **203**, 235
    inductive, 177, 203, **235**, 278
receptiveness to learning, 17, 21, 30
reciprocal, 258, **286**
rectangle, 286
rectangular coordinates, **187**, 263, 280, 287
recurrence relation, *see* recursive
recurring decimal, 287
recursive, 224, 287
    formula, *see* recursive
    rule, *see* recursive
reduced
    fraction, 288
    row echelon form, 288
reference for math terms, *see* crib sheet
reflection, 288
reflexive property, 288
regression, 249, **288–289**, 310
    coefficient, 191, **199**, **288–289**
    line, 288–289
    linear, 249, **288**
regular (adjective in geometry), 289
relative, **170**, 250, 289
    direction, 182
    proportions, 308
    sound intensity, 203
    velocity, 243, 260, **289**, 301

remainder, 192, 221, 227, 245, 256, 275, 276, **289**
    theorem, 289
renormalization, renormalize, *see* normalization, normalize
repeated root, 290
repeating decimal, *see* recurring decimal
residuals, 290
resultant (of a vector), 290
rhombus, 290
Riemann sum, 290
right
    angle, 232, 287, **291**
    circular cone, 291
    triangle, *see* right-angled triangle
right-angled triangle, 172, 263, **291**
rigid body, 291
Romberg integration, 291
root mean square (r.m.s.), 291
root, roots, **194**, 205, 280, 286, 290, **291**
rose curve, 292
rotational symmetry, 292
rounding, 292
rows (of a matrix), 206, **252**, 264, 266, **292**, 300, 309

saddle point, 237, **293**
sample
    random, 182, 261, **284**
    statistical, 293
SAT, 112, 113, 141, 144, 150
scalar, **293**, 317
    product, **293**, 317
scale factor, 61, **261**, 296
scalene triangle, 293
scatter plot, 60, **293**
scientific notation, 222, 251, **294**
sec, *see* secant
secant, 176, **294**, 313
sector, 294

segment, 62, 254, 255, 272, **294**
semicircle, 294
semilatus rectum, *see* latus rectum
semimajor axis, 294
semiminor axis, 294
sequence, 295
    infinite, *see* infinite series
series
    arithmetic, 178, 192
    binomial, 183
    infinite, *see* infinite series
    Maclaurin, *see* Taylor series
    sum of a, 197, 210, **303**
    Taylor, 305
set(s), set theory, 295
side-side-side, *see* SSS
sigmoid function, *see* logistic function
significance (statistical), 199, 200, 288, **295**, 299
significand, **251**, 294, 295
significant figures, 171, 251, 292, **295**
similar
    figures, 296
    triangles, 296
simple
    harmonic motion, 229
    interest, 296
simplify, simplification, **162**, 172, 184, 242, 286, **296**, 303, 309
Simpson's rule, 291, **297**, 310
simulated exams, *see* exams, simulated
simultaneous equations, *see* equation(s), simultaneous
sin, *see* sine
sine, 176, 190, 200, 201, **297**, 298, 305, **313**, **366**
    rule, 297
singular matrix, 241
sinh, *see* hyperbolic functions
sinusoid, 298
skills

estimation, 34–37, 43, 146–147, 163, 339, 352–353, 358–361
    for studying, *see* study skills
    graphing, 59–84, 113–114
    mental, *see* mental skills
    mental arithmetic, 37, 38, 44
slope, 227, 298
slope-intercept form, 298
software tools, **20**, 41, 42, **44**, **71**, 83, 84
speed
    definition of, 298
    in exams, 50, 138, 151, 157
    linear, 249
    of a moving object, 170, 171, 230, **249**, 260, 284, 293, **298**, 315, 317
    with mental arithmetic, *see* mental, arithmetic, speed in
sphere, 206, 215, 230, 244, 250, 273, 283, **299**
spheroid, 299
spline, 299
spurious correlation, 289, **299**
square
    (power), 38, 193, 267, 279–281, **299**, **300**, 316, **348**
    (shape), 201, **299**
    matrix, 206, 233, 241, 266, **300**
    perfect, 269
    root, 38, 194, 226, 242, 283, 291, **300**, **349**
SSA, 300
SSS, 300
standard deviation, 210, **300**, 316
standard position, 301
standardized exams, tests, *see* exams, standardized
static, 301
    friction, 243, **301**
stationary point, 237, **301**
statistic (model-fitting), 301

statistical
    error, **301**, 302
    fluctuations, *see* random fluctuations
    sample, 293
    significance, *see* significance (statistical)
statistics, 302
statute mile, 302
stem-and-leaf plot, 302
step function, 302
strategies for
    communication with your child (about math), *see* personal interaction
    exam preparation, *see* exams, studying for
    studying, *see* study skills
Student's t-test, 232
study
    skills, 53–55, 123–127, 135
    techniques, *see* study skills
studying
    active, 31–37, 123–125, 130–133, 135
    for exams, *see* exams, studying for
    strategies for, *see* study skills
subset, 192, **303**
substitution, 214, 297, **303**
    property, 303
sum of a series, 197, 210, **303**
sum to inifinity, 303
supplementary angle, 303
supplies check, 52
surface area, 304
syllogism, 304
symmetric property, 304
symmetry, 304
    axes of, *see* axis of symmetry
    axis of, *see* axis of symmetry
    line of, *see* axis of symmetry
    rotational, **292**, 304

synthetic division, 289, **304**

tan, *see* tangent (trigonometric function)
tangent
    (line), 305
    (trigonometric function), 176, 305, 313
tanh, *see* hyperbolic functions
tautology, 305
Taylor series, 305
teachers
    as a valuable resource, 6, 20, 21
    dedication of, 24
    extraordinary, 21, 24, 85
    passion of, 6, 21
teaching
    challenges, 11–16
    classes, 11–16
    philosophies, 6
    strategies, 11–18
techniques for studying, *see* study skills
term(s) (in an equation), 306
terminal side, 301
terminating decimal, 287, 306
terms (math reference), *see* crib sheet
tessallation, 306
tests, *see* exams
tetragon, *see* quadrilateral
tetrahedron (plural tetrahedra), 306
theorem, 199, 226, **306**
    central limit, 187
    De Moivre's, 204
    intermediate value, 240
    linear factorization, 221, **248**
    midpoint, 255
    Pythagorean, 279
    rational root, 286
    remainder, 289
third quartile, *see* quartile
third-degree polynomial, 307
three-body problem, 307

388

tools
- general, 3, 89
- software, *see* software tools
- teaching, 86

topologically equivalent, 307
topology, 307
torque, 174, 256, **307**
trace (of a matrix), 307
transcendental number, 307
transformation, 308
transitive property, 308
translation, 308, 309
transpose
- an equation, 309
- of a matrix, 266, **309**

transversal, 309
transverse axis (of a hyperbola), *see* major axis
trapezium, *see* trapezoid
trapezoid, 309
- isosceles, 242

trapezoidal rule, 262, 291, 297, **310**
tree diagram, 310
trend, 310
trial (probability), 310
triangle, 310
- acute, 171
- centroid of, 188
- circumcenter, 190
- congruent, 196
- cosine rule, 200
- equilateral, 215, 216
- hypotenuse of, 232
- incenter, 234
- inradius, 237
- inscribed (in a circle), 237
- inscribed circle, 237
- isosceles, 242
- median of, 254
- oblique, 263
- obtuse, 263
- orthocenter, 265
- Pascal's, 268
- right-angled, 172, 263, 279, **291**
- scalene, 293
- similar, 296
- sine rule, 297
- sum of angles, 198, **310**

triangular
- matrix, 311
- number, 311
- prism, 276

triangularization of matrices, 311
triangularize, 311
triangulate, 311–312
trichotomy property, 312
trigonometric
- addition formulas, 312
- cosine rule formula, 200
- double-angle formulas, 211
- function, 73, 175, 176, 190, 200, 201, 211, 217, 229, 294, 297, 305, 312, **313**
- half-angle formulas, 229
- identity, 313
- sine rule formula, 297

trigonometry, 105, **312**
trinomial, 313
- perfect square, 269

truncated decimal, 313
truth table, 313
tuition, *see* tutoring
turning points, **237**, 253, 255, 313
tutor
- experience level, 86, 88–90, 141
- how to find, 96–103
- how to interview, 98–103
- independent, 86–90, 94, 95, 98–103
- qualifications of, 100–103
- with an agency, 86–89

tutoring
- affordable, 85–93
- agency, 86–89

anecdotes, 25–29, 116–119
checklist of criteria, 93
cost of, 85–87
frequency of, 112–113
general, 85–120
goal setting and planning, 104–105
graphing calculator, help with, 113–114
ideas for reducing cost of, 85–93
joint, 93
optimal use of, 33, 86, 104–116, 119–120, 148, 151
targeted, 104–116, 141, 148, 151
two's complement, 193
two-body problem, 313

unbiased, 293, **314**
    distribution, 284, 314
    sample, *see* uniform distribution
unbounded, 185, **314**
uncooperative students, 11, 13, 15, 20, 39, 40
underachieving, *see* performance, poor
underperforming, *see* performance, poor
uniform, 314
    distribution, 284, 293, 314
union, 314
unit matrix, 233, 253, 258, 266, **315**
unit, units, 315
universal set, 315
unknown (variables), 195, 215, 297, **315**
unlike terms, 315
upper quartile, *see* quartile

variable, 172, 199, 200, 205, 207, 223, 224, 226, 230, 237–239, **267**, 268, 303, 313, **316**
    dependent, **205**, 233, 235
    independent, 205, 219, 233, **235**

random, 276, **284**
variance, 316
varies directly, *see* direct variation
varies inversely, *see* inversely proportional
vector, 170, 251, **274**, **290**, **316–317**
    analysis, 317
    components, 316–317
    cross product, *see* vector product
    dot product, *see* scalar product
    inner product, *see* scalar product
    product, 317
vectors
    basis, **181**, 266
    orthogonal, 182, **265–266**
velocity, 205, 216, 243, 260, 289, **298**, 316, **317**
Venn diagram, 317
vertex, 172, 173, 208, 237, 254, 267, 291, 311, 312, **318**
vertices, *see* vertex
volume, 187, 205, **318**

wall sheet, 125–127, 135
Watt, 275, **319**
websites, *see* internet, websites
weight, 252, 319
weighted average, *see* weighted mean
weighted mean, 319
wikipedia, 3, 9–10
word problems, 28–31, 115
work
    (in applied math, physics), 274, 319
    dating, 50–51
    organization of, 50–51, 124, 125
wrapping function, 319

x-axis, 321
x-intercept, *see* intercept

y-axis, 321
y-intercept, *see* intercept

z-axis, 321
z-intercept, *see* intercept
zero
    factor theorem, 322
    matrix, 322
zeros (of a function), 322
zoom settings on graphing calculator, 74–82

About the Author

Dr. Tahir Yaqoob is an astrophysicist, and obtained a BA in physics from the University of Oxford, England, and a Ph.D. in astrophysics from the University of Leicester, England. He has over a quarter of a century of experience in tutoring and mentoring math and physics across the entire academic range, from students at elementary school to those in Ph.D. programs. He has also trained postgraduate students and postdoctoral researchers to become established scientists and professors in physics and astrophysics. Dr. Yaqoob has published over a hundred research papers in peer-reviewed international journals and works on NASA-funded astrophysics research projects. He is also a member of the editorial board of the international peer-reviewed journal *ISRN Astronomy and Astrophysics*. Dr. Yaqoob currently lives in Baltimore, USA, with his wife, Rehana, and two children, Humza and Aazam.

www.ingramcontent.com/pod-product-compliance
Lightning Source LLC
Chambersburg PA
CBHW022057150426
43195CB00008B/173